GIRL GROUPS

The Story of a Sound

by
Alan Betrock

45 RPM

DELILAH BOOKS
DISTRIBUTED BY
THE PUTNAM PUBLISHING GROUP
N E W   Y O R K

A Delilah Book

Delilah Communications Ltd.
118 E. 25 Street
New York, New York 10010

ISBN: 0-933328-25-7
Library of Congress Catalog Card Number: 81-71010

Manufactured in the U.S.A.

First printing 1982
Second printing 1983

Photo Credits

All photos are from the collection of Alan Betrock with
the exception of the following:

Tom Carlucci	p. 10
Kevin Dilworth	pp. 95, 116, 117, 139, 140, 141
Cook Friedman	pp. 73, 74, 160
James Jamerson	pp. 158, 159 (top)
Peter Kanze	pp. 93, 94, 155
Michael Ochs Archive	Front cover (Angels). pp. 8, 9, 11, 21, 61, 153

Photo on page 111 taken by and courtesy of David Dalton.

Special thanks to Penny Stallings for her contributions to
the Motown chapters.

Book Design by Ed Caraeff

Contents

Maybe 6

He's A Rebel 22

The Locomotion 38

My Guy by Aaron Fuchs 56

South Street 70

Chapel Of Love 84

Out In The Streets 98

It's My Party 112

Be My Baby 120

Easier Said Than Done 142

Nowhere To Run by Aaron Fuchs 156

Where Did Our Love Go 172

There are 1000 Girl-Group Records: 174
Here are 131 of The Best . . . .

This book is dedicated to Isidore & Gertrude Betrock for all their love & support over the years.

Acknowledgments

THE TASK OF PUTTING *GIRL GROUPS* TOGETHER COULD NOT HAVE BEEN POSSIBLE WITHOUT THE CONTRIBUTIONS AND HELP OF MANY PEOPLE.

Deepest thanks must go to Ellie Greenwich, Mary Wells, James Jamerson, Gladys Horton, Ronnie Spector, Joseph Alexander, Wanda Rogers, Mary Wilson, Harvey Fuqua, Mickey Stevenson, Lesley Gore, Richard Gottehrer, Freddy Gorman, and Martha Reeves.

Special thanks extended to: Eli Fontaine, Kevin Dilworth, Penny Stallings, Bruce Pollack (for *When Rock Was Young*,) Adam White, Elliot Hubbard, Jane Berk, Cook Friedman, Lenny Kaye, Phil Spector Appreciation Society (Hi to Mick, Carole & Keith), Bruce Solomon, David Dalton, Peter Kanze, Michael Ochs, Rob Finnis, Ralph Newman, Richard Williams, and Chris Capece.

My personal thanks extended to Aaron Fuchs for his diligent efforts in writing the two Motown Chapters, "My Guy" and "Nowhere To Run."

To all the performers, writers, producers, and musicians who created this lasting body of music, my eternal thanks for your creative genius, your heartfelt emotions, and your honest guidance.

And of course my appreciation and much credit goes to all the wonderful people at Delilah Communications for their support, ideas, hard work, and belief.

And finally, to Marilyn Laverty goes my love for her understanding and inspiration. Without her, this book would simply not exist.

THIS IS NOT A BOOK ABOUT "WOMEN IN ROCK,"
AND
IT IS NOT EVEN A BOOK ABOUT "GIRLS IN ROCK."

More accurately it is the story of a sound, and of a time and place that brought a unique combination of performers, songwriters, producers, musicians, and businessmen together. No one aspect outweighs another in its importance to the whole; success was simply not possible with even one weak link in the chain.

While providing a comprehensive overview of all the major contributors, I've also chosen to chronicle in depth one person who best exemplified each link in the chain: The Producer; The Songwriter; The Group; The Singer; The Record Company; and so on. Here we can see why and how people created what they did, and what the results and consequences of their actions were. In a larger sense, perhaps, this story also traces the transition of rock 'n' roll from what it once was, to what it has become today. It is a picture of both musical and personal triumphs and failures, which after all, is what the soul of rock 'n' roll is all about.

Alan Betrock

MANY FOLLOWERS OF ROCK 'n' roll history believe that the true spirit of the music died in the late fifties, and that the first few years of the sixties were filled with mechanized and bleached pap heralded by the arrival of the so-called "teen-idols." The usual rationale for such a theory revolves around the "death-of-rock" angle: Elvis Presley served in the Army from March 1958–March 1960; Chuck Berry was charged with violation of the Mann Act in 1959 and served time in prison in 1962; Little Richard left the rock fold in 1959 to serve the Lord in a more traditional manner; a North Dakota plane crash took the life of Buddy Holly, Ritchie Valens, and The Big Bopper in February 1959; and Jerry Lee Lewis felt the wrath of public indignation following his marriage to a fourteen-year-old cousin in 1958. Although this series of events taken as a whole certainly points to a significant loss of momentum, to cut off rock 'n' roll's developments and triumphs for this reason alone is both limited in scope and short on perspective.

During his two years in the Army, Elvis had fourteen records hit the American Top Thirty; roughly one every seven and a half weeks. Included were such songs as "Wear My Ring Around Your Neck," "Hard Headed Woman," "A Big Hunk Of Love," and "Stuck On You." Ten of his releases reached the Top Ten, so Presley's hitch in the service, though possibly inhibiting his artistic growth, did little to keep the Presley rock 'n' roll sound off the airwaves or out of the record stores. Chuck Berry's absence was more pronounced, but this was due in some part to the overly repetitive and somewhat substandard nature of his releases. In the year *prior* to his arrest, for instance, Berry had ten chart singles, and not one broke into the Top Thirty. Both Buddy Holly and Ritchie Valens meant more to the public after they had died. As a solo artist, Holly had only one Top Thirty hit before his death (as the leader of The Crickets he had four Top Thirty hits, but his name was not a household word, by any means), and Ritchie Valens had only scored one Top Forty hit (and that, "Donna," was certainly more of a "teen-idol" type song than a rock 'n' roll raveup), before he perished.

One doesn't wish to underestimate the toll these developments took in the history of rock 'n' roll, but their impact should not be overstated either. To think that rock 'n' roll just died at the end of the fifties is to forget about the continuing success and emergence of these artists: The Drifters, Ray Charles, The Coasters, Sam Cooke, The Miracles, Beach Boys, Ben E. King, Jerry Butler, Gary U.S. Bonds, Solomon Burke, Dion, Stevie Wonder,

Lloyd Price, Gene Pitney, Garnett Mimms, Isley Brothers, Chuck Jackson, Roy Orbison, Marvin Gaye, Jackie Wilson, Del Shannon, Everly Brothers, Contours, Four Seasons, Little Anthony, Marv Johnson, Jan & Dean, and many others. An integral part of rock 'n' roll during this pre-British Invasion period was the sound and impact of the girl groups, so called because they were for the most part, both groups and girls. Their story is not one of *females* in rock 'n' roll (for there were hundreds of female stars who had nothing to do with the girl-group sound), but of a musical setting, lyrical direction, and business organization that added up to the creation of a unique genre—a style that would prove to be as significant, trendsetting, and lasting as almost any of rock 'n' roll's many permutations.

With the exception of the teen-idols (Fabian, Frankie Avalon, Bobby Rydell, Paul Anka, et al), girl groups were the only truly distinctive genre to blossom fully in the early sixties. Others, like Motown, surf, and folk-rock were just in their formative stages and they evolved over a period of years, while in comparison the girl-group sound developed and peaked rather swiftly. The mid-fifties had brought us clearly delineated categories like rockabilly, rhythm & blues, doo-wop, and just plain rock 'n' roll, while such early sixties hit-makers as Sam Cooke, Gary U. S. Bonds, Roy Orbison, and The Everly Brothers were not so easy to label.

If any one event *can* be blamed for the departure of wildly raw rock 'n' roll from the charts, it was not the untimely demise or departure of a handful of performers from the scene, but rather the payola investigations which erupted in 1959. It was these investigations, combined with increasing adult charges concerning rock 'n' roll's alleged delinquent effects on teenagers, that led to an image and musical change among record companies and disc jockeys. Maybe harsh attacks could be leveled by elders against Jerry Lee Lewis, Little Richard, Bo Diddley, and Elvis Presley for their "salacious" antics and lyrics, but who could complain about Bobby Rydell, Connie Francis, or The Beach Boys (or, for that matter, Sam Cooke, Little Anthony, The Drifters, or Jackie Wilson)? Concurrent with rock 'n' roll's attempt to clean up its image came the advent of programming, playlists, and the resulting Top Forty format. In the past, small labels scored regional hits by reaching a certain area or market, while the new playlists usually resulted in a record being either a national hit or a relative stiff. "Go national or go broke!" was the cry heard throughout the land. Heavy usage of formulaic imitation and watering down swept the

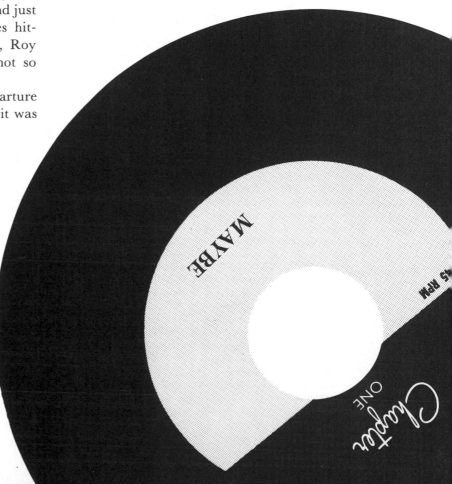

business, in an attempt to reach this new mass audience. Many smaller labels that had been doing just fine with their regional sales were not able to compete financially on a national scale, and they soon went out of business. Television, and the rise of mass magazines (also attempting to reach the widest range of consumers) played up the big hitmakers and forgot about the rest. A pie that had once been split up into many little pieces was fast becoming a pie of fewer big pieces. (Ironically this world of the haves and have-nots actually increased the intensity of payola, because the pressure to be added to a national playlist was that much greater, and the potential rewards were that much larger. . . .) In an attempt to fuse the urgency, creativity and honesty of rock 'n' roll's roots into a style that could be widely accepted on this newly emerging national Top Forty network, a handful of writers, producers, singers, and businessmen soon created what would come to be known as the girl-group sound.

★ ★

In the early 1950s, dance hall proprietor George Goldner formed a record label in New York to cater to fans of Latin music. The label, Tico, was successful, and soon George began to be intrigued with the newly emerging rhythm 'n' blues group sounds that echoed from neighborhoods throughout the city. His new label, Rama, broke nationally in 1954 with The Crows' recording of ''Gee,'' one of the first r&b records to have an across-theboard impact. His cousin, Sam Goldner, joined the company and soon new labels were started up. There was Gee (Frankie Lymon & The Teenagers, The Cleftones) and then Gone (The Dubs, The Isley Brothers), along with a series of less successful ventures (Juanita, Mark-X, Goldisc, Cindy). The Goldners had one label almost exclusively dedicated to the ''Flying Saucer'' records of Dickie Goodman called Luniverse, and they also had a hand in the early days of Roulette and Jamie Records. George Goldner could spot talent and brought a tremendous amount of nascent rock 'n' roll from obscurity to national prominence, but his free-wheeling and often exploitative business practices saw fortunes come and go, often at others' expense, several times over.

The Chantels.

Artistically, one of the prime reasons for the success of Goldner's labels was Richard Barrett. Barrett, a Philadelphia native, began hanging around Goldner's 42nd Street office, and sold some original songs to George. Barrett was a natural singer, songwriter, and producer; soon his group The Valentines achieved a steady success on Goldner's Rama label. In 1956 Barrett brought Frankie Lymon & The Teenagers to Goldner's attention, and shortly thereafter the group had become one of the biggest recording and performing sensations in the country.

★★★★★★★★★★★★★★★★★★★★★★★★★★★★★

One night, backstage at an Alan Freed Show, a young group of girls waited to meet their idol, Frankie Lymon. While they waited, they began to sing, acappella, an original song (called "The Plea") written by one of the girls. Frankie Lymon didn't get to hear it that night, but Richard Barrett, performing on the same bill with his group The Valentines, did. He was captivated by their sound, and brought the group to George Goldner. Goldner balked at first, saying that groups of young girls were just not saleable in the rhythm & blues market. Barrett disagreed and stood by the group, telling Goldner that he would not write or produce for the other acts if the girls were not signed. Goldner knew what the loss of Barrett's talents could mean, so he belatedly gave the go-ahead. Barrett rehearsed the group for two months, and they were then ready to make their debut recordings. The quintet was known as The Chantels.

The Chantels were all classmates at the Saint Anthony of Padua School in the Bronx. The group had been organized by lead singer Arlene Smith, who had been trained as a classical singer and had performed solo at Carnegie Hall when she was twelve. All the girls sang in the school choir, where classical music was interspersed with Latin hymns. At the time Barrett met them, the group consisted of Lois Harris, Sonia Goring, Jackie Landry, Rene Minus, and Arlene Smith, and they ranged in age from thirteen to sixteen. Goldner decided to start up another label, End, with The Chantels being one of the first groups on the roster. (The Chantels name, by the way, was inspired by a rival school, Saint Francis de Chantelle—it was certainly better than calling themselves The Anthony's, or worse yet, The Padua's. . . .)

With Barrett honing the arrangements and overall sound, The Chantels entered the studio for the first time, and recorded two songs: "He's Gone," and "The Plea"; both written by Arlene Smith, then fifteen. "He's Gone" described a broken romance, and "The Plea" was based around a Gregorian chant Arlene had learned at school. This first release set the tone for most of the Chantels recordings: Richard Barrett hammered out the chords, while a solid distant echoey snare kept the beat; Arlene Smith's vocals wailed plaintively above it all. There were other instruments used—a bass, occasional horns, and organ, as well as the chorale-type vocal support of the rest of the group—but all that really mattered was the piano, the snare drum, and Arlene's voice. "He's Gone" did relatively well for a new group on a new label with a new sound, reaching #71 nationally. It also made a significant impact on the r&b charts. In early 1958, The Chantels released their second record, a Richard Barrett song called "Maybe," and this would come to be the recording against which all future Chantels' efforts would be measured. Upon its release, the record literally

The Chantels' debut album.

exploded—its impact and appeal were simply undeniable. Barrett kicks off the record with a series of piano triplets, a wailing vocal chorus jumps in, and then Arlene tears your heart out with one of the most searing and honest vocal performances ever. It all came together here; the churchy-gospel influences meshed with a commercial rhythm & blues sensibility. Utterly convincing and profoundly moving, ''Maybe'' packs even more of a wallop when one realizes that Arlene Smith was only sixteen at the time of the recording session, and the record still captivated both teenagers and adults. The Chantels' records were not polished—their rough edges and even occasional wrong notes are there to hear if you search hard enough—but it was their utter intensity and atmospheric realism that carried them into a class all their own. ''Maybe'' *entered* the national charts at #55, and the next week had reached #32. Yet this incredible burst of popularity caused problems for Goldner and End Records, because they simply could not meet demand fast enough. In many cities bootleggers moved in, selling thousands of records before Goldner could fill the orders. Not only could the bootleggers press 10,000 records, pack them in a station wagon, drive around their territory, and sell them all that day, but they did so without such concerns as overhead, royalties, bill collecting, and shipping. In this fashion, they easily undercut Goldner's official prices. Because of these sales and order discrepancies, the record only reached #15 nationally, but it stayed on the charts for over a third of a year. Not only was ''Maybe'' one of the biggest selling records of its time, but its sound greatly influenced musicians and producers for years to come.

* *

Following the success of ''Maybe,'' The Chantels' next two releases were a relative letdown, both artistically and commercially. ''Every Night (I Pray),'' taken on its own merits, was rather moving, but coming on the heels of ''Maybe,'' was simply an inferior soundalike. Though it reached #40 in its second week on the charts, that was as high as it got, and it dropped steadily but slowly over the next eleven weeks. ''I Love You So'' provided a slight alteration in format, but it suffered a similar commercial fate, and many considered The Chantels' recordings to be too much of an ''earthy black r&b sound'' to be

. . . And then there were four.

continually successful on the pop charts. Still others believed that a group of young girls singing r&b was just a novelty, and that the success of ''Maybe'' was merely a one-time fluke.

At this point, a rift began to develop between the girls themselves, as well as with their record company. Royalties were rarely forthcoming, and while the groups' first four releases had made the charts, the next handful on the End label did not crack the Top 100. Goldner was still selling records, and Barrett, now an executive in Goldner's operations, also managed The Chantels. Publishing and writing credits usually fell their way as well. Throughout 1959 and 1960 the situation continued to deteriorate, with the girls becoming more and more disillusioned. As time went by the r&b sounds pioneered by most of Goldner's groups had gone out of commercial favor, and his organization seemed unwilling or unable to break new ground. Goldner's financial obligations eventually forced his label's activity to a virtual standstill, and he ultimately had to sell out to Roulette Records. Richard Barrett took The Chantels over to Carlton Records, but without Arlene Smith. She left the group and went out on her own.

With Barrett firmly at the helm, the new Chantels went all the way to #14 with their debut Carlton release, ''Look In My Eyes,'' and the follow-up ''Well I Told You'' reached #29. There was still the steady drumbeat and gospel-inspired chorale effect, but Barrett now glossed up the sound by adding soft strings and percussive effects which were layered over predominantly group vocals; the lead voice had almost totally disappeared. In fact, with Arlene Smith gone from the fold, Barrett occasionally utilized different ''Chantels'' on each recording; auxiliary members and even session singers were hired if the need arose. In the past Barrett had tried to capture and atmospherize an actual group sound, but now he was writing, arranging, and producing records first, and the actual group sound and personnel were of secondary importance. This development would prove to be a trademark for almost all of the girl groups to follow. When the next few Chantels' releases were not commercial successes, Barrett's priorities went elsewhere, and the group was cast aside and soon vanished from the scene.

Arlene Smith's first brush with the music

business left a bitter taste in her mouth, and she was no longer so anxious to devote her whole life to it. She continued her education, first at The Professional Children's School, and then at Julliard, and recorded only a couple of one-off singles for various labels. In early 1961 she signed with Big Top Records and recorded a single which was produced by a promising twenty-year-old who had come to New York to work for Jerry Leiber and Mike Stoller. The record, a remake of The Clovers' 1956 hit, "Love, Love, Love," was quickly forgotten, but its producer, Phil Spector, was not destined to meet a similar fate.

* *

Though The Chantels' chart impact had been short-lived, it nonetheless inspired others to follow in their footsteps. Such was the case with four close friends from Passaic, New Jersey. They began singing together in junior high, and by the time they entered high school were appearing regularly at local dances and talent shows. At one of these shows, a fellow classmate, Mary Jane Greenberg, heard them and convinced them to audition for her mother who "was in the music business." Florence Greenberg did get to hear the group eventually—they auditioned in her living room —and she signed them up to her small Tiara label. The contract not only bound the group to her for five years, but it also placed Florence Greenberg in the position of their manager. The group had composed a song called "I Met Him On A Sunday" which not only captivated their high school peers, but the Greenbergs as well. Florence took the group into a studio, recorded the song, and then pressed it on Tiara. It began to sell locally at first, then got some air-play, and the demand increased. Decca Records approached Greenberg, and picked up the master for national release. In the spring of 1953, the debut record by The Shirelles had a two-and-a-half-month chart run and reached #50.

The girls themselves didn't take this all too seriously. It was great fun to hear themselves on the radio and be local celebrities, but they were just friends who happened to sing, and anything else was gravy. And they were indeed friends. Beverly Lee, Doris Coley, Addie "Micki" Harris and Shirley Owens were virtually inseparable. They went to school together, sang together, worked together, ate together, went to shows together, and became a "family" together. In actual fact, they

were almost born together, amazingly enough, with Beverly, Doris, and Shirley born within seven weeks of each other (Micki was about a year older). Doris was primarily the lead singer at this point, and her father, a minister, had infused her with a strong leaning towards gospel music. After their initial success on Decca, they released a few more records but nothing happened. It might have ended right there, as it did with so many others, but Florence Greenberg had other ideas.

Free from her obligations to Decca, Greenberg formed a new label called Scepter Records and took a small office at 1650 Broadway, right in the middle of New York's bustling music business scene. It was here that she met Luther Dixon. Dixon had been a member of The Four Buddies (who recorded for RCA), but he left that group in order to devote his efforts to songwriting, and soon thereafter, publishing. Dixon was writing smooth songs for the likes of Pat Boone, The Four Aces, Perry Como, and Nat "King" Cole, and initially rejected Greenberg's request for material. His songs were going to "name" performers, and he saw no reason to give them away to unknowns. But Greenberg persisted, and after meeting the group, and making financial arrangements with Greenberg, Dixon hopped aboard. By agreeing to work with the group, Dixon had garnered some potentially lucrative concessions. Not only would he write for the group, but he would produce the records as well. Additionally, many of the songs would go through his Ludix publishing company, and if he created hits for The Shirelles, he would own part of Scepter Records. The deal was in place; now all he had to do was make it work.

Dixon's first effort with The Shirelles was a recording of "Dedicated To The One I Love," done originally by The Five Royales on King Records. The Shirelles' version was clearly patterned after the sound of The Chantels and did well in the New York area, but Scepter lacked the muscle to break it nationally, taking it to only #83. This was still a promising debut for the small Scepter label, but when the next record failed to chart, Luther Dixon decided that a change in direction was called for.

Dixon loved r & b music, but he felt that in order to succeed on Top Forty radio, he needed to sweeten up the sound. While others had just tried to water down the vocal tone or lyrical content, Dixon decided to keep the solid beat and vocal quality of r&b, and employ heavy use of strings in an attempt to reach a wider audience. His first effort was on a song that he and Shirley wrote called "Tonight's The Night." Some adventurous pop recordings of the day were incorporating sounds and beats found frequently in Latin and Spanish music, and Dixon flavored "Tonight's The Night" with a West Indian rhythm. He felt that there was a big market for that kind of sound in New York, and that city would be the first place to break the record.

"Tonight's The Night" was a wonderfully appealing record, from the intricate drum-string intro, to Doris' uniquely convincing vocals, both layered on top of the catchy melody and slightly suggestive "let's make love tonight" lyrics. Scepter at first started to get a strong reaction in New York, but then another group, The Chiffons, rushed out their cover version on the small-time Big Deal Records. Although The Shirelles' version was clearly better, having two versions out at once caused some confusion. Both versions entered the national chart the same week in September 1960, and The Chiffons actually led in the chart battle for the first three weeks, until The Shirelles began winning radio station polls (on which recording the listeners preferred). From there on it was no contest, as The Chiffons' version was universally forgotten. The Shirelles reached #39 on their healthy three-month chart run.

Luther Dixon was still writing songs for other artists, and spent time cutting demos and playing them for publishers and artists. People liked his demos so much that they often hired him to sing on theirs. This constant contact with songwriters and publishers let Dixon hear many new songs before any of his competitors, and he would often bring songs to The Shirelles the day demos were cut. While at the offices of Don Kirshner's Aldon Music, he heard a piano-voice demo of a new song called "Will You Love Me Tomorrow," written and sung by Carole King, a recent arrival at Aldon. Dixon liked the song immediately, and took it to The Shirelles.

"Will You Love Me Tomorrow" already had an interesting history by the time Dixon heard it. In its original form it ran some four and a half minutes, almost double the length of a typical pop hit of the day, and had a country and western flavor to it. After Kirshner persuaded Carole and her husband and co-writer Gerry Goffin to shorten it, Carole cut a rough demo and Kirshner began to shop it around town. His big hope was to get Johnny Mathis to record it for Columbia, but Mathis' A&R man, Mitch Miller, listened to it and turned it down. When Luther Dixon played it for The Shirelles, they didn't like it either, and said it just wasn't right for them. Dixon felt otherwise and prevailed on the group to trust him, saying that when they heard his arrangement in the studio, it would be perfect for them. Dixon worked on the vocals with the group, and then had Carole devise an intricate musical arrangement. At the session, things were sounding good, but Carole couldn't get the drummer to play the way she wanted, so she went in and played the kettle drums herself.

In one bold stroke, Dixon, King and The Shirelles, this time with Shirley on lead, made musical history. The strings swirled precipitously while the snare drum inverted the traditional rock beat and added on a slight rhythmic shuffle. "Tonight you're mine completely. . . ." So moving, and sung so honestly; here was a record that you felt—that carried you on effortlessly to totally warm and secure terrain. It was a record that you could hear again and again and again. For the next year or two, many, including Phil Spector, Leiber & Stoller, and even Carole King herself, would try to incorporate and enlarge upon its techniques. It also made clear to many that the right song—with the right singer and the right arranger and the right producer—was the way to succeed.

In late 1960, "Will You Love Me Tomorrow" entered the Top 100 at #88 and didn't stop until it reached #1. It also went to #1 on the r&b charts, and was a hit all over the world. It remained in the national Top Forty for almost four months, and made The Shirelles' sound so much in demand that their first Scepter release, "Dedicated To The One I Love," jumped back onto sales and air-play reports. It was soon officially re-released, and joined "Will You Love Me Tomorrow" in the Top Ten. On February 20th, 1961, "Will You Love Me Tomorrow" stood at #3 on its way down from #1, and "Dedicated To The One I Love" rested at #9 on its climb to #3. (Carole King wrote and arranged an answer record called "Not Just Tomorrow But Always" which she had a young Tony Orlando sing [under the name Bertell Dache]. The

The Shirelles receive a gold record for "Will You Love Me Tomorrow," while Wilt Chamberlain looks on.

United Artists release failed to chart, probably because it sounded so similar to the original; it was perceived as more of a cover version rather than the answer record it really was.) Not only did The Shirelles have two records in the Top Ten at once—a rarity for any artist—but they were also the first girl group to reach the #1 spot. There had been solo females at #1, or mixed groups with female lead singers, but since the onset of rock 'n' roll, this was an all girl-group first.

Once this fact sunk in among record biz types, the rush was on. "Gimme a girl group; gimme a love song; gimme a beat; gimme some strings—please, gimme a HIT!"

The girls were still in school, but this sudden surge of success forced them to drop out, and services of tutors were called upon. During Christmas week 1960, they appeared at The Brooklyn Paramount with Ray Charles, Dion, The Drifters, Neil Sedaka, The Coasters, Johnny Burnette, Chubby Checker, Bobby Vee, Little Anthony & The Imperials, and many more. At Easter they were back again with The Marcels, Carla Thomas, Del Shannon, Chuck Jackson, Isley Brothers, Freddie Cannon, Ben E. King and others. These shows were continuous round-the-clock affairs with each artist

The Shirelles with Murray The K.

With two records in the Top Ten simultaneously, The Shirelles became overnight sensations. Their following was particularly strong in New York. They seemed to capture perfectly the thoughts and moods of their listeners, and their records pulsed with the rhythms of the street. Murray The K was a particularly enthusiastic supporter, and his powerful WINS radio station played The Shirelles incessantly. He booked them into his week-long rock 'n' roll shows, and the listeners responded in kind—The Shirelles were voted Most Popular Group in almost every poll the station had between 1961-1963. An uncle had joined The Shirelles' family.

doing only about three or four songs. Sometimes, if a group just had their first hit, they performed only that—and were gone. Both the performers and audience were completely integrated racially, and the shows were wildly successful. The audience cheered and clapped and screamed. The performers responded by communicating with the audience and giving them energy and emotion. The Shirelles were a direct, warm, and soulful act. They loved what they were doing; they were joyous; and they fed off the audience's support. On their first tour of England in 1963, however, where they were not so well known, their first appearance almost left them in shock. It was a package tour where The Shirelles were billed under Little Richard and Duane Eddy. Opening night was at

The Edmonton Regal and there were two shows scheduled, at 6:40 and at 9:00. The first house was only half-full and had given the British opening acts a lukewarm reception at best. When The Shirelles came onstage, they were lacking in confidence and only performed a perfunctory four-song set, and this did not include "Will You Love Me Tomorrow," their only British hit. Then Duane Eddy came out and told the audience he couldn't perform because his guitars and amplifiers had not yet arrived from his previous dates in Europe. This obviously did not sit well with the crowd, and Little Richard, who followed, felt the ice in the air and couldn't break through. During intermission, Eddy's equipment arrived; the second show was sold-out; disgruntled patrons from the first show were re-admitted free, and the place was packed. The groups talked backstage, and decided to go all out at the second show.

When The Shirelles came out and the second house responded warmly, the girls came alive and let loose. They opened with "Everybody Loves A Lover" and segued right into "Will You Love Me Tomorrow" which brought great cheers. Doris and Shirley alternated lead vocals, and each one tried to top the other. Next came "Tonight's The Night," a wild "Twist And Shout," and then a lengthy version of "The Saints" brought the audience to its feet. On "The Saints," their musical director and guitarist Joe Richardson stepped out from the background and played several electrifying solos while the girls danced all around the stage, leaving the crowd whistling and cheering. The Shirelles had just been themselves, and that's all the crowd wanted.

Back home in New York, the group felt exalted. Their records were selling, their shows were packed, but most of all they felt like a tight family at Scepter. The girls were closer than ever; Florence Greenberg was their supportive mother taking care of business and looking after their career; Luther Dixon was their father who protected them, and always searched for just the right song and just the right production. Everyone was happy.

Flushed by their success with The Shirelles, The Scepter operation expanded quickly, until a second label, Wand, was established. The Scepter/Wand complex broke new ground time after time and fostered a new brand of urban-pop soul. Hits came with Chuck Jackson, Maxine Brown, The Rocky Fellers, The Isley Brothers, and Dionne Warwick.

By employing the new breed of adventurous songwriters, arrangers, and producers, the Scepter/Wand organization was constantly on the charts. The Shirelles' success continued as well with Luther Dixon's "Mama Said," a plaintively rocking song which developed the "lonely girl will find true love some day" theme. It went to #4. In late 1961, a talented pop craftsman, Burt Bacharach, brought The Shirelles a song called "Baby It's You." Bacharach had been writing, arranging, and occasionally producing for artists on Scepter/Wand, and had also cut elaborate demos and peddled his songs all around town. "Baby It's You" was one of those. Bacharach had actually recorded it as a demo with different lyrics and a nondescript female vocalist singing. It was called "I'll Cherish You," and when Dixon heard it, he flipped, and had Bacharach and his collaborators come up with new words. They took the original vocalist off the tape and added on The Shirelles, keeping Bacharach's original musical tracks intact. (They even left on some *male* backing vocals that had been on the original recording.) It became The Shirelles' next single and went all the way to #8. It was a marvelously atmospheric record, carried along by the intricately delicate snare–tom-tom–tambourine percussion and the utterly emotional vocal performance.

"Soldier Boy," a Luther Dixon-Florence Greenberg song that was originally intended as an album filler, came next. It was recorded at the tail end of a session—in only five minutes on the very first take. It was simpler and more tame than previous Shirelles recordings, with almost a white-pop kind of flavor to it. Perhaps that's what helped it go so far, as it became the group's second #1 record. Three more Top Forty releases followed, and then Luther Dixon stunned everybody by announcing that he was leaving Scepter/Wand, and The Shirelles as well. He felt he could do no more with them—he had accomplished what he could, and he wanted to pursue other offers. He was writing and producing continuously at Scepter —dozens and dozens of records—singles, albums, demos and on and on. He was carrying the whole company and it became too much for him. Capitol Records had offered him a lucrative production deal, and he accepted their proposal. In addition, he would issue records on a variety of his own labels, distributed through a series of companies.

The Shirelles carried on, and their first non-Luther Dixon supervised record, "Foolish Little

the SHIREL

FOOLISH LITTLE GIRL

ES

SCEPTER
RECORDS   511

WHAT A SWEET
THING THAT WAS

By GERRY GOFFIN

CAROLE KING

Recorded by
THE SHIRELLES
on SCEPTER Records

Price 60¢

02602   ALDON MUSIC, INC. • NEVINS-KIRSHNER ASSOCIATES, INC.

Sole Selling Agent: KEYS-HANSEN INC., 119 West 57th St., New York 19, New York

Girl,'' went all the way to #4, but the white-pop sensibility was becoming stronger and their emotional, churchy, gospel strengths were being downplayed. The next few releases didn't fare as well, and without Dixon, the group lacked the direction and adventurous creativity that had become their trademark. Florence Greenberg was spending more and more time with her other successful acts at Scepter, most notably Dionne Warwick (who had become a major star under the writing and producing wing of Burt Bacharach). Doris and Shirley of The Shirelles had gotten married, becoming Mrs. Doris Kenner and Mrs. Shirley Alston, and Dionne Warwick had gotten her start by subbing for them when family matters called them away. (Warwick had appeared at live shows, taking any missing Shirelles' place in the group, and she also sang backup on some of their records. But now she was becoming a ''big star'' and solo performer, and she could be molded more easily into a public focal point. Her records were more adult-oriented, and this resulted in a wider range of television and live show exposure, than The Shirelles received.)

Scepter began to cut corners and pay less attention to creative work. When The Shirelles needed some cuts to fill an album, Scepter took Chuck Jackson's vocal off his classic single ''I Don't Want To Cry,'' and added The Shirelles' voices onto it. How much cheaper and more quickly could an album be created than by the use of an already existing cut? When a group of young males called The Rocky Fellers hit it big with ''Killer Joe,'' their album was filled with The Shirelles' hits like ''Foolish Little Girl'' (here it was called ''Foolish Little Boy''), and ''Will You Love Me Tomorrow.'' They were the original Shirelles' tracks with new Rocky Fellers vocals added on. The Shirelles were then forced to add *their* vocals to two hastily recorded Rocky Fellers tracks, covers of ''Lonely Teardrops'' and ''Runaway,'' for release on Shirelles' albums. Then *both* The Rocky Fellers and The Shirelles were handed The Isley Brothers track to ''Twist And Shout'' and added their voices for the albums. It was a mess. What had been a uniquely creative and supportive environment was fast becoming a shoddy assembly line. Publisher Aaron Schroeder brought the group a song called ''He's A Rebel,'' which Greenberg turned down because she was afraid that it would cause problems in the South. The Crystals then recorded it and it went to #1.

When the girls turned twenty-one, they were expecting large sums of money that they had been told were being held ''in trust'' for them. The girls were surprised to find the cupboard less than full, and believed that financial wheeling and dealing, and contractual fine points had cost them dearly. They had placed all faith and trust in those around them, and now they felt betrayed. They tried to leave Scepter, but court cases left the group unable to record for another label. Old cuts were released as singles on Scepter, and repackaged old material began to appear at regular intervals.

Although Scepter continued to push the group as though they were still with the label, The Shirelles never broke into the Top Fifty again. Their ''father'' had left them; their ''mother,'' they felt, had exploited and deceived them; and their ''family'' was no more. As Shirley Alston later told writer Bruce Pollack in *When Rock Was Young*: ''During the proceedings I found out things that tore me apart. Things I was innocent of. We didn't know we were being treated this way by the people there, because we loved everyone. Our feelings were sincere and theirs evidently weren't. We took to our manager, Florence Greenberg, like a mother. She gave us that mother routine, and being kids, we fell for it completely. We never questioned anything she did, not one thing. They supposedly had a trust fund set up for us, but when we got to be twenty-one, there was no money for us. We never saw it like they said we would. They should have invested the money for us properly. Being the top female group in the country, we should have made a lot of money, and we didn't . . .''

It wasn't only the money, it was the pain that followed the realization of deception from those they trusted. The group continued together, because as Micki said, ''We always loved and respected each other,'' but by early 1964, when The Beatles were releasing *their* versions of hits like ''Baby It's You,'' and ''Boys,'' The Shirelles themselves were appearing at the Brevoort Theatre, at Bedford and Fulton Streets in Brooklyn, on a bill with The Coasters and Dee Clark. They did four shows a day; the audience saw films of the Liston/Clay fight in between; early arrivals were admitted for just one dollar. The Shirelles had pioneered the girl-group sound, look and lyric— but now others who had been watching from the sidelines saw an opening and moved in. There were new battles to be fought.

The Shirelles in happier times.

Chapter TWO

45 RPM

HE'S A REBEL

"YOU KNOW, THERE ARE ONLY two types of people in this world," Phil Spector stated matter-of-factly to his newly signed recording artists, The Righteous Brothers. "There's winners and losers. Some people are born to win and some are born to lose." That Spector believed totally that he was a winner was obvious to the duo, but even if Bobby Hatfield and Bill Medley had not been in the room, Phil Spector would've made the statement anyway, as if to reinforce his own clarity of belief. Intellectually, to Phil, it was a black and white world, clear cut, one way or another, with nothing in-between. Emotionally, however, there was a vast array of colors to be dealt with. Ultimately, it was this black and white versus color dichotomy that would lead Spector to the creation of records that would not only revolutionize the trends, scope, and techniques of popular music, but actually alter the very way we saw, heard, and *felt* sound.

Born in New York on December 26, 1940, Harvey Phillip Spector traveled west to Los Angeles in 1953 with his widowed mother Bertha and sister Shirley in the search for the promised land within the promised land. In this new world there were new rules, and the Bar Mitzvah boy was given a guitar which Phil studied with the intensity that others before him had devoted to the Torah. In 1955, the fifteen-year-old Spector was jolted by the rhythm & blues and resulting rock 'n' roll explosion that rattled the nation. Los Angeles, and its diverse surrounding neighborhoods that sprawled for miles in all directions, was a hotbed of churning, jumping, and powerful rhythm & blues music. Each week new groups and new labels would burst from the streets to the clubs and onto the airwaves: Imperial had Fats Domino, T-Bone Walker, and Smiley Lewis; Aladdin spun out Shirley and Lee, The Five Keys, Thurston Harris, and Amos Milburn; Modern and its various subsidiaries boasted Elmore James, John Lee Hooker, Etta James, The Cadets, and Richard Berry; and Speciality Records, right there on Sunset Boulevard—barely a mile from Spector's own home—unleashed the raw sounds of Larry Williams, Don & Dewey, and the ultimate rock 'n' roll icon, Little Richard.

Many of these (labels and) artists however, were not "discovered" until they had been working for as long as ten years, and a large percentage were strictly blues or rhythm & blues artists who adapted slightly or whose stylings came into favor when rock 'n' roll became popularized. The new exposure of what was previously called "race" music to younger, whiter audiences inspired these new listeners to emulate, imitate, and ultimately mutate these roots into ever-growing branches, reaching out into ever-widening musical and geographical territories. Whereas many of these Los Angeles labels had been releasing records by artists based in cities all over the country, now the newer Los Angeles based and staffed labels began to emerge, and they often championed solely local talent. Suddenly, Liberty Records went national with Eddie Cochran; Del-Fi and Keen hit with Ritchie Valens and Sam Cooke; and there were Challenge, Era, Class, Arwin, Rendevous and dozens and dozens of new, young, and more often than not, white kids, singing, playing in bands, recording, and having hits, regional or otherwise. A fast, young, interchangeable circle of talented and hungry music business performers and hustlers evolved: Bruce Johnston, Frank Zappa, David Gates, Lou Adler, Terry Melcher, Gary Paxton, Herb Alpert, Sonny Bono, Lee Hazelwood, Jan & Dean, Kim Fowley, Jack Nitzsche, Sandy Nelson. On the perimeter of it all stood, at five feet four inches, Phil Spector. When you're young and full of ideas, with no previous positions to defend, things start to happen in new ways. Here in Los Angeles in the late fifties, the freedom—and sometimes necessity—of doing things in fresh ways was rampant, and it was fast becoming time for the young to sweep out the old.

One month after graduating from high school, Phil became obsessed by a song he had written for his amateur high school group. "To Know Him Is To Love Him" was inspired, as legend would have it, from the inscription on his father's tombstone ("To Know Him *Was* To Love Him"). At the same time, Lew Bidell and Herb Newman, owners of the more pop-oriented ERA label, decided to start up Dore Records, purely as an outlet for rock 'n' roll material. After hastily auditioning Phil's trio, they offered to finance a recording session. Gold Star Studios, known for its classy demos and widely acclaimed echo chamber, was chosen as the site. Phil and his group (Marshall Leib, Annette Kleinbard, and last-minute-recruit Sandy Nelson) recorded the song in three hours, at fifteen dollars per, bouncing each track back and forth from one mono tape machine to another, each time adding a new layer of sound, while the previous layer degenerated slightly each time it was copied. In the end, the thin, soft, and simple trio (what Phil would later call "honest"—"There's a big difference between simple and honest," he declared, "and I make *honest* records. . . .") was transformed into an atmospheric, moody, and haunting entity. If honest is what he wanted—honest is what he got. The record was released early in August 1958, and it wasn't until a full two months later that the song

broke open in Minneapolis (when the call came in from a distributor for twenty thousand copies, everyone, including Phil, thought it was a joke), and soon spread across the country. The Teddy Bears' "To Know Him Is To Love Him" stayed in the Hot Hundred for a massive twenty-three weeks, resided loftily in the Top Ten for eleven of those weeks, and commanded the #1 position for three weeks, until it was finally toppled by the enormously popular novelty item, "The Chipmunk Song." In all, the record sold 1.2 million copies in the United States alone, hit #2 in England, and fought off a cover version rushed out by Capitol, the major label, by one Evelyn Kingsley. At age seventeen, in his first time in the recording studio, Phil Spector had written, arranged, played, sung, and produced the best-selling record in the country. Total cost: forty-five dollars.

The Teddy Bears had signed a contract for 1½ percent royalty (when the industry average was 3–4 percent), but even at the penny-a-record the 1½ percent equaled, The Teddy Bears were due some twenty thousand dollars in sales and air-play royalties. Somehow, all they ever got was three thousand dollars, and although Spector was technically out of school, he was now learning the most important lessons of his life. New rules were constructed by Phil, and these rules, he decided, were not to be broken. Phil Spector's new commandments were as follows:

The Teddy Bears...

WHEN YOU'RE DAFFY ABOUT MUSIC, IT HELPS

★ This is the year for teen-age talent . . . and the Teddy Bears have come along to prove it. The three Los Angelenos soon discovered they had something in common: all were daffy about music and singing. Sweet-faced Annette Bard, 16, Marshall Leib, 18-year-old athlete, and Phil Spector, 18, known as "Mr. Music" to the other students, recorded a tune written by Phil: "To Know Him Is To Love Him," and zoomed to the Hit Parade. "We've got the feel for young music," says leader Phil, "and we think we can contribute to it."

#1. MUSIC MUST BE EMOTIONAL AND HONEST.

#2. CREATE A SOUND ON RECORD THAT NO ONE CAN COPY OR "COVER."

#3. MAKE SURE YOU GET YOUR MONEY.

#4. THERE'S NEVER A CONTRACT WITHOUT A LOOPHOLE.

His heart and soul innately followed rule #1. He was constantly dreaming and devising the solution to rule #2. He had a hard time figuring out rule #3. And rule #4 was executed cleanly when he walked out on Dore's Lew Bidell, stating precisely and firmly that (A) The Teddy Bears were minors; (B) Their contract was neither signed nor approved by their parents or court of law; and (C) Therefore, Mr. Record Company Owner, your contract is clearly, and totally, null and void.

After their hasty departure from Dore, The Teddy Bears signed with the more established and respected Imperial label (this time the contract was court approved), but Spector quickly realized that he was not in charge. Control of the recording sessions was taken away from him and put in the hands of Jimmie Haskell when it was determined, by record company executives, that Spector was too laborious in the studio, and "wasting" too much of their money. The records turned out to be harmless, well recorded soft pop, rather sterile, but with some nice touches, and, fittingly enough, did not sell. In addition, Phil didn't relish making the public promotional appearances required of him as a "Teddy Bear," and he longed to devote his time and energy to self-produced records. None of the Teddy Bears' Imperial releases had been successful chartwise, and Phil was not satisfied with his lack of either commercial or artistic progress. After all, a year ago he had had the #1 record in the country, and nothing since. A chance meeting with Lester Sill resulted in an offer for production work with less interference. Phil dissolved The Teddy Bears and went to work for Sill, and Sill's recently acquired partner, Lee Hazelwood.

Lester Sill was a great spotter of talent and a swift deal-maker. He helped bring Jerry Leiber and Mike Stoller into prominence when he financed and promoted the L.A.-based Spark label for them. He managed black vocal groups like The Coasters, and had his own publishing companies. Lee Hazelwood first made his mark in Phoenix as a local deejay, and then as producer of "The Fool" by Sanford Clark, a record that reached #9 in the summer of 1956. Hazelwood next found a young guitar player named Duane Eddy; he and Sill formed the Jamie label for him, with Philadelphia distributor Harry Finfer and *American Bandstand* host Dick Clark brought in as partners. The Clark connection and resulting exposure for Eddy cer-

tainly didn't hurt, and Duane racked up fifteen Top Forty instrumental hits between 1958 and 1960. Spector began his Sill-Hazelwood association by sitting in on those sessions, fascinated by Hazelwood's use of different echoes and delays, which gave Eddy's records their distinctive flavor—the ultra "twangy" sound that no one else could accurately copy. A result of long and often tedious hours of trial and error, the sound was created by combining a variety of echoes and delays—some at different speeds, some from chambers, some from the room, some from tape and so on—until they were all blended together, producing a totally unique sound. Record history was being made, and Spector sat there, soaking it in.

With things going well for themselves, Sill and Hazelwood formed a new label, Trey, which was distributed by Atlantic. (An earlier S/H label, East-West, had also been distributed by Atlantic during 1958 and '59 without viable success.) For Trey, Spector formed a group called, modestly enough, The Spectors Three, which tried to recreate The Teddy Bears' hit sound, and failed to do so. He also wrote, played, and arranged several other commercially unsuccessful Trey releases, though a few exhibited a large measure of flair and creativity. So once again, fearing a dead end, Spector wanted to move on, and persuaded Sill to arrange for him to go to New York and work under the wings of Sill's former proteges, Jerry Leiber and Mike Stoller. They were then regarded as the country's most talented and successful writing–production team.

In May 1960, Phil arrived in New York, and immediately immersed himself in the great Atlantic music machine under the aegis of Leiber & Stoller. Within weeks of his arrival in New York, he played guitar on records by The Coasters, The Drifters, and LaVern Baker, and began to absorb the techniques and musical settings of these adventurous recordings. If the L.A. music scene was competitive, Spector soon found out that the New York action was positively frenetic by comparison. Everywhere you went, you were assaulted by hipsters and hucksters. The Brill Building at 1619 Broadway was crammed with dozens of publishers, record companies, producers, songwriters, agents, managers, and outright sharks. All of them paced the halls and rode the elevators, auditioning

ASSOCIATED
Recording Studios
723 SEVENTH AVENUE   at 48th St. CI5-7640

45 RPM

" YOUNG BOY BLUES "

HILL & RANGE

One of Phil Spector's New York demos, circa 1960.

groups and material, cutting demos, stealing songs they heard being played in the office next door, forming labels, and preying on young kids. Many prospective music business talents entered the Brill Building with a hopeful gleam in their eyes, and an armload of songs under their arm, and left a few hours later without either. But what many occupants of the Brill Building loved most was making deals. To many, making ''the deal'' was more significant than the actual end product. Make enough deals, the theory went, and sooner or later one would pay off. Deals were made in offices, in recording studios, in restaurants, in elevators, in bathrooms, in taxis, in subways, on backs of envelopes; any space two humans could squeeze into was fair turf for the deal-makers. And everybody wanted a piece of the action. I'll give you this, you give me that, we'll give this to him, he'll give that to them, and on and on. It was a tangled web of interlocking interests brought about by a vibrant, hungry, often talented, success-oriented group of people. All wanted that first big hit, and then the hit after that, and where the gravy train would stop next—or if it would stop at all—was anyone's guess.

In his first year in New York, at the age of nineteen, Phil Spector did the following: he signed to the prestigious Hill and Range publishing house and cut demos and wrote songs with several collaborators including Doc Pomus; he created Ben E. King's beautiful ''Spanish Harlem'' and later follow-ups; he composed and produced numerous records at Atlantic for the likes of Billy Storm, Ruth Brown, LaVern Baker, and many new acts; he produced records for the just-formed Dunes label, including Ray Peterson's ''Corinna Corinna'' (which hit #9), and the fabulous ''Pretty Little Angel Eyes'' by Curtis Lee (which reached #7). Spector was on his way to becoming a winner, and Leiber & Stoller, sensing paydirt, signed him to Trio Music, their new publishing company. They placed his songs, and got him work producing Johnny Nash, Sammy Turner, Arlene Smith and others. (Soon after, Phil invoked his rule #4 and informed Leiber & Stoller that he was a minor and his publishing contract with them was invalid. Paul Case of Hill and Range said: ''Phil never wanted to get involved, get tied down. He just wanted to do whatever he wanted wherever possible. . . .'') With the help of Leiber & Stoller, Phil produced numerous demos for Elvis Presley—demos cut so well that Presley often copied them note for note. Lester Sill financed independent sessions for Spector which were licensed to labels like Jamie and George Goldner's Goldisc. Spector met more and more musicians and arrangers, kept trying out new techniques, and cut early songs by Gerry Goffin and Carole King, Doc Pomus and Mort Shuman, Tommy Boyce, Jeff Barry, Barry Mann, Bert Berns, and Gene Pitney. It was a busy year.

Gene Pitney was three months younger than Spector, an aspiring songwriter and singer. Pitney's manager, deal-maker and music publisher Aaron Schroeder, formed the Musicor label primarily in an attempt to sell Pitney to the public. Their first release in late 1960 had done well for an unknown artist and untried label, and scraped its way into the Top Forty nationally. The follow-up, however, failed to even crack the Top 100. Now what to do? What else, Schroeder reckoned, but to make a deal. Aldon Music, headed by Don Kirshner, was the most promising publishing house in the record business, and they had a great demo "that would be just right for Gene," written by Goffin and King. Spector had cut other Aldon songs before and was regarded as a hot talent and hip producer. Pitney was a young and good looking singer with one Top Forty hit to his credit. Put it all together, and pooft! the magic deal. But when deals are made, everyone jockeys to protect their interest—their "piece"—and often the end product winds up being an uneasy compromise of divergent ideas and goals, rather than the work of one particular vision. Sometimes it works; more often than not it doesn't.

Schroeder and Pitney set up a meeting with Spector, and Gene remembers it vividly: "We went down to the House of Chan on the corner of Seventh Avenue and Fifty-third Street, off Broadway; a Chinese restaurant. Phil then had long hair, no loot, and little success. He was a kind of angry young man, undirected but not mixed up. He was full of ideas. . . ." The deal was finalized over spare ribs, with all concerned getting a piece of something. Pitney continues: "It turned out to be the most ridiculous session ever. Although Phil wanted to experiment, he didn't have enough control—not to the extent he had later—and there were too many people at the session making com-

ments. To add to it all, I had a wicked cold and was croaking—I sang the whole thing in falsetto. . . ." In an era when the average song cost five hundred dollars to record, Phil Spector spent *fourteen thousand dollars* producing a total of four sides. "For the first three hours, the musicians got regular scale, the next thirty minutes they got time and a half, and after three and a half hours they got double scale. Most people would just do three-hour sessions, and if they weren't finished, would start fresh again the next day. It was a lot cheaper that way. But not Phil," says Pitney, "he kept on and on. In the end there were only two usable tracks, for fourteen thousand dollars. It was unbelievable." The result was "Every Breath I Take," a marvelously constructed record, but not the ultimate for commercial sensibilities. After its release, it moved slowly, finally reaching #42, which probably meant that everyone just about broke even. More importantly, it solidified the relationship between Spector, Kirshner, and Pitney, both of whom were to figure very prominently in Phil's future. It also gave Spector new reasons to enlarge and cement his ever-expanding list of rules to play by. "Phil really went over the limit, but we dug him," says Pitney. "Phil was very talented inspirationally, but was more prone to studio conditions and psychological conditions than almost anyone else back then." If his peers and deal makers on the scene thought that this was the limit for Phil they were wrong. This wasn't the end—it was just the beginning.

Out on the West Coast, Phil Spector's creative headway and growing commercial acceptance did not go unnoticed. Lester Sill called on Phil to return to L.A. to produce a session with a trio of young sisters, Priscilla, Albeth, and Sherrell, known collectively as The Paris Sisters. Phil went back to Gold Star with two songs he had written, and arranged and produced "Be My Boy" and "I'll Be Crying Tomorrow." The result was an atmospheric ballad, with Priscilla's hushed lead vocal played against a sparse, moody backdrop. The recording utilized some of the same qualities of The Teddy Bears' hit but neither the song nor the lead vocal were as riveting. Sill attempted to sell the master to a major label, but was turned down wherever he went, so Sill and Hazelwood formed another new label, Gregmark, and issued the record themselves. It first gathered air-play on

the West Coast, where Sill's contacts were strongest, and entered the chart at a promising #80. But an unknown label with limited clout couldn't do much to build upon that base, and after a short five-week run, the record dropped off the charts, having peaked at #50. It was at this point that Spector became adamant about needing greater control of his recording projects. Sill ultimately concurred; he realized that when Spector was given free rein, the results were costly, but highly effective. Over the next few months, in and out of the studio, Sill would learn just how costly. Spector would run up bills totaling one hundred thousand dollars learning, by trial and error, how to create on tape the sounds that whirled about his head.

Phil's next move was hastened when he heard a demo of "I Love How You Love Me" in Don Kirshner's Aldon offices in New York. The song was written by Barry Mann and Larry Kolber, and Spector sensed something magical after only hearing a rough guitar–voice recording. He flew out to Los Angeles and shacked up with arranger Hank Levine. Together the two wrote and re-wrote the string parts, making revisions for hours and hours, trying out different angles and the slightest modifications, until they finally were satisfied. Spector then gathered up The Paris Sisters and sat around the piano in the studio working on the vocals over and over again, first coaxing Priscilla into a sultry and believable lead, and then blending in the numerous backup vocal parts. With this extensive pre-production rehearsal, itself an innovation for the time, the recording went rather smoothly, but this time it was to be the mixing, not the recording, that would test everyone's endurance and convictions.

Spector would do a mix, concentrating his attention on the intricate string lines, and then listen to it ceaselessly. Sometimes he would listen alone in the dark at very low levels, and others entering the room thought he was asleep. Then he would remix it again. And again. And again. Upon completion he kept the tapes at home for a week, until he decided the record should be pressed. After the pressing, he listened to it for days before he gave the go-ahead for actual release. (This *has* to be my greatest record, Phil decided, but it only became the first in a long string of "*has* to be my greatest record" attempts. . . .) At this point, ironically, Sill signed a distribution agreement with Herb Newman at ERA Records, the very man Spector had previously walked out on when he was under contract with The Teddy Bears. Friends and enemies alike would turn up time and time again to both help and haunt Spector in the future.

Upon release in August, 1961 the record that Phil had lived with for months moved slowly, gaining only five positions between its first and second weeks on the chart, but suddenly it became a heavily requested item, and then began to sell like crazy. Over the next 4 weeks it jumped a massive 78 points to #12, eventually peaked at #5, and stayed anchored in the Top Twenty for 2 months. It sold over a million copies. To Phil this was vindication for all he had believed and worked for. Left to his own devices, in full control of the material, arrangements, musicians, and production, he alone would bear the responsibilities if a costly project failed, and likewise felt that only he should get the credit and the benefits that entailed if it were a success. "I Love How You Love Me," was Spector's biggest hit since "To Know Him Is To Love Him" three years before. "I Love How You Love Me," was unlike anything else then being done. It absolutely convinced Spector that he could do it all. What remained was to prove it to the rest of the world.

Spector's return to New York prompted a flood of offers. The most appealing came from Stan Shulman, owner of Dunes Records, where Phil had produced hits for Curtis Lee and Ray Peterson. Shulman's proposal was short and to the point. He would finance a new label, Spector would choose and produce the acts, and each would own 50 percent of the company. Lester Sill heard of the offer, and persuaded Phil that he (Sill) could form a more potent company giving Phil full artistic control. Spector decided to go with Sill, and so Philles Records (Phil & Les) was born.

Shortly thereafter, while he was visiting Hill and Range Publishing, Spector was introduced to a group of young girls who were doing demo sessions while considering a possible recording future of their own. Their managers had some interest from both Big Top and Liberty, but knew that if Spector decided to produce, a significant contract would be easy to obtain. Spector said he was interested, but only if the group were to record for Philles, his new label. After some deliberation, the pact was agreed to, and Philles Records had its first recording act.

What Spector saw in these five young girls, (ages fifteen to seventeen), was a basic raw quality —talent that could be shaped and molded as he saw fit. It seems apparent that Spector chose to work with young, inexperienced girls because they offered little resistance on the creative end, and Phil could use their voices merely as one component in the complex and distinctive sound he wanted to create. They were disposable pawns in his gambit for creative freedom and chart domination, and if they would leave, there would be others ready and able to take their places. In short, he felt that they needed him far more than he needed them. Spector also realized that black artists offered him the best chance for honest and emotional vocal performances. He had grown up listening to black r&b records, and in his year in New York had almost exclusively produced black performers. His few white productions (Gene Pitney and Curtis Lee, for example) were clear attempts to mold those singers into an emotional black idiom. (Both Pitney's and Lee's Spector recordings scored high on the r&b charts as well as the Top 100). Spector later said: "All my records have a black flavor. If you go back in music history, you'll see that imitation of the black man is always the most successful form. Al Jolson did it. Stephen Foster was able to capture it. I don't like to record white artists. There's something unnatural about white artists doing it [soul] to me." So here was Phil, twenty years old, poised for attack with his own record label, and a vocal group with all the prerequisites he felt he needed to help him make his mark. "I picture sounds," he said later. "When I first began I pictured a sound so strong that if the material and the artist weren't that good, the sound would overcome it. . . ."

When he met them, the quintet of girls consisted of Dee Dee Kennibrew (Delores Henry), LaLa Brooks (Delores), Mary Thomas, Barbara Alston, and Pat Wright. Even at that point, though they were all high school students, deals had been made. Three of the girls were singing together after school ("Just for fun, we never thought we'd do any recording") when an aspiring songwriter, Leroy Bates, told the trio that if they wanted to use his songs, they'd have to take his sister-in-law into the group. That promptly made four. Dee Dee joined because her mother worked where the girls rehearsed; when the group decided they needed a fifth member, Mom stepped in and Dee Dee became number five. At first the group was going to be called The Five _____ (you fill in the blank), but that name implied more of a fifties doo-wop sensibility. Since The Chantels and Shirelles were reigning queens, the group went looking for a name along those lines. Leroy Bates had a young daughter named Crystal, and since that seemed a worthy omen, it was quickly decided they would be called The Crystals.

In May 1961, Spector took The Crystals into Mirasound Studios to record two songs. One was "There's No Other (Like My Baby)," originally written by Leroy Bates, and re-worked by Spector (who then shared writer's credits), and "Oh Yeah Maybe Baby," written by Spector and part-time Aldon songwriter Hank Hunter. Spector's new publishing company, Mother Bertha, published both songs. The A-side was "Oh Yeah Maybe Baby," a percussive and atmospheric song constructed much like a Drifters record, featuring their popular baion rhythm coupled with deep echoey drums, clangy percussive effects (castanets, tambourine, sand blocks, and triangle), and a soaring violin break with cello counterpoint. As far as Spector was concerned, the lyrics were almost as important. He realized early on that lyrics must paint a visual picture and relate a concise universal story. By sound and lyric Spector felt that the listener should be transported to a place where visual imagery and youthful emotions would mesh together in a warm, understanding, fantasy world. If parents, and even friends, couldn't recognize and sympathize fully with your problems; if an aching heart was your constant companion; well, for at least two and a half minutes you could close your eyes and escape it all. Spector wasn't pandering either—he was only twenty himself—and his work was emotional and honest. When the song, sound, lyric, and vocal all came together, the whole was much greater than the sum of its parts. If you accept the theory that acting out is therapeutic, many future psychiatric bills were saved right there.

Originally released in early October 1961, almost five months after it was recorded, the record appeared to flounder. It was rather adventurous sounding, and no one was quite prepared to hear girls in this intense lyrical setting, expressing attitudes previously reserved for male singers like the more established Drifters. It wasn't until deejays tried out the flip-side that the record began to gain acceptance. (In their defense, perhaps "Oh Yeah Maybe Baby" had Barbara Alston's lead vocals mixed down too low, obscuring the wonder-

An inauspicious trade ad for the Philles debut release.

ful lyrics, and the *baion* rhythm's *boom, boom-boom* beat was handled rather crudely on the chorus. In all, it seems rather rushed, and not as perfect as Spector probably would've desired.) Six weeks after release the record entered at #92, then moved slowly but steadily over the next month and a half until it peaked at #20. Although by all outward signs this was a most promising beginning for Philles, Spector was confused and let down. His creative side had been rejected, replaced by "There's No Other," a more fifties-flavored song that successfully imitated earlier Chantels records. It was a plaintive ballad with good string accompaniment, and a strong wall of background vocals, but Phil felt he, and others, had done that all before . . . and better. There were only two worlds Phil related to: the *best*, and *all the rest*, and this "hit" fell into the latter category.

There were new problems he hadn't foreseen. Helen Noga, the manager of Johnny Mathis, was brought in to finance the first Crystals record, and in return she owned a piece of the proceeds. Before the second Crystals session, Spector had bought her out. Other liaisons were not so easy to deal with. Lester Sill had sold 25 percent of Philles to Harry Finfer and Harold Lipsius, Philadelphia distributors and promoters (of Jamie Records fame), and Sill had hired his son, Chuck Kaye, to fill the spot as head of Philles promotion. Other pieces were taken—Lester Sill became The Crystals' manager, and he and his son ran Philles from Los Angeles, although their distribution emanated from Philadelphia, and Spector himself was in New York.

On top of all the business entanglements, Sill started to produce records for Philles out in Los Angeles. After the first Crystals record was released, three of the next four Philles records came out of Sill's West Coast office. They were all throwaways—groups of Sill's L.A. session men doing novelty instrumentals, or lame nondescript pop records. Apparently issued as favors of one kind or another, their chart potential was negligible, and needless to say, none of them sold enough to fill a shopping bag. To Phil, the supposed artistic head of Philles, this was a personal affront.

Spector felt, artistically and commercially, that "every record Philles releases should be a hit. If it's not a hit, why bother to put it out? If I don't have the right song, I'll just wait for one to come along." The fact that Philles had issued some throwaway sides via Lester Sill ate at Phil's conscience as well as his pocketbook. He had struggled for years to be in control of his destiny and now, even at his own company, he found he was not master of his fate. He disliked having several partners with conflicting ideals and goals; he couldn't condone spending (his) money on Sill's throwaway sessions and records; he didn't relish the use of "promotion" money which lined a variety of pockets; he didn't enjoy being dependent on publishing houses for new song material; and he didn't even feel the need to spend money on trade advertisements for Philles Records. "I felt if a guy doesn't like the record, that's it. You don't take him to dinner, you don't send him something in the mail. If he doesn't like it, that's the way it is."

That may have been the way it was for Spector, but that wasn't the way it was for almost everyone else in the business. Spector was rocking the boat, and the music industry captains and their crews already safely on board didn't enjoy having their ride disturbed. Realistically though, Phil lacked the power to alter the situation at this point. Power came from money, and money came from having your own hits. As a freelance producer he had merely been paid a fee for his work. If the record were a hit, he rarely shared in the profits. If he did manage to secure a royalty, it was a minimal amount; his songwriting and publishing income was limited as well, since few of his chart records

had been written or published by his company; and royalties actually due him took months and months to arrive, if they ever did at all. By owning your own record company and controlling pressing and distribution, you were taking a bigger financial risk, but the potential *profit* on each record sold was at least sixteen cents. Write and publish the songs on both sides, and you gained another four cents. Multiply twenty cents times a million copies sold, and your profit was two hundred thousand dollars, perhaps not much by today's inflated industry figures, but certainly a huge sum for a small company with low overhead back in 1961. On the heels of the hit would come the album, the air-play royalties, and the follow-up singles. But Spector wasn't seeing anything like this kind of money. He had only one hit on Philles (and that only reached #20); he had several partners dividing the spoils; there were unnecessary records released that "wasted" promotion money, and so on. If he were going to have his own record company, it would have to be all his, and Spector set off on a course designed to do just that.

Stop number one was the reliable Aldon, where he convinced Barry Mann and Cynthia Weil that their new song, written for Tony Orlando, was meant to be sung by a girl. (Orlando was coming off three consecutive chart records, and none of his next eight Aldon-sponsored releases even dented the Top 100. Perhaps if he had recorded this new song, history would've taken a different turn. . . .) In order to get the song, Spector had to record another Aldon tune for the flip-side, "What A Nice Way To Turn Seventeen," an undistinguished piece of fluff by Larry Kolber and Jack Keller. In contrast, the A-side, "Uptown," was majestic and brilliant, even to the deafest of ears. Opening with a spoken vocal over a mood-setting mandolin, the song breaks into an emotional mini-symphony. Lyrically, it relates the story of a young man who has to endure a demeaning existence downtown trying to eke out a living during the day, but then he can come uptown "where no one's his boss" and be a real man, "a king." The lyrics and internal rhymes are stunning, the visual imagery is breathtaking, and the vocal phrasing alternates beautifully between descent and ascent. Spector complements it with a tremendously innovative arrangement. There's a downbeat *pizzicato* musical setting and tone to the "downtown" verses, and a completely different uplifting quality to the "uptown" sections. With the complex string arrangements, background vocals, castanets, and mandolins blended together into a three-dimensional mural, few listeners noticed the complete absence of drums on the record. It had become common practice for producers like Leiber & Stoller, Bert Berns, and Spector to do away with cymbals and snare drums on many of their records, but there had always been tom-toms or tympanis. In this song, a bass and rhythmic sand blocks took their place, letting the strings and mandolins drive along and soar without obstruction.

"Uptown's" lyrics were the strongest reflection to date of struggling urban youths' desire to climb up the social ladder. It hit home for blacks in ghettos, as well as those actively fighting for their rights down South. Its underlying meaning also capsulized the frustrations of the young and presaged the violence that exploded across America during the street riots of the summer of 1967. (The hard-hitting imagery was not surpassed by the imitations it spawned—the best of these being The Drifters' "Up On The Roof" and "On Broadway." Both of those songs came from the Aldon stable, and were produced by Leiber & Stoller. At that point, Leiber & Stoller were following in Spector's footsteps—just one significant indication of Spector's growing creative influence.) In contrast to the teen-idol fodder crowding the charts, "Uptown" came as nothing short of a revelation. For Spector himself, it clearly represented his desire to break free of the creative and economic shackles holding him down, and the need to be in command of his future.

The commercial fortunes of "Uptown" are significant in several ways. Upon release, *Billboard* said: "Girls sell both sides with emotional impact and sincerity . . . dual market wax with appeal for both pop and r&b buyers," while *Cashbox* added: "Highly original sounding Latinish date . . . excellent material." Within two weeks, on March 17th, the record had registered strong initial sales in Los Angeles, and two weeks later entered the Top 100 at #80. From there it moved briskly to #68, then #56, and then #43, each week marked by a red star, or "bullet," indicating strong sales and air-play. On April 28th it only registered a six-point gain, to #37, and lost its bullet. Phil realized he was still playing the music business' game by

their rules, and took out a half-page trade ad for the record, and miracle of miracles, the next week the trades showed a 13-point jump to #24, with a bullet. The following week it only moved 4 points to #20, again without a bullet. Phil countered this time with a full-page ad to help grease the wheels, and the next week it moved to #17 with a bullet, and then to #13 for 2 weeks, and when no more trade ads appeared, it began a quick downslide and disappeared totally from the Top 100 just 3 weeks later. It's also interesting to note that the record did not even enter the r&b chart at all, even though during that time similar records by Dee Dee Sharp, Mary Wells, and The Shirelles all reached the r&b Top Ten, and such widely diverse (and often worse selling) records by King Curtis, Chubby Checker, Bobby Gregg, Acker Bilk, and Bruce Channel all scored heavily. (The Crystals' previous release, the less popular "There's No Other," had hit the r&b Top Ten.) With pay-for-play coming under heavy federal scrutiny, it seemed that pay-for-chart-action was still in full swing, and chart action was often the key to additional air-play and sales. But Phil was secure in the knowledge that he had handily executed the first part of his plan. He had scored a major hit with The Crystals on their second Philles release. Now the game was going to be played in his ballpark.

What happened next surprised most observers and stunned those close to Spector. As "Uptown" was scurrying up the chart, Phil Spector accepted a position as head of New York A&R for Liberty Records, offered to him by Snuff Garrett. For Phil to go to work in such a restrictive corporate setup, just when Philles was enjoying its own greatest success, was a double-edged shock. Garrett provided Spector with his own set of offices, and a hefty twenty-five thousand dollar salary. All Phil had to do was turn out some hits. In order to obtain Spector's services, Garrett made one major concession: Phil could still produce the acts he was currently working with outside the Liberty setup. But Phil decided to do nothing. Absolutely nothing.

His partners at Philles didn't know what to do. Sure they had the company and The Crystals, but what good was that without Spector? They began to sweat while Spector sat in his spacious Liberty offices all day and played with a hockey game on his desk. In Los Angeles, Lester Sill had parted ways with Lee Hazelwood in order to monopolize

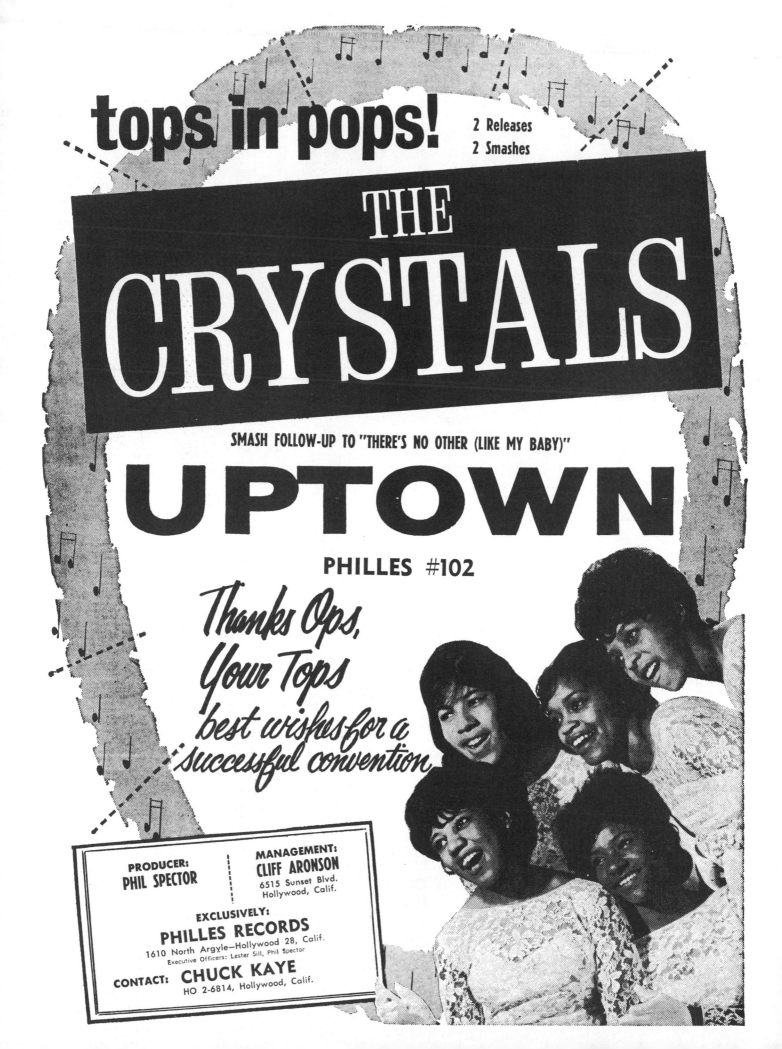

UPTOWN

Words and Music by BARRY MANN and CYNTHIA WEIL

on PHILLES Records

Recorded by **THE CRYSTALS**

SCREEN GEMS-COLUMBIA MUSIC, INC.

the services of Spector. Hazelwood got Duane Eddy and a promising arranger–producer–songwriter named Jack Nitzsche, while Sill got Spector and what was left of The Paris Sisters. Spector did produce a few Paris Sisters follow-ups for Sill, but his heart wasn't in it and each one did progressively worse saleswise, until both Gregmark and The Paris Sisters disappeared. Sill had cast his lot with Philles, but Spector was playing hard to get.

For a short time it was a stand-off, and then abruptly Harry Finfer made the first move. Finfer was a shrewd man who rode out the payola investigations of 1960, even after admitting to a Congressional committee that he had paid money to Tom Donahue, Lloyd "Fatman" Smith, Joe Niagra, Hy Lit, and other disc jockeys in relation to his part-ownership of Jamie Records. (Paying money to deejays was not a crime at the time, so admitting it did not place Finfer in any legal jeopardy.) In June 1962, Finfer suddenly sold his interests in Jamie Records and Universal Distributing to his associate Harold Lipsius, in return for Lipsius' share in Philles. Finfer now owned 25 percent of Philles outright, and issued a statement to the press saying he "would run the Philles label, and Sill and Spector would make masters for the firm. . . ." The next week Spector and Sill fired back with their own version: "The statement by Harry Finfer that he will be in charge of Philles is erroneous. Lester Sill and Phil Spector, executive officers of Philles, will continue to run the company. Sill and Spector have been in charge of the Philles label since it was started and they are not making any changes in management." Finfer had made a serious miscalculation, and was now a very silent partner.

At the end of July, Spector issued a new Crystals single, "He Hit Me (And It Felt Like A Kiss)," which told the tale of unfaithfulness and an ensuing sado-masochistic relationship, building up to the line "He hit me and I was glad. . . ." Even though the trade papers gave the record favorable reviews, it seems impossible to believe that Spector seriously thought this record could be a success. More likely he issued it in an attempt to scare his partners off even more. (Harry Finfer, perhaps sensing his days at Philles were numbered, soon started up two new labels, Arlen and Lanar. Both promptly fled into obscurity. . . .) On "He Hit Me," the lead vocal is unnaturally upfront, so that

each and every word is clearly audible. One can picture Spector lurking somewhere in the background rubbing his hands with glee and laughing out loud. Barbara Alston, who sang lead, recalled: "We didn't like that one. After we cut it, we absolutely hated it. Still do. Phil was so particular about the arrangement and sound that we had a terrible session. What made it worse was that after a few weeks had gone by and the record was issued and started selling, the kids at school started singing it and their teachers heard them. They didn't like the title and the lyrics, so the P.T.A. got it banned." Did Spector actually expect anything less? Even The Crystals' Dee Dee Kennibrew was left in the dark: "At the time we were all just kids and weren't aware what was happening behind the scenes."

In his five months at Liberty Phil had produced a total of five sides, none of which exhibited much committment to excellence . . . or hits. When Phil found out that Garrett was planning to cut a new Gene Pitney song for Vicki Carr out in Los Angeles, Spector listened to the demo and flipped. He suddenly called Garrett and told him he was quitting Liberty, making up some story that he was "taking an extended European vacation, and was undecided whether to continue in the music business. . . ." With the notorious "He Hit Me" just issued, and his non-productive and abrupt departure from Liberty, Phil was further cementing his image to those in the business who thought he was "crazy." Jerry Leiber said, "Yeah, Spector's crazy allright . . . crazy like a fox."

Instead of leaving for his "extended European vacation," Spector caught the next plane to L.A. armed with Gene Pitney's demo of "He's a Rebel." Snuff Garrett was putting the finishing touches on his version for Liberty when Spector arrived at Gold Star. Spector's usual engineer, Stan Ross, was on vacation, so Spector had to work with Ross's nephew, Larry Levine. On top of that he needed an arranger, and Sill recommended Jack Nitzsche, who had been working freelance and for Lee Hazelwood as a partner in Hazelwood's latest venture, Eden Records. Sill called Nitzsche, Nitzsche asked Hazelwood if he could work for Spector, Hazelwood said yes, and that was that.

Time was now a major factor. Spector gathered up musicians he had known from previous work at Gold Star, as well as newcomers that Sill and Nitz-

sche suggested. They were younger and more open to experimentation than many of the older, go-by-the-book New York players. Everything was in readiness, except for the fact that The Crystals weren't there. Spector said they were afraid to fly; Sill indicates that they wanted to save money on airfares, hotels, and the like and not fly the girls out; others suggest that scheduling conflicts and the need to record that very day made it impossible for The Crystals to attend. In all likelihood it appears to be a combination of all these factors. But why Spector flew to L.A. to record, instead of doing the session in New York, remains unclear. Perhaps with Sill basing Philles in Los Angeles it was the quickest and safest thing to do in order to keep pace with Liberty; perhaps Spector wanted to stay on top of Liberty or hear their version; perhaps Gold Star had been lucky for him in the past; perhaps it was a hunch or just a flight of last-minute whim.

Unlike other Spector sessions, often drawn-out affairs with instruments recorded one day, strings another day, and vocals on still another day, all the recording for "He's A Rebel" was completed in one session. The vocalists for the session were The Blossoms, a black female vocal group that performed backgrounds on dozens of records made in L.A., and also cut their own mildly successful records for a variety of labels. Darlene Love, the lead vocalist, and Fanita James, were joined by Gracia Nitzsche, Jack's wife and a part-time Blossom.

Both versions of "He's A Rebel" were reviewed favorably by the trades on August 25th, 1962. ("He Hit Me" was still bubbling under the Top 100, having only been released a few weeks before.) Liberty's release was heralded by a full-page ad which proclaimed in bold headlines: "The Original!! The Hit!!" There were no ads for the Philles release. The next week, the brass at Liberty Records partied in Chicago at a celebration for the opening of their new branch distribution center. On hand, along with three hundred other record distributors, dealers, Liberty artists and employees, and deejays, were Liberty president Al Bennett, National A&R head Snuff Garrett, and national promotion manager Bob Skaff. While they partied, Spector tended to business, and the next week The Crystals' "He's A Rebel" appeared at #98. Two weeks later it had broken open and stood at #66, while Vicki Carr's version made a belated appearance at #120. That same week Philles' distributors received a letter from Spector which said:

I am pleased to advise that I have acquired complete and absolute control of Philles Records Inc. I have purchased all other interests in this company. Lester Sill and Harry Finfer are no longer associated with Philles Records. I am assuming immediate direction of the entire company . . . I will be devoting my full time to producing and recording for my company Philles Records . . . I have the utmost confidence that I will continue in the hit making tradition . . . I realize that certainly you, as my distributor, will play an important part in my success, and I implore your utmost cooperation in promoting my forthcoming releases. Thank You for all past and future considerations in my behalf . . .

Three weeks later The Crystals stood at #11, while Vicki Carr's version dropped off a cliff, and 21 more days passed until "He's A Rebel" vaulted to #1, beating out such competition as Bobby "Boris" Pickett's "Monster Mash," The Contours' "Do You Love Me," and Gene Pitney's "Only Love Can Break A Heart." "He's A Rebel" also stood at #2 on the r&b charts.

What Spector had accomplished in a few hectic weeks was shattering. He left Liberty, produced a cover version of their record, and beat them handily on the charts; the record was recorded in one session with an arranger, musicians, and vocalists he had never worked with before; he bought out Lester Sill and Harry Finfer and assumed total ownership of Philles; and to top it off, he had the #1 record blaring out from every radio in America. Snuff Garrett couldn't show his face; Sill and Finfer were in a daze; the "real" Crystals were left totally confused. At age twenty-one Phil Spector looked down from his office on East 62nd Street and smiled. He had finally gotten what he wanted.

Phil Spector, late 1962.

Chapter THREE

THE LOCOMOTION

THE ASPIRING SONGWRITER SAT down in the publisher's office and asked: "Which comes first, the words, or the music?" The publisher lifted up his head and quickly replied: "The check." Along Tin Pan Alley, that story, or others played along a similar theme, soon passed from joke to fact to legend. Put that fifty bucks in my hand and by god, I'll write you a hit on any subject you want. Perhaps it was the conflict between old art and new commerce that transformed the revered craft of the Gershwins, Porters, and Berlins into the hustling churn-'em-out world of Teen Pan Alley, but as Phil Spector and the burgeoning number of his hopeful contemporaries discovered, this was a new game with new rules. Don Kirshner, once an aspiring professional basketball player, also knew about playing games: "We were just a different breed of ballplayer. We may have looked a little different or unorthodox, but the ball went in the basket the same way, and that's what mattered."

Although Don Kirshner and his Aldon publishing company were thought of as the arche-

typical Brill Building organization, the Brill Building sound really emanated from the stretch along Broadway between 49th and 53rd streets. Aldon was at 1650 Broadway, and other centers of activity were found at 1674 and 1697. The Brill Building itself (named after the Brill brothers whose clothing store first inhabited the street level corner, and who later bought the building outright), was at 1619 Broadway. Soon after its completion in 1931, the landlords were forced by the deepening Depression to rent space to music publishers, since there were few other takers. The first three concerns, Southern Music, Mills Music, and Famous-Paramount, were soon joined by others, until in 1962, the Brill Building contained 165 music business listings in the lobby directory. That doesn't actually mean that there were 165 different music business *offices*; some companies had two or three, or even a dozen different spinoffs or "subsidiaries" under the same roof. Every unsuspecting relative or gullible out-of-town investor who threw a couple of hundred bucks into the pot became a partner in a grand new venture. Besides, the multitudes of corporations could help turn a huge tax bite into an insignificant nibble. And if you would offer to name the prospective goldmine after one of the investor's young offspring, you could almost be sure to raise even more capital. "Yessiree, when it's time for college, we'll have Debbie Music Inc. as a nice nest egg for the kid. . . ." Sometimes, when the new companies became too plentiful, or the corporations came and went too swiftly, it was almost impossible to keep the multitude of names on the door up-to-date.

That was often a serious mistake, because when Uncle Ralph from Manhasset dropped in unexpectedly one day to see how his corporation was flourishing, and Debbie Music Inc. was not permanently engraved on the door, it took a glib and utterly convincing speech to keep Uncle Ralphie in the music business. That's why the Brill Building was so popular. The elevator door opened directly into the offices. No door engraving to worry about.

By the early sixties, the Brill Building was a classic model of vertical integration. You could write a song there, or make the rounds of publishers with one until someone bought it. Then you could go to another floor and get a quick arrangement and lead sheet for ten bucks; get some copies run off at the photo duplication office (our quick-copy world had not yet arrived); book an hour at one of the demo studios in the building like Audiosonic; round up some musicians and singers who hung around; and finally cut a demo of the song. Occasionally the demo even turned out to be a finished record. The musicians, singers, and studio time each ran about fifteen to twenty dollars an hour. A trio of musicians, a singer, and an hour of studio time would run you about a hundred dollars. All *you* usually came up with was a rough demo, but the musicians and singers who did a couple of sessions a day could be taking home three or four hundred dollars a week, which was good money in 1962. It wasn't *their* problem that you never got your song to Frankie Avalon, or that your record returned more than it shipped. There were always others waiting in line to take your place. Then you could hustle your demo around the building to record companies, publishers, artists' managers, even the artists themselves. If you made a record deal, there were radio promoters on call to peddle your wares. If no deal was made, well, there was always tomorrow.

It was this scene that first greeted Don Kirshner when he arrived in New York, and Kirshner soon decided that young blood, creative control, and a lot of hustling were the essential keys to success. A native New Yorker, Kirshner spent most of his late teens in East Orange, New Jersey when he attended Upsala College. While working as a bellhop in the Catskills during one summer, he wrote his first song, and while carrying bags for Frankie Laine, tried to sell it to the popular star. Laine declined, but explained to Kirshner where and how to get a demo cut. Kirshner followed his advice, had the song published six months later, but no one ever recorded it. (Kirshner later repaid the favor by giving Laine a Mann–Weil song, ''Don't Make My Baby Blue,'' which provided Laine with a chart record after a *seven-year absence* from the Top 100.)

THE LOCOMOTION

Chapter THREE

Back in New Jersey, a mutual friend introduced Kirshner to Robert Walden Cassotto in a local candy store, and after hearing Robert play and sing his original material, Kirshner decided they should be a team. It took a long year for a deal to come their way, and the first few records stiffed, but Robert Cassotto, known professionally as Bobby Darin, would soon develop into a highly creative and incredibly successful recording star.

During these early years, 1956–58, Kirshner penned some supremely forgettable songs like "Go To School," and "Warm Up To Me Baby." With Darin, the compositions improved slightly, but "Wait A Minute," "Lost Love," "Delia," and "I Want To Spend Christmas With Elvis" still failed to catch the public's imagination. The duo also composed local radio commercials, like the one for a New Jersey clothing store that went: *For values you can't beat/ just direct your feet/ hop a bus and come with us/ to 205 Main Street.* The singer on some of those commercials was one Concetta Franconero, a New Jersey friend of Kirshner's. As Connie Francis, she would later help Kirshner more than he ever could have imagined at the time.

In 1958, at age twenty-one, Kirshner met Al Nevins, a successful composer, musician, and recording artist, who had numerous pre-rock era hits as a member of The Three Suns. Kirshner told Nevins that publishing new material for teenage record buyers could be an extremely profitable venture, and Kirshner's conviction and persuasiveness overwhelmed any reticence on Nevins' part. In May 1958, Aldon Music was born.

Rock legend would have us believe that Aldon burst out from nowhere, discovered a slew of unknown but extremely gifted songwriters, and ran up a huge string of hits overnight. Close perhaps, but not entirely accurate. One of Aldon's first signings was the team of Neil Sedaka and Howard Greenfield. The duo had been turned down all over town in their attempt to get on-staff salaries, and when Doc Pomus at Hill and Range politely passed and suggested they see Nevins and Kirshner. Kirshner was captivated with their material. But Sedaka and Greenfield were not inexperienced chickens ready for a fast plucking, and Aldon had no track record of its own to speak of. As a writing team, they had several songs published and recorded by Atlantic Records for LaVern Baker, Clyde McPhatter, The Clovers, Micky and

An early Aldon demo.

Kitty, and The Cookies, and had sold other songs to Tryton Music and Benell Music. Sedaka had recorded with a youthful Brooklyn group, The Tokens, and had also cut solo records with Decca and Guyden.

Kirshner wanted to sign the team to a long-term deal, but Sedaka and Greenfield wanted to give eight new songs to Aldon for three months. If one of them charted, they would sign. Aldon got four months, but even that relatively short length of time was unnecessary. A few days after the four-month contract began, Kirshner took Sedaka out to New Jersey to play his songs for old friend Connie Francis, who now had two Top Forty hits to her credit. She picked one for her next single, and by October 1958, "Stupid Cupid," written by Sedaka and Greenfield and published by Aldon Music, stood at #17. Sedaka and Greenfield signed with Kirshner, and in less than a year had scored two more hits with Connie, "Fallin'" (#30), and "Frankie" (#9).

Al Nevins (left) and Don Kirshner of Aldon Music in 1962, alongside a few of their hit records.

In short order, Aldon signed Barry Mann, who had over two dozen songs recorded in the two years before he signed with Kirshner, including some national hits; Jack Keller and Hank Hunter, also with track records to their credit; Cynthia Weil, an aspiring actress who also worked as a lyricist for Frank Loesser's publishing house; and several other writers. Most were experienced to one degree or another, but what they really held in common was their age—they were all extremely young. (By 1962, Aldon had eighteen writers on staff, aged nineteen to twenty-six.) Most of the writers were not brought in as teams, as is commonly assumed, but wrote in various configurations. Eventually, though, teams began to solidify—alliances were primarily cemented by personal ties as much as by professional or artistic merits. For instance, in his first two years at Aldon, Barry Mann not only wrote songs by himself and with Cynthia Weil, but also with Larry Kolber, Art Kaplan, Hank Hunter, Leiber & Stoller, Howard Greenfield, and several others. Gerry Goffin and Carole King were brought in as a team, but Goffin also wrote with Jack Keller and Barry Mann, while King collaborated with Cynthia Weil, Howard Greenfield, Jack Keller, and Art Kaplan. The Goffin–King team also occasionally shared writer's credits with third parties like Weil, Artie Ripp, Greenfield, and Phil Spector.

The Aldon office was broken up into tiny cubicles, each filled with different writers banging out songs at the same time. Sometimes they would get a specific assignment from Kirshner, like ''Brenda Lee needs a follow-up, and she's looking for a ballad. . . .'' The groups would then retire to their spaces, compose, cut demos, and come back and play them for each other at the end of the day, making comments, suggestions, and criticisms as they went along. Kirshner usually had the final word. Don had a good ear and commercial pop sensibility, but was far from infallible. There were such early Aldon teams as Harrey and Martin (''Someone In Heaven''), and Hershenson and Strassberg (''Three O' Clock Rock''), who quickly fell into the abyss filled with pop unknowns. He did, however, provide an objective, demanding ear, and a rewarding, though ultra-competitive environment. He also took care of business with authority, something the writers alone were often unable or unwilling to tackle.

After Aldon's first few hits as publishers, Kirshner became increasingly dissatisfied with the two-cent mechanical his company received for each record sold; one cent went to Aldon and one cent went to the songwriter(s). So Nevins and Kirshner became independent producers, supplying finished masters to major labels. They picked the songs, arrangements, musicians, etc.; produced the record, and helped package and often manage the artist. They signed Neil Sedaka to RCA where he had a long string of hits; they discovered Tony Orlando, placed him with Epic, and scored Top Forty hits with his first two releases; and Barry Mann went to ABC-Paramount (''Who Put The Bomp'' reached #7).

With this arrangement, Aldon was able to place its songs on both sides of the record, thereby doubling their mechanical income, and also got a royalty on each record sold. With their growing track record as leverage, Nevins and Kirshner could command about a 10 percent royalty, with half going to the artist and half going to Aldon. Here too there were failures. Massive campaigns were launched for Tina Robin (Mercury), and Kenny Karen (Columbia), among others, to no avail, but the rewards of the successes far outweighed the losses incurred by the failures.

With all their songwriters churning out hits, near hits, and total misses with increasing frequency—in 1962, there some three hundred Aldon songs recorded, an average of six per week—air-play and mechanical moneys flowing in; royalties on their independent productions continuing steadily; and other benefits accruing as well; one would think that everything was rosy. Perhaps it was, but not rosy enough for Kirshner, who in mid-1962 announced the formation of Aldon's own record label. Within two months there would be three Aldon labels, and by the end of the year, a fourth was added. Only one of these really took off, but as with most of Aldon's successes, when something took off, it didn't just go for a ride, it went into orbit.

In June 1962, The Dimension Label was formed, distributed by Al Massler's Amy-Mala complex. Then came Companion, also distributed by Amy-Mala, which quickly changed its name to Motion to avoid conflict with an already existing Companion label. Next was Plateau Records, distributed by Bernie Lowe's incredibly successful

Carole King, Paul Simon, and Gerry Goffin at an early demo session, circa 1960.

Cameo-Parkway machine, and finally Chairman, distributed by the American London group. Apparently, the initial conception for these labels was to issue records from Aldon's elaborate demos, or masters rejected by other companies or artists. The Aldon family took such pride in their demos that they were often superior to the records that tried to copy them.

Plateau Records was an outlet for the newly signed team of Koppelman and Rubin. It lasted for only one release. Motion was an outlet for the production work of Jack Keller. It lasted for just two releases. Chairman was the label of last resort, issuing records only when no one else, including Aldon's other labels, wanted them. Everyone got to make a record here. There were eight Chairman releases, and these were produced by the likes of Jack Keller, Howie Greenfield and Helen Miller, Steve Rappaport, Sylvester Bradford, Koppelman and Rubin, Feldman–Goldstein–Gottehrer, and even Goffin and King. But it was Dimension Records, a label created almost exclusively to

showcase the work of Gerry Goffin and Carole King, that would leave a major imprint on the girl-group sound, blossoming into one of the top three labels of the genre, alongside the already established Philles, and the trendsetting Red Bird, which would soon follow.

Carole King, born Carole Klein on February 9, 1941, learned the piano at age four, and by her early teens was writing songs, hanging out with local band members, and forming her own groups, among them an amateur high school vocal aggregation dubbed, appropriately enough, The Co-Sines. Carole was fourteen at the time. She became close friends with neighbor Neil Sedaka, and followed him into the New York music business by cutting demos of her own songs, as well as playing piano, singing backup, and occasionally informally helping to arrange other sessions. While she was enrolled in Queens College, she met chemistry major Gerry Goffin, three years her senior, who had been writing songs since the age of eight. They meshed immediately, as Carole considered herself "a musician who wrote bad lyrics" while Gerry called his early songs "lyrically interesting, but sung over inane melodies. . . ." In 1958 and 1959, Carole, with Gerry's aid, recorded some harmless solo records for ABC-Paramount and RCA, and placed other material with Columbia, ABC, and Atlantic. When Neil Sedaka took his "Oh Carol" into the Top Ten in late 1959, Carole went into the studio to cut an answer record, "Oh Neil," for the tiny Alpine label. Attending that session was Don Kirshner. He later recalled: "I heard Carole playing the piano, and after just a few minutes, I knew she had a great natural talent—just tremendous. I ran down to a chemistry lab in Brooklyn where Gerry Goffin was working, grabbed hold of him and said, 'Listen, you and Carole sign with me. I'll give you fifty dollars a week, and make you the biggest writers in the country. . . .' "

Carole and Gerry, now Mr. and Mrs. Goffin, said yes, and joined the expanding Aldon family. During their first year and a half at Aldon, they provided the company with some of its biggest hits: "Will You Love Me Tomorrow" (not only a #1 pop record, but also recorded by fifteen other artists during the first year and a half of its release), "Take Good Care Of My Baby," "Go Away Little Girl," and "Up On The Roof." At the BMI Awards ceremony in January 1962, Aldon Music received more Citations Of Achievement (read: most played and bought records), than any other publisher in the business, garnering a total of twelve awards. Gerry Goffin received four, and Carole King received two. (Two of Goffins' hits that year were written with other collaborators.) The next year, Aldon won again, with Carole leading the way with four awards and Gerry with three.

Kirshner favored this particular team, not only because of their commercial successes, but more importantly because of their adaptability and willingness to write "commercial teen material." Others, most notably Barry Mann and Cynthia Weil were not as happy to sublimate their artistic goals and ideals, and were more interested in writing what they called "message songs" like "Uptown," "On Broadway," and "You've Lost That Lovin' Feelin' " (although they did score repeatedly with well-crafted pop fodder as well). Barry says, "When we were writing back then, we really did think we could change the world." This differing outlook often put them at odds with Kirshner's basic philosophy, and while many of the Brill Building habitues were busy hanging out at their favorite eateries, (Jack Dempsey's, The Turf Bar and Restaurant, The Maulers, Al & Dick's Steak House, and Lindy's were the most patronized), Mann and Weil usually stayed away, preferring contemplation to idle conversation.

* *

Back home in New Jersey, Carole King and Gerry Goffin were sitting around the piano working on new material. As was usually the case, their newly hired babysitter danced and occasionally sang along with the songs as they developed. One day, as the babysitter danced with strange up and down movements, Gerry said to her: "Y'know, what's that funny dance you're doing. It looks like a locomotive train. . . ." The image was quickly set into motion, and soon the Goffins had come up with a song called "The Locomotion." As babysitter Eva Narcissus Boyd had been such an inspiration, they took her to New York and cut the demo with her singing.

With new dance crazes hitting the charts every week, Aldon first pitched the song to Cameo–Parkway label-mates Dee Dee Sharp and Chubby Checker. It was turned down, but Kirshner had such faith in the song that he decided to release it himself. It became the first record on the newly formed Dimension Records. They went back into the studio, added an overdub or two, polished it up, and it was ready to go. Released early in 1962, Dimension's debut offering first entered the charts on June 30th at #85. A week later, Little Eva, as she was now known professionally, appeared on Dick Clark's *American Bandstand* lip-syncing the song and demonstrating "The Locomotion." The response was immediate, and greater than anyone could have reasonably predicted. The next 3 weeks saw the record move from #71 to #13, an amazing gain of some 58 points. The next week it jumped into the Top Ten where it would remain for the next two months. It ultimately knocked Aldon's own production of Neil Sedaka's "Breaking Up Is Hard To Do" out of its #1 perch, stayed in the Top Five for 6 weeks, and was also a monstrous r&b hit, holding down the #1 spot for 3 consecutive weeks. First time artist, first time label. It set the industry on its ear.

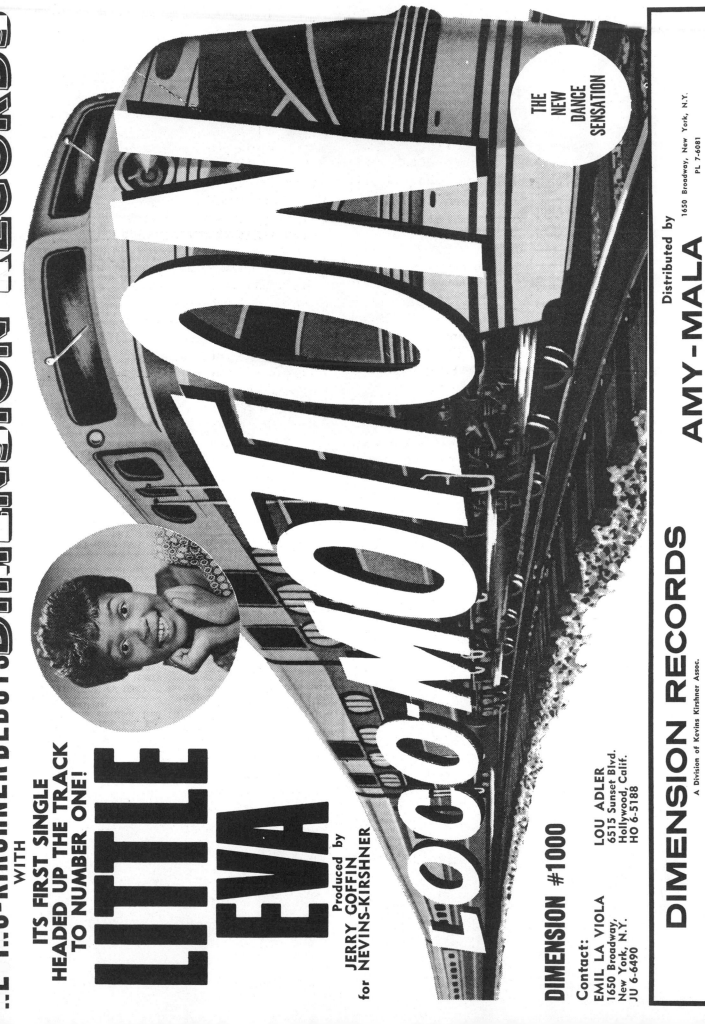

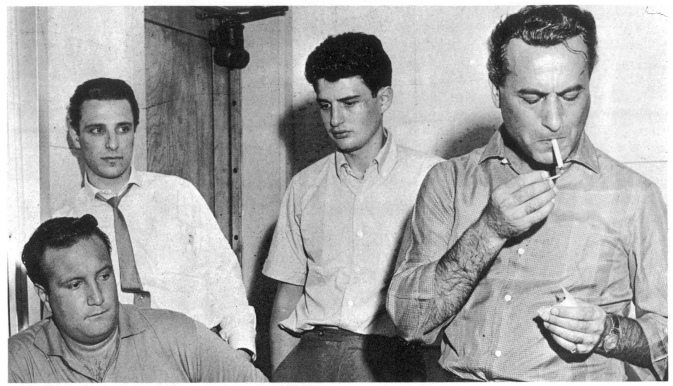

Late 1962 (L-R): Don Kirshner, Barry Mann, Gerry Goffin and Al Nevins.

Eva Boyd was born in Belhaven, North Carolina in 1946, one of thirteen children. She was only 16 when "The Locomotion" hit #1. Her salary as the Goffins' babysitter was thirty-five per week. Her earnings from "The Locomotion" were reported to be around thirty thousand dollars. She appeared on television shows and in numerous magazines. She performed live on package tours of the U.S. (Dick Clark's Caravan Of Stars), and did several tours of England where "The Locomotion" reached #2. In France, her live show and demonstrations of different dance steps caused a sensation, and in the U.S. a record called "Little Eva" was released by a group called The Locomotions. Listening to "The Locomotion" only once, it's easy to hear what all the fuss was all about.

From the moment the opening drum figure kicks off, the song drives along incessantly, with a beat so strong and solid that your body just cannot stay at rest. The great backup vocals, loose but effective sax break (courtesy Art Kaplan), and percussive hand claps are all rolled together into one unique sound. In actual fact, though most people remember the song as a powerhouse "wall-of-sound" recording (it has been said to have inspired Bruce Springsteen's "Born To Run"), the musical track consists only of drums, saxophones and a bass. The fact that these records were usually recorded and heard in mono placed everything on top of each other and resulted in the distinct and powerful mix. Heard in stereo, many of these tracks lost their jolt when each instrument (and there weren't many) was separated and heard too clearly and too cleanly. Painters who use green and red themselves just have green and red, but combining the two creates a totally unique shade.

Carole arranged all the Little Eva tracks, while Gerry would produce. In truth it was a team effort, but Carole usually was in the recording room, going from musician to musician working out individual parts and polishing the string arrangements, while Gerry sat in the control room and got the sounds down on tape. Carole had no great illusions about what she was creating, as she told an interviewer in 1961: "The sound that clicks with the vast teenage audience is the sound that sells. . . ." The fact that Carole's work was superior in conception and execution to others in the field was all gravy, but one gets the feeling that if her often adventurous arrangements and structures were not "clicking with the teens," she may have turned to something else that would've. (A group of songs with weird lyrical angles like "He Hit Me (And It Felt Like A Kiss)," "Please Hurt Me," and "He's A Bad Boy" were recorded, flopped, and that direction was quickly abandoned. . . .) While she certainly was the most successful young female in the business, King didn't find that so strange: "Is it surprising that a teenager should write songs? To me it seems like the most natural thing in the world." As a teenager writing for teenagers, King's songs cut deep with an edge of truth and sincerity. Others who tried to mimic these sounds and themes usually fell far short of capturing the essential emotional impact the originals evoked. Said Carole: "To me, a successful song should turn on emotion. That's what I look for. . . ."

Little Eva, remembered by most as a "one-hit wonder," was actually deserving of more than that. Her voice had a sullen edge to it, an edge that worked best when she played the hurt, abandoned girl, and for an inexperienced sixteen-year-old—she had previously only sung in church and school—she possessed a unique knack for phrasing. Her follow-up to "Locomotion," "Keep Your Hands Off My Baby," told the story of a close friend who tried to move in on her boyfriend, and musically it was a bit more sophisticated, adding acoustic guitars and piano to the initial formula. It reached #12 on its 3-month chart run, and bode well for her future. Yet Kirshner, and to a lesser degree Goffin and King, had a weakness, and that was an over-utilization of the soundalike, follow-up mentality. If record "A" was a hit, then record "B," sounding just like it, will also be a hit. So the theory went. That kind of thinking may work once, but more often than not, the fast-paced music scene could just pass you by. Producers like Phil Spector would always at least add variations to keep the public's imagination riveted, but Aldon, in both music and lyric, would too frequently try to mine a vein for all it was worth—although if the original was good enough, the vein may have already been exhausted.

Little Eva's third record was a case in point. "Let's Turkey Trot" was another "dance craze" tune that stood scant chance of surpassing "The Locomotion," and did not, reaching only #20. (Interestingly enough, at this time, the team corraled one of Little Eva's sisters, Idalia Boyd, onto Dimension for a single entitled "Hula Hoppin."
It was a catchy dance novelty recording, but did not puncture the Top 100, and Idalia never got a second chance.) As if this declining rate of success didn't clue the Kirshner team into the fact that

YOUNG HOLLYWOOD GOSSIP

Little Eva backstage at an ABC television show. Carole King and Gerry Goffin (right) look on.

Little Eva (left) returns from a tour of England in early 1963. Eva's sister, Idalia Boyd (above) didn't fare as well with her recording career.

soundalikes had run their course, Little Eva's next record was a clichéd combination of "On Top Of Old Smokey" and "The Locomotion," entitled "Old Smokey Locomotion." It only reached #48 in its short 6-week chart life. Although Little Eva was to release four more records on Dimension, the damage could not be repaired. She was perceived as a one-hit artist, and none of her future releases even entered the Top 100. Little Eva did continue to cut demos, and one duet with Big Dee Irwin ("Swingin On A Star," featuring Eva's great vocals) reached #38, but as a viable recording artist, her career was over.

As a rock 'n' roll genre, the girl-group sound was one of the most successful, and ultimately one of the most influential. It was also one of the few where there was no such thing as "artist development." In essence perhaps, the true artists were the writers, producers, arrangers, and musicians. The artist listed on the label provided a vocal, and occasionally a visual image, but if a release or two didn't click, or the writer's or producer's interests went elsewhere, in most cases the career was over. Little Eva was one of the first girl-group performers to find that out. She certainly wasn't the last.

Little Eva with deejay "Cousin" Bruce Morrow.

Singing backup on almost all of Little Eva's recordings, from "The Locomotion" onward, was a vocal trio known as The Cookies. The founding member of the trio, Dorothy Jones, was born in South Carolina, but as a youngster she moved to Brooklyn. At age seven she had joined the choir of the First Baptist Church in Coney Island. She continued singing, drifted into backup session work, and later brought Brooklyn friends Earl-Jean Mc-Cree and Margaret Ross into the business. Earl-Jean was born in North Carolina, moved to Brooklyn at age two, finished high school, and was working as an IBM operator when Dorothy brought her into the record business. (To bring the story full circle, it was Earl-Jean who recommended Little Eva to the Goffins as a babysitter.) Together, they became The Cookies, and made their public debut at The Apollo Theater on Amateur Night, winning the contest. There, they were spotted by an employee of Atlantic Records, who brought them to the label for vocal sessions. It was during their tenure at Atlantic that Neil Sedaka found them, used them on some of his early RCA hits, and later recommended them to Carole King for backup work on Tony Orlando's recordings. While working on the Orlando sessions, they were improvising around the piano, and Don Kirshner asked Dorothy Jones if she wanted to do a record for Aldon. Carole King and Gerry Goffin wrote, arranged, and produced the session. The result was "It's Unbearable," released on Columbia in July 1961, a rather intense ballad which boasted a dizzying string arrangement and torrid vocals. It didn't chart, but an ongoing professional relationship began.

The Cookies soon became staples on most Aldon-sponsored sessions. Besides Orlando, Sedaka, and Little Eva, the trio was featured on records by Big Dee Irwin, Ben E. King, Eydie Gorme ("Blame It On The Bossa Nova"), and Mel Torme ("Comin' Home Baby"). Their first Dimension release, issued late in 1962, was "Chains," a typically smooth and classic Goffin–King creation featuring a shuffling drum beat, handclaps, and wonderful vocals which alternated between straightforward sung verses and sultry, almost hoarsely whispered choruses. The record reached #17, and was later brought to even greater public attention when the Beatles recorded it. (The Beatles actually recorded five American girl-group songs on their first two albums: "Chains," "Devil In Her [His] Heart," "Please Mr. Postman," "Baby It's You," and "Boys." How's that for influence?)

"Don't Say Nothin' Bad About My Baby" was the next Cookies release, and it took their smooth shuffle beat to its peak with almost effortless ease, sporting beautifully honed lyrics and vocals, a highly memorable chorus, and an occasionally tougher lyrical stance highlighted by the almost impromptu "girl you better shut your mouth" tag line. This one hit #7, but the follow-up, "Will Power," struggled to reach #72 in its brief 5-week chart run. Deservedly so, as it was merely a vastly inferior imitation of its predecessor. The Cookies' B-sides were often more interesting than their later, over-formulized A-sides, exhibiting traits used most notably on records by The Shirelles and Crystals. One of these, "Only To Other People," was planned as an A-side, but gave way to an earlier recorded song, "Girls Grow Up Faster Than Boys Do," at the last moment. "Girls . . ." coupled their now familiar shuffle beat with a rhythm reminiscent of "Breaking Up Is Hard To Do," and added some deep-throated vocals for good measure. This was originally a demo for another girl group, but when it wasn't recorded, The Cookies issued it. In the process, it became their last chart record, reaching a respectable #33. One final Dimension release slipped out virtually unnoticed, and, as they say in the music business, that's the way the Cookies crumbled. . . .

During 1964, Goffin and King wrote and produced two solo records for Cookie Earl-Jean, the first of which, "I'm Into Something Good" kept the basic Cookies sound intact, while slightly modernizing it. Once again, it was a demo for other Colpix artists to consider, but it never found a taker. Though it was a lovely record, it only reached #38, but Herman's Hermits' cover version went to #13 only 4 months later. (It was Herman's Hermits' first hit, setting the group up for a massive run of Top Ten records, and it also hit #1 in England.) In late '64 and early '65, Goffin and King made one last attempt to revive the Cookies' sound, writing and producing two marvelous records for The Honey Bees (most probably The Cookies or some variation under a pseudonym), but although the records had made a noticeable progression, apparently they were still too dated for programmers, and their efforts fell on deaf ears.

The Cookies in the recording studio.

During the early days at Dimension, Carole King had three records issued under her own name. The first, "It Might As Well Rain Until September," was originally recorded as a demo for Bobby Vee, for whom Goffin and King had previously written the #1 hit, "Take Good Care Of My Baby," as well as several follow-ups. This new offering, in lyric and sound, had "Bobby Vee '62" stamped all over it, but when Vee delayed record- ing it, Kirshner slated it as the first release for Aldon's new Companion label. (When there was some difficulty in using the Companion name, it was switched onto Dimension.) Pleasant enough, with a bouncy arrangement and Carole's double-tracked lead vocals, the record did surprisingly well, reaching #22 in the fall of 1962. It did even better in England, where numerous recordings of Goffin-King tunes by British artists were fast becoming a lucrative new source of income for Aldon, reaching #3. The follow-up, "School Bells Are Ringing," was more in the Dimension girl-group mold, though sung in what can best be described as a Jamaican interpretation of the Little Eva vocal style, with background vocal support provided by the reliable Cookies. It didn't crack the Top 100. Carole's final Dimension release, "He's A Bad Boy," was in a soft folk-protest vein, with acoustic guitar and prominent harmonica, and only reached #94 on its short 3-week chart run. The problem with these recordings was that they possessed no sense of distinct style, no focal point, and no continuity. It was a disjointed set of releases, and certainly lacked the brilliance that had marked Carole's work with The Cookies and Little Eva. It seems doubtful that Carole wanted to have a recording career of her own with all the en-suing public exposure. At age eighteen, she had married Gerry Goffin and by twenty had two children, Louise and Sherry. She rarely appeared in public, and only had one official photo of herself circulated during her first four years at Aldon. She much preferred the behind-the-scenes activities, and continually writing, arranging, and producing with great success satisfied her creative goals. Her own records, issued as apparent afterthoughts, were often no more than rejected demos, and their release showed little regard for the public or Carole's own artistic profile or integrity. Aldon's British licensee, London Records, refused to issue her second and third Dimension recordings, even though the first, "It Might As Well Rain Until September," had hit #3. A spokesman for London Records said at the time: "These recordings are very substandard, and are by no means worthy follow-ups. . . ."

A hastily issued LP, *Dimension Dolls*, featured three other King recordings, as well as cuts by Little Eva and The Cookies, and is interesting to hear, if only for the demos and interpretations of such Aldon standards as "Up On The Roof," "Uptown," and "Breaking Up Is Hard To Do." Carole apparently didn't care to create girl-group style records for herself, and didn't find the time or inclination to work on developing a unique direction best suited to her talents and aspirations. Perhaps the real truth was that she had no goals whatsoever as a recording artist—hence the haphazard nature of the releases—and she simply acquiesced to Kirshner (who wanted the records issued).

Although they did have their shortcomings, the "demo years" provided the charts with some brilliant recordings, the result of a distinct division of labor. When properly meshed they resulted in American pop at its best. With the machinery well conceived and executed, the songwriters worked long and hard on their compositions; the musicians and arrangers toiled over sounds and details; the artist provided a distinct image and vocal styling; and the producer created a sympathetic and at-mospheric setting. Later on, when such boundar-ies disappeared, and almost every artist decided that they could be songwriter, arranger, vocalist, musician, and producer, the results were often so ego-laden and pedestrian that they sound incred-ibly embarrassing today. In contrast, many of the "Brill Building" records, although older and recorded without the benefits of modern techno-logy, frequently stand the test of time, and the songs themselves are continually re-recorded.

The benefits of the system cannot be ignored. Could Little Eva have written, "The Locomo-tion," or The Cookies composed "Chains"? Could The Crystals have produced "He's A Rebel"? Would The Drifters or Coasters have scored fifty chart records between them without Leiber & Stoller? One honestly thinks not. On the other hand, where would Barry Mann and Cyn-thia Weil have been without The Righteous Brothers to sing "You've Lost That Lovin' Feel-ing"? Or Luther Dixon without a Shirelles, or Phil Spector without a Darlene Love? Creative freedom is fine if you have the talent to back up the bravado. Del Shannon, The Miracles, and Gene Pitney were a few of the artists from this period who did write most of their classic hits, but taken purely as records, to say they are better or more important than, say, The Drifters, Everly Brothers, or Ronettes, who did not compose, is simply ludicrous.

Was Little Eva exploited when she received thir-ty thousand dollars for "The Locomotion"? No more or less, one guesses, than when Del Shannon received thirty thousand dollars for "Runaway." People were cheated out of money. People were given bad career advice, or none at all. People were cast aside after a flop or two. People were ex-ploited. But these emotional and financial thefts

The Aldon family in January 1963 at the BMI Awards dinner (Top, L-R): Jack Keller, Artie Levine, Lou Adler, Al Nevins, Mr. and Mrs. Don Kirshner, Emil La Viola, Larry Kolber, and Howard Greenfield. (Bottom, L-R): Barry Mann, Cynthia Weil, Gerry Goffin, Carole King, and Neil Sedaka.

cut across all race, religion, age, and gender classes. The Brill Building scene and the girl-group genre in particular was not any worse in this respect than any other period in popular music, and in many ways the system was superior and more straightforward. You do your job, I do mine, he does his, she does hers, and we share in proportion. That's the pact and that's the promise. There were honest, creative, and caring people; there were unscrupulous backstabbers; and there were many somewhere in-between. Music business participants from the top to the bottom both prospered and starved, some rightfully and some wrongfully. In truth, some twenty years later, not all that much has changed. In fact, with the stakes so much higher, pretention and seriousness running rampant, low regard for public taste, an industry devoid of spontaneity, and one-hit-wonders exalted to the level of ''superstar,'' a strong case could be made for a return to ''the old days.'' It was this developing trend, and the desire for more money, more power, total control, and more lowest-common-denominator pandering which would pervert and ultimately undermine the foundation that the Brill Building process had been built upon. A formula was soon extracted, ex-

tracted from what was essentially a complex creative process; those who made the format forgot the essential fact that a formula is only as good as the ingredients it contains. Use inferior elements and the golden formula quickly becomes little more than fool's gold: the ultimate triumph of formularized form over creative content.

Aldon was clearly the most successful songwriting and publishing house in the business; their independent productions flowed constantly to the major labels; and the first year of operation for Dimension Records had produced ten chart records out of thirteen releases, with eight reaching the Top Forty. Suddenly, in early 1963, rumors circulated that the Aldon complex was up for sale. On April 12, 1963, it became official; all assets of Nevins' and Kirshner's publishing and recording interests were taken over by Columbia Pictures–Screen Gems. Aldon received some two million dollars in cash and Columbia Pictures stock; Don Kirshner was named Executive Vice-President in charge of all Columbia Pictures–Screen Gems publishing and recording activities; and Al Nevins was named as consultant.

This must have come as a shock to the Aldon ''family'' who were now working for a huge international entertainment complex, but to Kirshner it was just good business. He assured his writers that Dimension would continue; that Screen Gems Music would pursue recordings of their compositions as aggressively as Aldon had; that Colpix Records would be developed into a powerful "major" label; and that new leverage and opportunities for movie and television writing was now at hand. What actually happened fell far short of these promises. For one, Kirshner devoted his strongest recording efforts to the Colpix label. Of the next 15 Dimension releases, only one made the charts, and Goffin and King, responsible for 95 percent of the first 13 releases, only worked on about 20 percent of the next 15. After that, new producers were brought in, outside masters were purchased, and records not good enough for Colpix were passed onto Dimension. Another twenty or so releases were issued over the next year, with only a few written or produced by former Aldon hitmakers, and not one of the twenty reached the Top 100. Officially, the label was quietly shut down in mid-1965, although it had lingered comatose since the end of 1963, when Kirshner's priorities went elsewhere.

Colpix, meanwhile, churned out some of the most mediocre teenage pap fodder imaginable, with television and movie performers making numerous records, alongside a heavy dose of adult-oriented MOR crooners, instrumentals, novelty items, and theme songs from various television, film, and Broadway shows. (The few decent Colpix releases, most notably those by Freddie Scott and Earl-Jean were the work of, not surprisingly, Goffin and King.) Kirshner did keep former Aldon songwriters busy composing and producing at Colpix, but their work was tailored to the lowest, most banal, and saccharin tastes. The same went for the promised television and film work. (Writing the theme for "I Dream Of Jeannie," "The Farmer's Daughter," and "The New Interns" was not exactly the challenging and artistically satisfying work most writers had envisioned.)

The atmosphere was not a happy or a particularly successful one. In 1962, Goffin and King, for example, had seventeen Top Forty hits with their songs. In 1964, the first full year of their employment for Kirshner at Screen Gems, they scored only five. The restrictive and non-creative environment, coupled with swiftly changing public tastes

and decreasing chart impact, contributed greatly to the decline of the Brill Building era. It also put the nail in the coffin of the girl-group sound as formulated by Aldon and Dimension Records. It led to disunity and dissolution of the previous levels of high-spirited competition, and also added to the writers' disenchantment with their personal lives. Kirshner was soon named President of Screen Gems–Colpix, and re-signed most of his Aldon staffers to long-term contracts, but these victories were rather empty and disheartening. Financial security was obtained, but at what cost?

It's a pity that Kirshner's personal goals, short-sighted vision, and condescending opinion of public tastes took precedence over the creative, emotional, and frequently innovative work he had helped nurture during Aldon's early days. (His financial gain, hefty for the day, would have increased several times over, had he held out for a few more years. . . .) We'll never know what the writers and producers could have achieved with artistic support and understanding during the mid-sixties. It then fell to others to race for the throne so carelessly abdicated by those who had once struggled so hard to sit upon it.

45 RPM

MY GUY

GIRL-GROUP MUSIC IS NOT THE first sound that comes to mind when Motown Records is discussed. The pounding, drill-press groove that Motown pioneered so relentlessly in the sixties emerged as such a completely unique idiom that none of the parts comprising its sum—be they girl-group, doo-wop, gospel, pop or otherwise—could justly describe the idiomatic unity that resulted.

By the same token, girl-group music—both in terms of the specific sound of the genre, and in the marketing sensibility that accompanied it—was very much responsible for putting Motown on the map. Much of the label's earliest chart success came with artists like Mary Wells, Martha & The Vandellas, and The Marvelettes, whose recordings were firmly in the girl-group mold, while The Supremes, led by Diana Ross, with their highly stylized brand of popsoul, and their endlessly spiraling upward mobility, were the single greatest personification of the label. Without the girl-group sound, and The Supremes in particular—Motown's biggest commercial success—the

Detroit soul sound of the sixties just may never have materialized. In the process, the girl groups were also the actualization of the dreams of every producer who thought he was maximizing his chances of pop penetration by taking pliable young women into the recording studio.

What is particularly noteworthy about the success of Motown, embodied by its dominating president, Berry Gordy Jr., is that girl-group music sprung from its macho milieu. Detroit was unlike New York and Los Angeles, which had long standing black pop traditions and had fostered prototypical girl groups as early as the doo-wop era: New York had The Chantels, The Deltairs, and group leaders Pearl McKinnon of The Kodaks and Lillian Leach of The Mellows; Los Angeles had The Six-Teens, The Dreamers, and Rosie Hamlin of The Originals. In contrast, there is almost no record whatsoever of a precedent for girl-group sounds from Detroit. The characteristic sound of that city was a harsh strain of blues cum r&b. Its roots could be traced to the very rough recordings of John Lee Hooker for the Sensation label, and extended through the '50s with gospel-sounding groups like The Falcons, whose very raw recording of "You're So Fine" is credited by many as marking the beginning of more commercial modern soul music. Even in the sixties, when Motown had its profound impact on pop music, the soul explosion, a parallel development in black music whose raw, unadulterated gospel-derived sounds stood for the diametric opposite of Motown, was spearheaded by Detroit-bred artists like Wilson Pickett and Aretha Franklin.

But the Motor City music scene of the '50s was undergoing dramatic changes that would create a sympathetic environment for the rise of a Motown. The two agents for change were rock 'n' roll, the music through which blacks were accepted in the white community, and doo-wop, the music through which women were accepted by men in the black community. Both nationally and locally, doo-woppers altered the course of Detroit music; nationally, the popularity of young Frankie Lymon, the Michael Jackson of his day, became as much an inspiration for aspiring female artists as it did for males of similar inclination. Lymon's youth—he was thirteen when he hit—and his remarkably precise diction made for an image not perceived in either racial or sexual terms; locally, The Diablos, led by the falsetto-styled vocals of Nolan Strong, who sounded as female as he did male, strongly challenged traditional notions of lead male vocalizing. (Nolan Strong was to become a major musical influence on Smokey Robinson, who would later write and produce records for Motown's girl groups.) The emergence of local rock 'n' roll/r&b radio, like WJLB, helped spread the message further. Gradually, the doo-wop groups that used to gather at The Madison Ballroom on Woodward Avenue to compete in "battle of the group" affairs began acquiring female members. By the time the sixties dawned, Detroit numbered The Del-Rhythmettes, The Andantes, The Primettes, and The Del-phis among its all-female groups.

Another new path to white audience crossover for the Detroit black music scene came through rock 'n' roll. While the city did not produce any Little Richard-styled wild men, it had a number of witty lyricists in the Chuck Berry/Leiber & Stoller mold. The fifties saw the emergence in Detroit of Coasters-type clown acts like The Fabulous Playboys, Mad Man Taylor, and perhaps the most consistent local influence on the Motown scene, the recordings by singer–writer–producer Andre Williams (songs like "Bacon Fat," "Mean Jean," and "Pullin' Time").

It was into this arena that Berry Gordy Jr. made his first entry. The diminutive but Napoleonic Gordy had first tried his hand as a lightweight boxer, and after a fair but short-lived career, he quit the sport, and opened up a jazz-oriented retail outlet, The 3-D Record Shop. The shop was not successful, and Gordy lost a substantial amount of money lent him by his father, Berry "Pops" Gordy, Sr. The defeated Gordy, by this time divorced and with child support payments to consider, worked on a Chrysler assembly line and wrote

songs in his spare time. Gordy's fortunes turned sharply for the better when a friend from his boxing days, Jackie Wilson, landed a contract and recorded a number of tunes that Berry had written with his sister Gwen. The tunes, "Reet Petite," "Lonely Teardrops," and "I'll Be Satisfied," resulted in a string of hits that turned Jackie Wilson into a major rock performer and secured Gordy's niche as a songwriter. Branching out from writing to producing, Gordy sought to take greater control of both the sound and potential financial gains earned by his work; he once received an impossibly low royalty check of $1.98 for a record by The Miracles, "Got A Job," that he had placed with New York's End Records. Eventually, he had a string of hits with Marv Johnson on United Artists, among them "Come To Me," the big hit "You've Got What It Takes," "Move Two Mountains," and "I Love The Way You Love." Finally, in 1959, Gordy launched his own Motown Record Corporation and Tamla Records with "Way Over There" by The Miracles.

It was not until after the company had its first few hits, and accumulated the necessary capital that one of Motown's most striking characteristics would evolve: what Gordy would later label "quality control." From his experience at Chrysler, Gordy learned the value of mass production and interchangeable parts. He soon cultivated the legendary rhythm section of Benny Benjamin on drums, James Jamerson on bass, and Earl Van Dyke on Piano, and kept them working constantly, recording tracks suitable for any one of a number of barely distinguishable artists. He kept releases to a minimum, issuing only a fraction of the body of work laid down in the studio, and concentrated on promotion. This way, every release stood a greater chance of becoming a hit. To enhance and customize the impact of live performances, he set up a number of finishing school-type classes in choreography, voice control, general polish. Gordy also personally oversaw the booking and management of the groups in an attempt to maximize the cross-marketing effects of recorded sales and performance revenues. He further controlled live appearances by packaging seven or eight of his acts on one self-contained "Motortown Revue" show, approving arrangements, song choices, billing, dress, and so on. It was a smooth assembly line.

As a man in his thirties who ran the company with the assistance of his three sisters and two brothers, Gordy used to his advantage the precious role of "father" of the patriarchal extended family to an artist-writer-producer roster of would-be stars in their teens and early twenties. Writer was pitted against writer to turn out the songs most valued by the hottest producers, who were in turn pitted against each other to produce the tracks that Gordy deemed most worthy of release, thereby proffering his paternal approval. Another aspect of Gordy's formula for success was his ability to choose the right person for the right task. Though Gordy himself, like many other black producers of his era, had next to no background in creating music by women, he was able to mobilize a staff of black men unequaled in their ability to produce music sympathetic to women artists. Led by Smokey Robinson, who wrote and produced hits for Mary Wells and The Marvelettes; the writing-production team of Eddie and Brian Holland and Lamont Dozier, who created hits for The Supremes and Martha & The Vandellas; the Motown staff turned out the most successful and satisfying body of women's music ever produced by black men. In this overall scheme of things, it's not surprising that Motown's first female artist of note, Mary Wells, was signed and initially produced by Berry Gordy on the strength of her ability to write and sing a tough Jackie Wilson-styled r&b song, but that her development into a classically feminine and popwardly mobile singer was architected by Smokey Robinson.

Wells' upbringing, like so many other artists, was deeply suffused with gospel music. Born into a family of "ministers and missionaries," Wells sang in church from the age of three, absorbing the gospel sounds that would shape her style. As a teenager she participated in the doo-wop fever that swept Detroit. A self-styled tomboy, she sang in all-male groups who, she remembers, "Didn't want me in there, but I was persistent." She considered Jackie Wilson her idol. In fact, Wells came to Tamla's door not to audition her voice for Berry Gordy the record manufacturer, but to see Gordy, the man who wrote songs for Jackie Wilson. Wilson was the artist for whom one of her new compositions, "Bye Bye Baby," was intended. Mary Wells' liaison to Tamla was Robert Bateman, whose vocal group The Satin-Tones en-

Berry Gordy outside Motown's Detroit headquarters, 1965.

MOTOWN

THE ONE WHO REALLY LOVES YOU
I'M GONNA STAY MT-1024

MARY WELLS

joyed early local success on Tamla with their recording of "Motor City." Like all members of the Motown organization, Gordy encouraged Bateman to diversify, and he had become chief engineer at the firm's recording studio. Wells knew Bateman through a mutual girlfriend, and he in turn provided access to the big man, Gordy. Armed only with an arrangement in her head, Wells auditioned the song for Gordy acappella; he signed her on the spot; in a matter of days he was personally supervising the recording of the tune in the converted garage that served as Motown's studio. Still working off the arrangement in her head, Wells relayed the parts to the musicians: Benny Benjamin, James Jamerson, and Earl Van Dyke (who were beginning to coalesce into the greatest rhythmic hitmaking machine of the '60s.) Background vocals were sung by The Andantes, Detroit's front-running female backup group; Berry Gordy personally worked out the vocal lines; his wife Raynoma wrote the charts. The Jackie Wilson roots of the song were evident—with its jerky, fragmented beat, the record seemed like an intensified reworking of "Lonely Teardrops," or another Gordy production, "Marv Johnson's "Come To Me." It also reflected the increasingly mechanized groove that would soon become a Motor City trademark. "He really knew what he was doing," Wells remembers of Gordy. "He made me sing the song twenty-two times, and then

when my voice got really hoarse, he considered that we had a final take." Like many other Motowners of this period, Wells' first session was her most pleasurable; its live-in-the-studio execution allowed her to "completely feel it."

The record was a fair-sized hit for the label in the early part of 1961, reaching #45 on its 11 weeks on the chart. The record also reflected another trademark of Berry Gordy: if he believed in a record he would promote it as much as possible. Many Motown records would begin to slide down the charts after a few weeks, and then Gordy would apply whatever leverage he could muster, and the record would often pick up air-play and sales for several more weeks. Wells' release had actually dropped off the charts after six weeks, but then jumped back in and broke into the Top Fifty.

While Gordy urged Wells to continue writing songs, the young singer, "scared by the success that came on me so fast," wanted to concentrate on expanding her command of performing beyond the family circle-type situations that had been her only previous experience. Never one to falter, Gordy called together his writers and producers and came up with a body of some fifty songs for Wells to record. After it was all over, Smokey Robinson emerged victorious. Wells' follow-ups to "Bye Bye Baby," "I Don't Wanna Take A Chance," and "Strange Love" failed to break her out of the mold of a mid-chart artist, but then the Robinson-penned and produced "The One Who Really Loves You" swept into the Top Ten in early 1962. This marked the beginning of the reign of Motown's first superstar, and also charted the course of the label's first long term artist–producer collaboration. In the threshold year of 1962, Mary Wells would score three of Motown's six Top Ten chart records.

Robinson had long ago acquitted himself as Berry Gordy's number one son. Robinson was involved with some of Gordy's earliest writing and production endeavors. As lead singer of The Miracles, Robinson was featured on masters sold by Gordy to Chess, Gone, and End, and he fronted the record with which Gordy bowed his Tamla label, "Way Over There." Much as he'd do with Eddie Holland later, Gordy recognized the potential chemistry that could develop between the loveman as producer, and the woman as artist. In any case, the chemistry that resulted from the two

Mary Wells, Motown's first star.

people who Wells described as "similar in mannerisms," and "like cousins who lived down the block from each other," resulted in five Top Twenty pop hits between 1962 and 1964. "The One Who Really Loves You" also inaugurated another Motown formula: following a hit with one soundalike hit after another until one finally failed to reach the Top Twenty. Here, "The One Who Really Loves You" was the prototype model; with its light, samba-like beat, it borrowed a page from the r&b axis of the Brill Building. Following success with imitation, Robinson (who would teach Wells the songs on the piano at the start of each session) cast her in a cool, seductive voice not dissimilar from his own. In the process he created Berry Gordy's first hit of 1962, Motown's first Top Ten hit ever (Gordy's previous hits had been on his Tamla label, and this was his *twenty-fourth* release on Motown), and Mary Wells' most successful record to date, peaking at #8. Following quickly was "You Beat Me To The Punch," cut from the same cloth, and it was a similar success topping at #9.

By this point, both Wells' onstage demeanor and voice was reflecting the emerging Motown-style polish. Before the year was out, Wells would again chart Top Ten on the strength of one of Robinson's most memorable compositions, "Two Lovers." Wells' voice was again so hoarse that "the words were barely coming out," but the record's lilting Latin-tinged groove was cast firmly in the mold of its predecessors. "Two Lovers" featured a set of Robinson's most captivating lyrics—it followed Berry Gordy's often repeated belief that "a song must tell a story." A tale of a woman in love with two lovers with polar personalities, the song as capped with a startling turn-around: both lovers were the two sides of one man's split personality. This twist made "Two Lovers" an R-rated thriller in an era of Top Forty bubble gum pop. Yet Robinson let the formula go on too long: the follow-up, "Laughing Boy," lost its momentum at #15 (no mean feat), but the next one, "Your Old Standby" failed to get past #40, not at all helped by the split air-play generated by the record's B-side, "What Love Has Joined Together."

It was at this point that the crack Holland-Dozier-Holland team stepped in. Like Smokey, Eddie Holland's relationship with Berry Gordy went back to Gordy's days as an independent producer; Berry had placed four singles he had produced on Holland with United Artists Records, while Gordy was making hits for Marv Johnson on that label. These 1959–60 recordings reveal the weaknesses Holland had as an artist—an excessive stylistic identification with others (in this case Jackie Wilson)—that he would later turn into strengths as a producer. Together with his brother, Brian Holland, and another artist–songwriter turned producer, Lamont Dozier, the trio turned into one of the most prominent hitmaking teams of the sixties. They became so adept at their craft that they would produce demos to be copied note-for-note by most of Motown's top artists.

At this juncture, the sound they were orchestrating melded equal parts of Phil Spector's wall of sound with tambourine shaking gospel fervor. They were successfully developing its use with Martha & The Vandellas, and had even nudged the charts with a no-hit group called The Supremes ("When The Love Light Shines"). The trio managed to interrupt Robinson's domination of Wells with their production of "You Lost The Sweetest Boy" (which, interestingly, included members of The Supremes and Temptations on backup vocals), and reached #22, but was hurt significantly by the air-play the flip-side received. This side, Smokey's "What's Easy For Two Is So Hard For One," actually reached #29 on its own, preventing either side from really breaking out.

Since her string of three Top Ten hits in 1962, Wells' next five chart placings had all failed to repeat those successes. Now almost five months since her last release had dropped off the charts, a new record was finally released. Gordy was tired of the series of mid-chart placings, and waited until he was sure he had a hit in hand. He went back to Smokey Robinson, who came up with "My Guy," a clear attempt to secure a niche for Wells in the pop market. "My Guy" had a light, slowly swinging groove—an arrangement that would not have seemed out of place with The Count Basie Band. The record shared a certain affinity with another nexus of the Brill Building crowd which was busy at that point redirecting former teen-idols into artists with adult appeal (i.e., Bobby Darin and his post-"Mack The Knife" material). "My Guy" was Mary Wells' greatest chart success for the label, and it became her first, and only, #1 record,

The amazing team of Brian Holland, Lamont Dozier, and Eddie Holland surrounded by their hit record awards.

nudging the red-hot Beatles from that coveted position. It was a monstrous hit, staying in the *Top Ten* for over two months.

Motown's wheels went into motion. After "My Guy," the label's very next release matched Mary with Marvin Gaye for a two-sided duet. Gaye had come to Motown when the label he was under contract to, Anna Records, was purchased by Berry Gordy. (That's one way to eliminate the competition.) An accomplished drummer, occasional piano player, and songwriter, Gaye had already scored hit after hit for Tamla with records like "Hitch-Hike," "Stubborn Kind Of Fella," "Pride And Joy," and "You're A Wonderful One." The match-up of the two hot artists resulted in "What's The Matter With You Baby," which reached #17, and "Once Upon A Time," which hit #19.

By this time Wells had become the reigning queen of rock 'n' roll; she was romanced by Jackie Wilson; idolized by The Beatles who took her on tour with them; and adored by fans on two continents. In mid-1964 she turned twenty-one, and it was time for her to renew the Motown contract she had signed when she was a minor. Wells had recently married a low-ranking Motown employee, Herman Griffin, once a former Motown artist produced by Berry Gordy. The urbane Griffin, like Gordy, was an adult in a community of teenagers, and it was not difficult for him to persuade Wells, who was already growing arrogant, that an offer of a five hundred thousand dollar advance for two years with a two-year option contract with Twentieth Century–Fox Records was more to her advantage than the measly 2.7 percent of retail (roughly three cents per record sold) that Motown was paying her in royalties.

The move was a disaster for Wells. Though Fox released numerous singles and several albums, none was able to come close to matching her previous successes on Motown. Her best charting was #34, and most of the rest barely clung to the bottom of the Top 100. Wells chooses her words carefully these days, but it's evident that she regrets her departure from Motown, even while harboring some bitterness regarding the circumstances that led to her move. She told a reporter that at the time of renegotiations with Gordy, she was "sensitive" and "hurt" about having information kept from her by the man who "helped raise me up." Be that as it may, while Wells refers to Gordy as a genius, there is a paragraph on the liner notes of her latest album dedicated to the inspirations of her career, and the name of Berry Gordy Jr. is most conspicuously absent.

By the same token, it appears too that Gordy was hurt by the departure of the woman whose rise to stardom he had created, and whose early hits had made Motown a viable force. Her abrupt departure must have been considered an embarrassment to Gordy in the music industry, and he vowed that other artists would not follow suit. Had this exit come sooner, it would have severely hurt the Motown operation, but coming as it did in 1964, the Motown assembly line was moving full speed ahead with an ever-growing roster of long-term hitmakers. Still other artists waited hopefully in the wings, and hit rhythm tracks already in the can, possibly for use by Mary Wells, would simply be utilized by others.

Mary Wells.

The Marvelettes were Motown's quintessential girl group. They were cute without being beautiful, innocent without being seductive, and vocally talented without being stylistically memorable. The group had two singers: Gladys Horton, who sang lead on most of the group's biggest hits; and Wanda Young, who sang lead on ballad-like flipsides such as "Forever," and occasional A-sides like "Don't Mess With Bill." Though careful listening does reveal the distinction between the vocal styles of the two—Horton was tougher—it is a measure so characteristic of the idiom that few people knew where Gladys left off and Wanda came in on their recording of "Locking Up My Heart." It is not terribly ironic, however, that the same innocent teenage qualities that made them so important to Motown's entry into the marketplace, also made them increasingly expendable in the face of Gordy's penultimate plans for Diana Ross as an adult solo attraction.

The Beatles visit Mary Wells backstage at a 1965 concert.

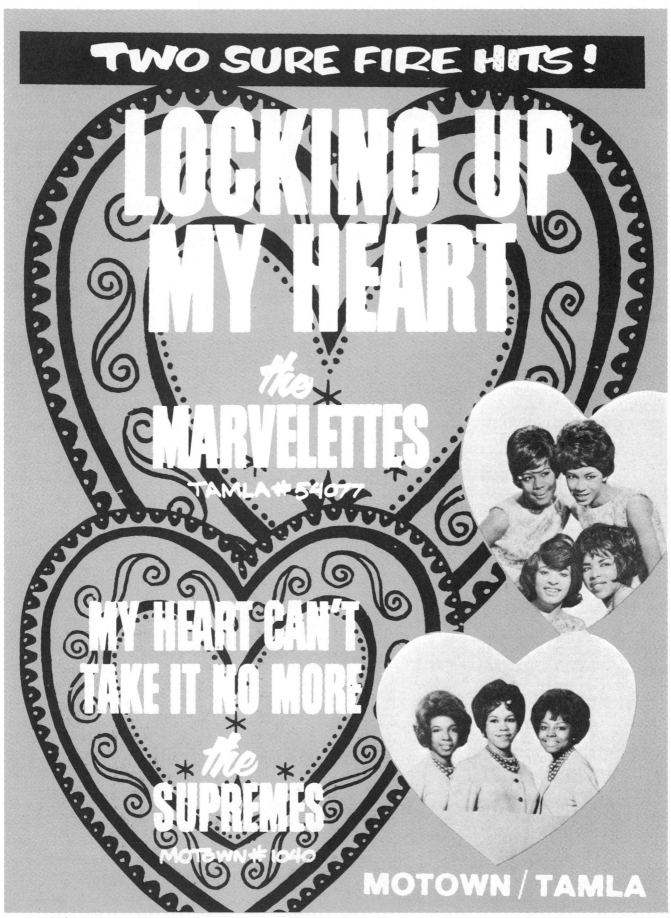

TWO SURE FIRE HITS!

LOCKING UP
MY HEART
the
MARVELETTES
TAMLA #54077

MY HEART CAN'T
TAKE IT NO MORE
the
SUPREMES
MOTOWN #1040

MOTOWN / TAMLA

The Marvelettes push their latest chart record, while an unknown group called The Supremes hope for their first hit.

Girl-group fever had barely hit Michigan when fifteen-year old Gladys Horton put together The Marvels in Inkster, Michigan, a tiny country suburb thirty miles outside of Detroit. With the exception of Wanda Young, who had just graduated and was considering a career in nursing, Horton and the other three group members, Katherine Anderson, Juanita Cowart, and Georgeanna Dobbins, were still students in Inkster High School. The impetus for starting the group was a school-sponsored talent contest, and the prize for the performers who placed in the top three positions was an audition with Tamla Records, the label in Detroit that was so hot with The Miracles. Rehearsing at Georgeanna's house, the group came up with an original song that got them no better than fourth place in the talent show. Still, the girls' teacher, Mrs. Sharpley, thought enough of their talent to include them among the auditioners for Tamla. As fate would have it, only The Marvels gained the approval of auditioner Robert Bateman, the man who had first auditioned Mary Wells.

While Bateman liked the group's rendition of The Chantel's "Maybe," he told them that nothing less than original material would be the key to their getting a deal. Overnight Dobbins wrote a ditty called "Please Mr. Postman." Only days later, the group—who had never performed as professionals—had a new name, The Marvelettes, courtesy of Berry Gordy, and found themselves in the Tamla/Motown studio. The session was an exciting one for the company. Although the song had

a simple doo-wop progression, it fit snugly into the imitation New Orleans, "Popeye" groove that was so popular at the label then, and the sheer youthful drive and exuberance of the group made the song notable in Motown history for the utter domination of the groove by vocalists. It was a great moment in Motown music, and everybody in the studio, from drummer Marvin Gaye up, felt that the record was a smash. It was. By November 1961, the *Billboard* charts listed "Please Mr. Postman" as the #1 pop record in the country, eclipsing the label's previous zenith, The Miracles' "Shop Around," which had hit the top spot some 8 months earlier. Gordy worked and worked on "Please Mr. Postman." After 4 weeks on the chart it started to fall off at #80, but then he pushed some more and took it to #30, where it began to drop off again. Another massive push sent it on its way to the top; its entire chart life was almost *six months,* long. Although doctor's orders forced both Georgeanna Dobbins and Juanita Cowart off the road, The Marvelettes carried on as a trio. The group's follow-up record, "Twistin' Postman," reached a barely respectable #34, but then they returned to the Top Ten with the "Postman" soundalike, "Playboy." The song, a Gladys Horton composition written in collaboration with Mickey Stevenson, Robert Bateman, and Brian Holland (whose writing and production work with The Marvelettes at this point was credited to the pseudonym Brianbert), reached the #7 position in June 1962.

On the heels of "Playboy" came another soundalike hit, "Beechwood 4-5789," which climbed to #17. The Marvelettes were now being put through the Motown star-making machine. They attended Motown's classes for choreography, voice, and charm. They were accompanied on the road by some of Motown's most experienced musicians, such as Andre Williams and Mickey Stevenson. Off the road they were rehearsed by Robert Bateman. Still, The Marvelettes were not to be Berry Gordy's entry to the white world. Even though the group was the hottest female act Motown had, neither of their first two albums featured the group's likeness on the cover, nor did a July 28 trade ad for "Beechwood 4-5789" sport a picture of the group. By contrast, the same ad showed a full, if doctored, shot of Mary Wells advertising "You Beat Me To The Punch," and, augering de-

A #1 record, and still no photo of the group on their releases.

The Marvelettes: Tamla's #1 girl group.

velopments to come, a photo of The Supremes —who had yet to chart at all—for their recording of "Your Heart Belongs To Me" (a record which did nothing to change their fortunes).

The Marvelettes had issued four records, and all had gone Top Forty, with two going Top Ten, but in early 1963, a precipitous slide would begin. The attention paid to the group seemed scattered. While most other favored groups at Motown worked with a set group of writers and producers, thereby developing a mutual understanding and craftsmanlike tailoring to each other's needs, The Marvelettes' songs were written by almost everyone on staff, and they were produced by William Stevenson, Brian Holland, Berry Gordy, Holland-Dozier, Smokey Robinson, Norman Whitfield, Freddie Gorman, Ivy Hunter, Clarence Paul, and others.

Following "Beechwood 4-5789" came "Strange I Know," which failed to crack the Top Forty. "Locking Up My Heart" only reached #44, and then a series of even less successful records was released: "Forever" (which featured an ingratiatingly tender lead vocal by Young, but only reached #78), "My Daddy Knows Best" (#67), "As Long As He's Mine" (#47), "He's A Good Guy" (#55), and "You're A Remedy" (#48). This painful slide lasted almost two years, and was particularly depressing for the group in the face of newfound and continuing success by many other Motown groups. In late 1964, the group bounced back somewhat with "Too Many Fish In The Sea," produced by Norman Whitfield, which reached #25, but with more attention to promotion it could have done even better. But new expectations for further success were squelched by the failures of "I'll Keep

Holding On," and "Danger Heartbreak Ahead," records that sounded like dress rehearsals for the tribal, marching-groove-sound perfected by Ivy Hunter, Hank Cosby, and Micky Stevenson on records like "Nowhere To Run" by Martha & The Vandellas, and "Uptight" by Stevie Wonder.

Even though "Too Many Fish . . ." sold records for The Marvelettes, group members still look back and second guess their choice of material. Wanda Young recalls that when "Lamont and Brian brought me 'Too Many Fish In The Sea,' they also brought me another tune. 'We want you to listen to this track,' they told me, 'and if you don't like it we'll give it to somebody else.' 'I don't like that tune at all' [she told them]. And when it was a hit," she remembers, "I could have kicked myself in the butt." The tune The Marvelettes rejected? "Baby Love."

The group's last fling with stardom came when they were assigned to Smokey Robinson for production. Even though he had deferred production of his own group, The Miracles, to the torrid team of Holland-Dozier-Holland (who expedited that group's re-entry to the charts with "Goin' To A-Go-Go"), Robinson proved once again that he had a unique ability to write and produce hits for women. Though Robinson's previous efforts with The Marvelettes included second-rate "Postman" imitations like "Paper Boy," he restored the group to the Top Ten for the first time in four agonizing years with "Don't Mess With Bill." The record had a slow, lightly swinging groove, accented by a bluesy Ray Charles-like organ, which effectively framed the bittersweet vocals of Wanda Young. With its "keep your hands off my baby" message, it seemed perfectly in sync with the girl-group ethos, but the soundalike follow-up, "You're The One," failed to breathe life into what was fast becoming an old form, and stopped dead at #48.

In 1967, Robinson's next production gave the group another hit, whose chart success they would not again eclipse. "The Hunter Gets Captured By The Game" climbed to the #13 position on the strength of some of Robinson's most cleverly metaphoric lyrics, which were layered on top of another lilting, bluesy groove. But though the group flirted with the Top Twenty through early 1968 with tunes like "When You're Young & In Love" (#23) and "My Baby Must Be A Magician" (#17), the group's career had lost its impetus. Once in the vanguard of Motown's hitmakers and America's musical trendsetters, the group had simply become another cog in the Motown wheel. Their career seemed vastly less important to the company's power structure than those of many others.

In 1969, two event conspired to effectively end the ostensible existence of The Marvelettes: first, Gladys Horton, the group's leader and main vocalist, left the group to get married and raise a family, and was replaced by Anne Bogan, who lacked her distinctive sound; and Wanda Young, who nominally became leader of the group, chose not to move to Los Angeles, isolating her from the mainstream of the company. She recorded a final album for the label, *The Return Of The Marvelettes*, using anonymous background singers, while two unidentified women veiled in mist posed for the cover alongside her. Gradually she, too, became estranged from the company, leaving The Marvelettes to share the fate of groups like The Drifters. Their memory and legacy were left to hastily put-together clones. It would be these outfits that would artificially perpetuate what had become an important, if faceless, legacy.

The Marvelettes: the name remained the same, but the faces changed.

69

Chapter FIVE

SOUTH STREET

45 RPM

THE GIRL-GROUP SOUND WAS primarily based in and around New York, because as a writer/producer medium, most of the well-connected writers, arrangers, producers, musicians, and studios were to be found there. Eventually, girl-group records were made in every city and town in America, but the most significant contributions (with the possible exception of Motown, which was a world unto itself), came from New York.

An adjunct to the New York scene, however, was that of Philadelphia; it became a secondary, though short-lived, focal point for several reasons. For one, major record distributors could rent the huge warehouse space they needed much more cheaply there than in New York, still only be ninety minutes away, and several even chose to base their own recording operations there. Secondly, as a continual black r&b stronghold, there was much promising talent around—talent that wouldn't be found by the New York Brill Building crowd. Most importantly, however, was Dick Clark's *American Bandstand*, whose daily telecasts

offered tremendous exposure for records and performers, and could literally make hits overnight.

The Philadelphia sound and *American Bandstand* in particular are probably best remembered for the teen-idols: Fabian, Frankie Avalon, Bobby Rydell, and their legion of imitators, but Philadelphia was also the home of some great soul artists during this same period: The Intruders, Spinners, Garnett Mimms, Patti Labelle and The Blue-Belles, O'Jays, Solomon Burke, Stylistics, Three Degrees, and Tymes. Philadelphia also offered up for mass public consumption a variety of acts like Danny and The Juniors, Len Barry and The Dovells, Freddy Cannon, Zacherle, and perhaps America's only black teen-idol, Chubby Checker. There were brilliant writers and producers who spent years working almost exclusively with Philadelphia acts and labels, including Thom Bell, Richard Barrett, Leon Huff, Bunny Sigler, Jerry Ragovoy, and Kenny Gamble. Most of these craftsmen worked in the soul idiom, many with their own labels, but it was left to the blander, more pop-oriented labels to achieve lasting national success. These were Cameo-Parkway, Chancellor, Jamie-Guyden, and Swan, and perhaps not surprisingly, Dick Clark, at one time or another, had some financial interest in each one of these operations. These labels made the biggest splash outside of New York with the girl-group sound.

The first star to rise was Dee Dee Sharp, born Dione LaRue on September 9, 1945. Dee Dee had sung in her grandfather's church choir and showed a flair for the piano at an early age. While in high school, she and two friends cut some demos, not as a group per se, but just to showcase their background singing and Dee Dee's piano playing. This ultimately led to work at Cameo-Parkway Records, Philadelphia's highly successful independent label complex.

Cameo, joined shortly by Parkway, was formed in 1957 by Bernie Lowe, a piano player and songwriter. He was quickly joined by songwriter Kal Mann, and Dave Appell, a musician and composer whose own band Dave Appell & The Appeljacks had scored some early instrumental hits, helping in the process to firmly establish Cameo as a national label force. The company was kept going with hits by The Rays (''Silhouettes'') and Charlie Gracie (''Butterfly''), but really broke open with Bobby Rydell, who scored a dozen Top Twenty hits between 1959 and 1962. Parkway was activated in 1960, and with Chubby Checker leading the way (aided by The Dovells and The Tymes) it was immediately successful. In his first two and a half years at Parkway, Checker had almost twenty chart records, with half of those reaching the Top Ten. In February 1962 Checker released a song called ''Slow Twistin','' which featured a duet with an uncredited Dee Dee Sharp. Within three weeks Checker's recording had jumped into the Top Ten, and Dee Dee Sharp's own Cameo debut was rush-released. This was not only because Cameo sought to capitalize on Dee Dee's massive exposure and acceptance via Chubby Checker's release, but also because Chicago's Checker Records (no relation) was putting a heavy push on one of their new releases, ''Mashed Potatoes,'' by Steve

Alaimo. Dee Dee's ''Mashed Potato Time'' was recorded the same day she sang the duet with Checker on ''Slow Twistin'.'' ''Slow'' was cut at four in the afternoon, then Chubby left and Dee Dee went out for dinner, returning at seven to cut her debut recording. There was probably only room for one ''mashed potatoes'' dance hit on the charts, and Cameo vowed that theirs would be the one.

''Mashed Potato Time'' was one of those classic concoctions that virtually leapt out of the radio and propelled listeners into immediate motion. Like ''The Locomotion'' (which took its cues from ''Mashed''), it was simple and rough, but as melodic and memorable as one could hope for. It would have been a hit regardless, but the day after Dee Dee drove crosstown and performed the song on *American Bandstand*, also sharing the floor for dance demonstrations with the *Bandstand* regulars, it simply skyrocketed. (These were the days when the *Bandstand* kids created steps, and records would be written around the existing moves, whereas later dances were manufactured on vinyl before

any such dance actually existed.) "Mashed Potato Time" took only six weeks to reach the Top Ten, and then stayed in the Top Three for almost two months. A truly monstrous record, it remained on the charts for over four months. Somehow it failed to reach #1 in *Billboard*'s Pop charts (it topped at #2—first kept out of the coveted spot by The Shirelles' "Soldier Boy," and then by Ray Charles' "I Can't Stop Loving You"). On the r&b charts the situation was reversed, with Dee Dee clinging to #1 for a full month. This was Dee Dee Sharp's first record, and she was all of 16 and a half the day it hit #2.

Unfortunately, the Cameo-Parkway complex had such short-sighted vision that they had Dee Dee repeatedly churn out one imitation after another of her debut hit. It's to the supreme credit of the original, Dee Dee's winning vocals, and Cameo's promotion that the next three follow-ups, "Gravy," "Ride," and "Do The Bird" all reached the Top Ten (spots 9, 5, and 10 respectively), but then the speeding train suddenly screeched to a halt. Dee Dee was cast as a maker of dance-craze hits, and was never able to break out of the mold. She frequently shared records, shows, and themes with Chubby Checker, but when the repetition became too wearing, and the dance crazes were manufactured like an unending series of bland breakfast cereals, the public got fed up. There were the dances (twist, fly, pony, popeye, and their innumerable variations), followed by the themes ("concept" albums were still a few years away), like calypso and limbo, traditional folk, spirituals, and classic standards, and each one appeared more desperate than the last. In her first eighteen months at Cameo, the company issued no less than six albums by Dee Dee, and she was also featured prominently on several other albums shared with Chubby Checker and various other Cameo hitmakers. This flood of vinyl, and the conflicting patterns of unrelentless imitation on one hand, and the widely disparate choice of album themes on the other, virtually washed away what could have been a promising career. Cameo's philosophy tried to make Dee Dee's singles appeal to the "teen market," while her albums were aimed at the "grownups." This tactic can rarely succeed, and in Dee Dee's case caused her Top Forty following to vanish—while her adult following never materialized.

Dee Dee possessed a strong emotional voice, and her live performances were animated and appealing. She was well-received on her tours of England, was a perennial star on the Dick Clark "Caravan" tours, and these live performances were well paced to show depth, avoiding the scattershot approach of her disjointed releases. A typical set on a package tour would have her open with "Twist And Shout" to get the audience going, knock 'em out with "Do The Bird" and "Wild" (her final Top Forty hit), and then have everyone sing along to "Rock Me In The Cradle Of Love." Then she'd throw in a popular girl-group cover of the day like "Da Doo Ron Ron," perform "Mashed Potato Time," and close with an emotional version of "Stand By Me." The crowd got their money's worth, and more.

Parkway Records

Dee-Dee Sharp
NATIONAL FAN CLUB
1405 LOCUST STREET • PHILADELPHIA 2, PA.

Personal Managers — HENRY COLT • KAL MANN

Dee Dee Sharp with her mom.

Cameo's other successful entry in the girl-group sweepstakes was The Orlons, actually a trio of girls, Marlena Davis, Rosetta Hightower, and Shirley Brickley, and a single male, Steve Caldwell. The original Orlons were a quintet of females who formed in junior high school, and then sang together for several years before going their separate ways. Shirley Brickley was then approached by a neighbor, Steve Caldwell, who wanted to start a professional group, and two "original" Orlons, Marlena and Rosetta, rejoined to complete the lineup. They were found about a year later by former schoolmate and then-current Parkway hit-maker Len Barry of The Dovells. He brought them to the label, where they not only sang backup on recordings by Dee Dee Sharp and Bobby Rydell, but also landed a recording contract of their own. Their first two releases, issued in late 1961 and early 1962, failed to chart, but the third, "Wah-Wahtusi," was a huge smash. (Watusi fans will remember that The Vibrations had paved the way for The Orlons a year earlier with their Top Thirty hit, "The Watusi.") "Wah Wahtusi" hit #2, "Don't Hang Up" then reached #4, and "South Street" then topped at #3. In less than eight months, The Orlons had released three singles and each had solidly broken into the Top Five. Chart-wise, the group was as successful as any of the competition during 1962 and early 1963.

All of The Orlons' hits were written by Kal Mann and Dave Appell. Mann and Appell also wrote some of Dee Dee Sharp's material, but most of Sharp's songs came from the pen of second-line Cameo writers, Jon Sheldon and Dave Leon. Whereas Sheldon and Leon had failed to do justice by Dee Dee Sharp, Mann and Appell outdid themselves with The Orlons. The first three Orlons hits were visual playlets, not as extreme as Leiber & Stoller's creations with The Coasters, but nonetheless full of spirit, wit, and an honest, shared-experience ring to them. They were street-wise and teenage foolish at the same time.

In addition, the inclusion of Steve Caldwell gave the group the opportunity to vary the overall sound from record to record, and the vocal interplay between Caldwell and the trio soon became an integral part of their appeal. (This is certainly a sub-genre of girl groups to be taken seriously, for along with The Orlons came The Raindrops, Exciters, and Bob B. Soxx and The Blue Jeans, each with a male playing a secondary, but significant role in the overall sound.) Besides the built-in sound and hook appeal to the ear, the records themselves could be bought by more people.

Girl-group records to this point had been purchased mainly by girls who could relate to the limitless variations of love themes of one sort or another offered up lyrically, and could also sing along with the girl or group in question—thereby fusing total unity between the music and its transfixed listener. Guys, however, couldn't sing along very seriously to "Soldier Boy," "It's My Party," or "My Guy" (although their current popularity in most bars along Christopher Street, for example, might make for critical-musical revisionism worthy of serious socio-sexual scientific study.) No, guys had to sing along with the like of Dion and "Runaround Sue," The Four Seasons' "Sherry," and Gene Chandler's "Duke Of Earl." But on The Orlons' records, the girls had a part, and so did the guys. Walking down the halls in school the girls would be singing "don't hang up" to themselves, and the guys would be singing "oh no" to themselves, and that's all they knew. The girls never sang or even realized there was a guy's part; and the guys were oblivious to the female vocals. Here then (at least as far as the record companies were concerned) was the ultimate: a record that

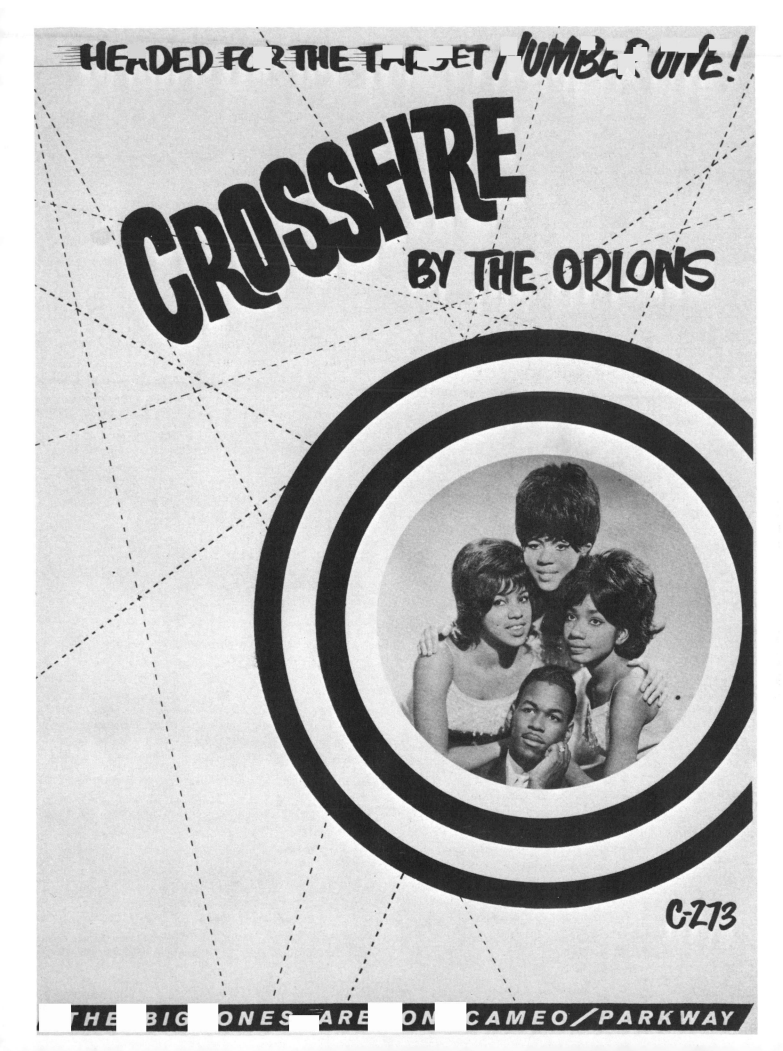

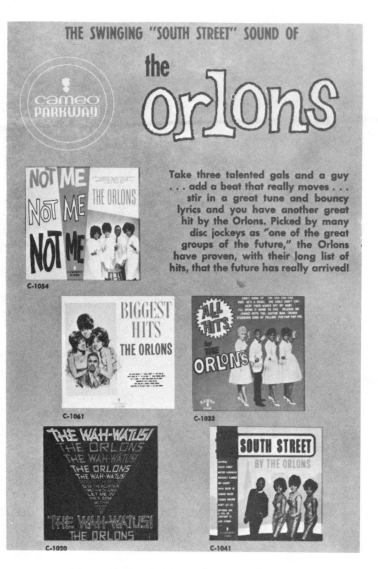

something layered across the top to keep you going. On their albums they chose popular songs of the day to cover, and they chose wisely. Sprinkled between their hits were songs by Goffin–King, Phil Spector, Marvin Gaye and Sam Cooke. (An obscure Orlons B-side, "Don't Throw Your Love Away," was later recorded by The Searchers, who took it to #1 in England.) The backing tracks on some of their album cuts, most notably "Chains" and "Keep Your Hands Off My Baby," are virtually indistinguishable from the originals, and might very well be Goffin and King's Cookies' backing tracks with the addition of slight variations. The Orlons' name was inspired by the new wonder fabric of the day which went by the same name. The trick also worked well for The Chiffons, but The Rayons and Nylons didn't wear quite as well with the public.

could captivate both males and females, without anyone knowing why, or even recognizing that it was happening. It wasn't studied, marketed, manufactured, researched, pre-sold, targeted, or labeled. It just happened. And that's what made it so much fun and naturally appealing. (Speaking of marketing, archivists of musical minutiae might note that Dee Dee Sharp had her own logo, two "flats" for her "D's", and a "sharp" for her "S". This could well have marked the birth of the important rock 'n' roll logo concept, now such a widely accepted and integral part of modern music. Dee Dee's was beautiful, brilliant, and quite literally, perfect. Merely one of the first and also the best.)

Musically, The Orlons' records were all drums and saxophones. There was some loose percussion, a tinny tambourine, or sloppy handclaps; always

One aspect of an interesting, if not unique group, is the fact that although they may have huge hits, their material is never covered or successfully revived. The re-recordings and continually popular success of songs like "Be My Baby," "The Locomotion," "Will You Still Love Me Tomorrow," and "Da Doo Ron Ron" makes the vinyl creations of The Orlons even more impressive. They achieved a unified totality that transcended a "good song." It was this song, this singer, this band, this studio, this production, and this one day in history that brought it all together— trying to recreate or surpass that moment would be sheer folly and doomed to utter failure. A case in point may be made for Philadelphia's other incomparable contribution to the girl group legacy, Claudine Clark's "Party Lights."

Claudine Clark was somewhat of an anomaly in the world of girl groups, often a hit-making world of the young, the naive and the inexperienced. Born in Macon, Georgia, she showed great talent on both the guitar and organ as a youngster, and after completing high school won a music scholarship to Coombs College in Philadelphia. There she not only became proficient on her instruments, but also gained valuable training in music theory and composition. After getting her degree in musical composition, she made two singles, one for Herald and one for Gotham, but nothing happened. She then came to the attention of Chancellor Records (home of Frankie Avalon and Fabian), who put her into the studio, hoping to use her talents and background as a springboard for a "serious" pop music career. The recording session was based around a ballad called "Disappointed," and the recording, arranged by Jerry Ragovoy, turned into a strong, emotional performance. Issued in May 1962, it appeared shortly thereafter to be a commercial failure, but then a deejay played the flip-side and got a strong listener reaction. By mid-June, the Chancellor promotion staff began pushing that B-side in earnest and on June 30, 1962, "Party Lights" entered the charts at #95. It began a long climb upwards, forging a trail that was somewhat unnatural by 1962 standards. One week it would jump fifteen points and be bulleted, and the next week it would move two or three points without a bullet. It took only a month to move from #95 to #32, which was quite good, but then took 6 weeks until it peaked a #5. For a hot record bulleted at

#32 to only average a 4 or 5-point gain each week for 6 weeks until reaching its peak is a strange course of events, but the record showed continued strength in its early markets, and could only pick up 1 or 2 new markets each week. Usually this kind of national impact happened much more quickly in those days, but for "Party Lights" it was a long, dedicated struggle.

"Party Lights," recorded quickly as a B-side to the intricately arranged and produced "Disappointed," benefits from the obvious looseness and spontaneity of the recording session. It kicks off with a solid drum roll and takes it from there, with an emotional Claudine lamenting her fate of being excluded from a party where all her friends are busy dancing the night away. Everyone is there but "momma just won't let me make the scene." Not only was the theme universal, but the music drove on relentlessly. Even if you couldn't get to *their* party, you could at least play the record at home and make your own party. It was a small consolation, to be sure, and even Claudine wails at the fade, "I wanna go, I wanna go, I wanna go." "Party Lights" was similar in construction to "The Locomotion" and "Mashed Potato Time," but as far as spontaneity, intensity and atmosphere go, "Party Lights" remains the greatest of them all.

To capitalize on the success of the single, Chancellor rushed out an album that was based almost entirely on the "party" theme. Besides "Party Lights," the album included "What Kind Of Party," "Party Time," "Havin' A Party," "Dancin' Party" and several others which played up every conceivable angle of the party motif. More interesting was the fact that Claudine Clark not only wrote "Party Lights," but also wrote three other songs on the album. Self-composed material by vocalists working in the girl-group genre was almost unheard of. Claudine also began preparing for appearances in legitimate plays, and also composed a rock 'n' roll operetta. The future looked bright indeed, but suddenly the glow dimmed markedly.

"Party Lights" had run its course by the end of September, and a follow-up to the Top Five debut should have been issued at that time. For some reason, Claudine Clark's follow-up was not released until mid-November, and when it did come out, deejays across the country were shocked to see its

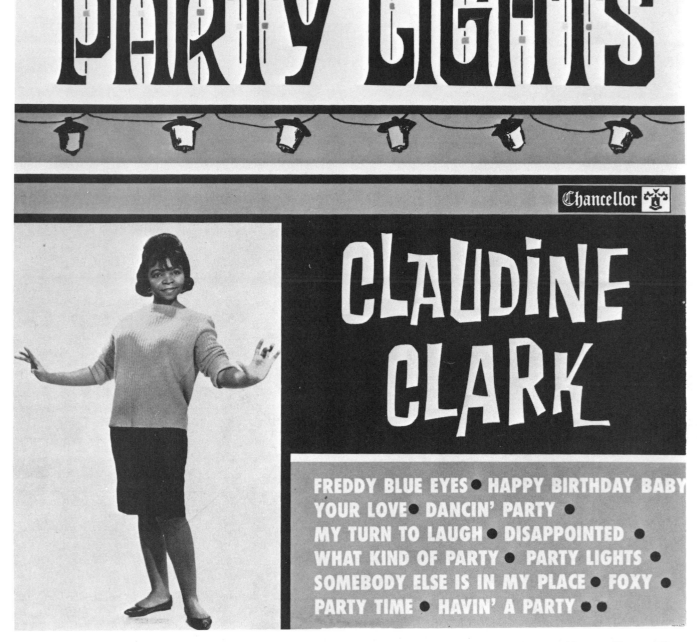

PARTY LIGHTS

Chancellor

CLAUDINE CLARK

FREDDY BLUE EYES • HAPPY BIRTHDAY BABY
YOUR LOVE • DANCIN' PARTY •
MY TURN TO LAUGH • DISAPPOINTED •
WHAT KIND OF PARTY • PARTY LIGHTS •
SOMEBODY ELSE IS IN MY PLACE • FOXY •
PARTY TIME • HAVIN' A PARTY ••

title—"Walkin' Through a Cemetery." Being upset about not going to a party is one thing, but walking through a cemetery is an entirely different matter. Could you reasonably picture any Top Forty deejay saying: "Yeah, that was The Four Seasons' latest and greatest 'Walk Like A Man,' and now the new one from that 'Party Lights' girl, Claudine Clark, 'Walkin' Through a Cemetery?'" No chance whatsoever, and the record was quickly laid to rest, failing even to *bubble under* the Top 100. A few months went by, and Chancellor tried to resurrect the initial formula with a song called "Walk Me Home (From The Party)," but Claudine's long-term absence from the charts, together with Lesley Gore's huge hit with "It's My Party," all but buried Claudine Clark's attempted comeback. It turned out to be her last record for Chancellor. She then went over to Philadelphia's Swan Records where she recorded under the name Joy Dawn, and next issued two final singles under her own name for TCF and Jamie Records. Claudine Clark may be a glaring example of a "one-hit wonder," but "Party Lights" should not be forgotten.

Philadelphia contributed other minor hits to the girl-group legacy, and these, more often than not, were more in the newly-emerging soul idiom; perhaps that's why they were not so widely accepted at the time. Cameo's Candy & The Kisses took a dance–rock composition of Kenny Gamble and Jerry Ross called "The 81" into the Top Fifty, and The Sapphires (produced by Jerry Ross and Joe Renzetti) reached #25 with "Who Do You Love" on Swan. Patti & The Emblems went Top Forty with "Mixed Up, Shook Up, Girl," and Little Joe Cook corraled his two daughters and two of their girlfriends into the studio as The Sherrys. Their biggest hit, "Pop Pop Pop Pie" reached #35, and despite heavy promotion they failed to build upon their initial success. Yvonne Baker and The Sensations, a Philadelphia group licensed to a Chess subsidiary, Argo, went all the way to #4 with "Let Me In," but numerous follow-ups for several labels went nowhere. The Blue-Belles (featuring Patti La Belle) took their wildly energetic "I Sold My Heart To The Junkman" to #15 for the fledgling Newton label, but although they continued to be popular on the r&b charts and in clubs, their Top Forty success was not repeated.

Meanwhile, back at Cameo-Parkway The Orlons and Dee Dee Sharp tried to make their sound more progressive by moving into the soul and Motown-influenced idioms, and working with Kenny Gamble, Jerry Ross, Thom Bell, and Leon Huff, chartwise at least, the efforts were fruitless. In mid-1964 Cameo was sold to record distributor Alfred Rosenthal, who moved Cameo's main office to New York, and actively pursued new British recordings in the wake of the on-going British Invasion. The girl groups (and for that matter most of the other Cameo-Parkway acts) were left to their own designs, and soon cast aside as has-beens.

Part of the problem was the obvious lack of support from their respective record companies, as well as the writers' and producers' constantly changing interests and priorities. But it was also a matter of mismanagement—a kind of mismanagement by omission, where you took what you could get when it came along, and any kind of image-making, publicity, or career planning was simply regarded as unnecessary work details that provided no concrete, immediate returns.

For most girl groups there was no such thing as a career build-up. In many cases, the group was only as important as their last record. Even worse was the understanding that "Hey, kid, there's plenty more out there waiting to take your place. If you don't like it, why don't you leave?" Most managers handled several acts at once, some upwards of a dozen. More often than not, the group's "manager" was also their producer or someone who worked for their record label. With this kind of set-up, the manager could not only control what the artist did, but also get another 20 percent of the performer's earnings—after the manager's "expenses" were reimbursed, of course. Some managers and record companies actually sought to keep the girls *out* of the public eye, and there were many reasons to rationalize that tactic.

For one, many girl groups were composed of session singers who did not want to go out on the road or appear on local TV shows. They were happier and more financially secure doing vocal ses-

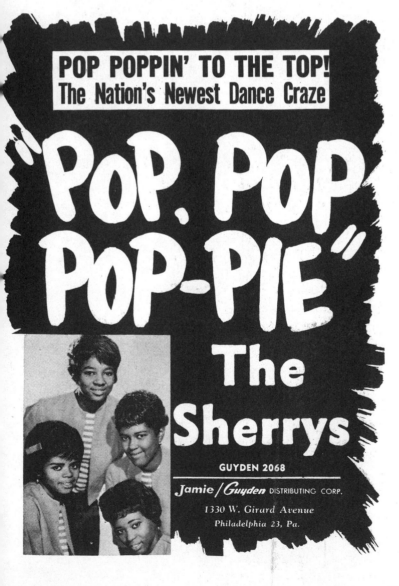

sions, whether as artists themselves or as backup vocalists on other records. Perhaps the girl group was not poised enough to perform live in front of thousands of people, or not strong enough to stand up to a grueling series of one-nighters strung out across the country. Perhaps they were in school and too young to travel. Perhaps they weren't "pretty" enough. Perhaps they were too "sexy." Perhaps they'd get married and leave show business. Perhaps they'd get pregnant. If the group's pictures weren't planted in every teen magazine in America, who'd be the wiser when two or three other girls took their places on the road? Some managers felt that the image or fantasy that record buyers visualized when they heard a specific record would be shattered when they saw the genuine article. And since most of the girl groups were black, teenagers would fail to identify with the performer, or more likely be brought back to a realistic world of black and white, a world of problems that most teenage record buyers were trying to escape from. No, managers figured, a record has no color—it's not black or white, and it's much safer to keep it that way.

While most male artists received intense publicity build-ups, girl groups rarely had press photos available. Images for male stars' albums were carefully conceived and executed, while girl groups did one quick session which would sometimes even suffice for their entire career. Pat Bennett of The Chiffons said: "For our LPs, they took us to the cheapest place in town to get our pictures taken. Pictures on record covers usually make you look better than you really look. Ours made us look like something out of the *National Enquirer*." The sheet music for "He's So Fine," for example, features an out-of-focus photo of The Chiffons that looks like it was taken in a Broadway photo booth and then blown up to size. Groups with five members would have cover shots with only three girls, and vice versa. Whatever was available at the time was usually used, despite the fact that it was often hopelessly outdated.

The powerful teen magazines did little to help matters either. Most of their covers and pages were filled with "teen-idols" like Fabian, Frankie or Bobby. Elvis was still a favorite for years after his chart popularity had waned. They were all featured in issue after issue, month after month, page after page. Any guy with a pompadour, or "a

look" could always get a "new star on the horizon" story, which would not only plug his likes and dislikes (Likes: shy girls with a sense of humor. Dislikes: parents who don't understand teenagers. . . .), but also his latest record and personal appearances as well. Teen magazines prospered on the theory that girls (who were the ones that bought them—guys bought *Mad* and car magazines) wanted to see big, hunky dreamboats, and not be confronted with threatening female competition. The only females who got any coverage at all were squeaky clean girls like Annette and Shelley Fabares, who were already known via television or movie exposure. But *their* role was to be as safe and reassuring as possible—with stories like "How to get the guy of your dreams," "Makeup tips for parties," and "My first love." Black artists of any gender, though highly successful on the charts, would rarely be featured, and girls in particular were just about banned altogether.

The competition to get steady and heavy coverage in teen magazines was fierce, and some publications would demand exclusives, prizes for readers, or other favors for featuring such and such an artist. (Occasionally these favors went so far as to include an under-the-table share of artist's royalties, or an outright upfront payment.)

The Blue-Belles, with Patti Labelle (upper right).

ZOW! **DION** COLOR PICS *tuesday*

25¢
AUG

Hi-TEEN

DION:
"HEY I'M
AN ACTOR"

★ THE ☆
STAR
MAKERS
☆
"They Made Me What I Am"

ANITA,
"Really Big" Ed
and **Hi-TEEN**

"JOEY DEE
CHOSE ME"
Jeri Lynne Fraser

MAKE DOWN
and
YOU!

BICYCLE
HOP!
Hi-TEEN
Hopsters
SWING OUT!

TONY ORLANDO
Song of Courage

Hi-Teen magazine. The early issues were little more than pro-Aldon propaganda handouts.

What to do if you couldn't get into the magazines posed a problem for many, and there were often unique solutions. Don Kirshner's Aldon complex, for example, helped get a new national teen magazine, *Hi-Teen* (later called *Teen Scene*) off the ground. *Hi-Teen's* first issue (cover date: August 1962), featured a full color cover shot and inside feature on "skyrocketing recording star" Tony Orlando, and also carried Tony's monthly column "Just Between Us." "Just Between Us" consisted primarily of news and pictures of Aldon artists, songwriters, producers, and other artists who had just recorded Aldon-published songs. (By the way, Tony O. was an Aldon artist.) There was also a feature on Aldon artist Tina Robin ("Miss TnT—Tiny 'n' Terrific" . . .), as well as Tina's own Hollywood gossip column, which ran in each issue. Finally, there was a three-page feature called: "The Starmakers: Nevins and Kirshner," which praised in-depth the entire Aldon operation, and ran photos of Carole King, Neil Sedaka,

Bobby Darin, Connie Francis, Tina Robin, Don Kirshner, Al Nevins, and even Aldon's "artist manager" Emil La Viola. Subsequent issues continued in this fashion, and even Aldon songwriters like Howard Greenfield had their own columns. When Aldon and Dimension were bought by Screen Gems in April 1963, however, the need for such exposure ceased to be a priority.

American Bandstand was the most open forum for girl-group performers, as managers realized that this appearance would plug the *record* more than the group, and other local TV dance shows were used as well. But there was a distinct lack of exposure for girl groups on the numerous prime-time variety shows which would always find room to feature male performers from every rung of the show business ladder. These were shows that would offer exposure that could make a performer more of a household name, broaden their audience, lead to better bookings, and basically legitimize an artist's existence and career. During the height of the girl-group sound's popularity on the charts (1960–1964), *The Ed Sullivan Show*, for example, featured regular performances by all kinds of male rock and roll groups, including The Everly Brothers, Jackie Wilson, Ray Charles, Gary U.S. Bonds, and The Four Seasons. Lesser chart successes like Bill Black's Combo, Mike Clifford (twice), and Cliff Richard (three times) also appeared. But during the entire four-year period, only two singers even vaguely associated with the girl-group sound, Linda Scott and Lesley Gore—both solo white artists—performed. Not a single girl group appeared on the show until October 1965, when The Supremes made their debut—and this only after the group had notched 5 #1 singles in a row!

The film industry, which churned out dozens of teen-oriented music-related films during the period, was just as "selective." Many solo male recording artists like Elvis Presley, Fabian, Frankie Avalon, Chubby Checker, Duane Eddy, Bobby Rydell and Paul Anka were featured actors in numerous films, and even male groups had speaking parts in films and television shows. Almost uniformly, however, the girl groups merely performed a song in the film and were gone. Plug the record, plug the sound, and disappear. The guys usually appeared in the bigger budget films, and the girls were thrown in at the last minute on quickie low-budget productions like *Beach Ball* (Supremes); *Bikini Beach* (Exciters); *Disk-O-Tek Holiday* (Chiffons); *Don't Knock The Twist* (Dee Dee Sharp); and *It's A Bikini World* (The Toys). Trying to find decent footage or print material on girl groups from this period is next to impossible, while scrapbooks on Fabian, for example (who actually only had five Top Thirty hits) could fill up a warehouse.

Public exposure for the girl groups was extremely minimal, hindered *sometimes* by the choices of the girls themselves, *usually* by their manager's lack of vision and conflicting interests, and *almost always* by society's own inbred and institutionalized exclusion of blacks—and girl-group performers in particular—from the mainstream mass media.

A rare girl-group theme issue published in early 1965 when the sound was already disappearing from the charts.

Chapter SIX

CHAPEL OF LOVE

YOU KNOW, ONE THING THAT was really true back then," declares Ellie Greenwich, "is that if you were an artist or a songwriter, and you had something to offer, you would get heard. If it was good, you'd get your shot. You might not make it, but at least you'd get your shot. . . ." Offering credence to that observation is Ellie's own career, a tale of talent that did indeed get heard.

Born in Brooklyn in 1940, Ellie Greenwich moved with her family to Levittown, Long Island in 1951, and she grew up there, listening to the radio endlessly, and attending every high school dance in sight. She was always interested in music, ("as far back as I can remember"), but her parents only let her play the accordian at home. After two years of nagging, her parents finally bought her a piano, and Ellie would play for hours at a time, learning by trial and error. She entered Queens College as a music major and then switched over to Hofstra University where she studied Psychology, English, and Education. An owner of a Hicksville record store took an interest in her, and through

his music business connections got her a record deal with RCA. Her lone RCA single, issued in 1958, consisted of two pleasantly harmless compositions, but Ellie Gaye's (as she was known on the record) recording career went no further. "I didn't want to use Greenwich because it was always being mispronounced. Besides, I didn't even think you could use your own name—I thought if you were in show business, you had to change it. I wanted to keep 'Ellie' because I thought it was cute, and had heard of a singer called Barbara Gay, so I kept the 'G' for Greenwich and made it 'Gaye.' I didn't know what it meant at the time, unfortunately."

Through the family grapevine she soon heard about one Jeff Barry, a cousin of her aunt, and they met one night at a dinner party. They spent the night talking about music, since Jeff was also a young recording artist and hustling songwriter. In fact, while trying to grab a recording contract for himself, the prospective label turned down Jeff Barry the artist, but bought the song he was singing. Ellie: "He told me that he had just written a song for Ray Peterson which was going to be a big smash. It turned out to be 'Tell Laura I Love Her,' and it was a huge hit."

Jeff and Ellie's friendship grew and soon Ellie was traveling into New York after school to cut demos of Jeff's songs. She remembers: "I would get my fifteen dollars and rush back home. I was really so excited." Jeff was making some headway as a songwriter, first with E.B. Marks Music and then in March of 1961 when he went on staff at the up-and-coming Trinity Music. From 1960 to

1962, Barry wrote an endless stream of songs, with almost a hundred of them finding their way on to record. Hardly any were hits, but Barry was learning his craft, writing, producing, arranging, cutting demos, and making connections. He worked with a wide variety of collaborators, most often Ben Raleigh, Beverly Ross, Artie Resnick, and Tony Powers.

Ellie, meanwhile, had graduated from college in January 1961, and began teaching high school but left after three and a half weeks to pursue a music business career. She recalls: "My parents had mixed feelings about this turn of events, but I was determined to give it a shot." Jeff and Ellie were dating seriously and planning to get married, but Ellie refused to get into the business on Jeff's coattails: "I wanted to do it on my own, or not at all. I just didn't want to be his wife, other half, or appendage. . . ." One day she had an appointment with John Gluck Jr. to play some songs and she met him at The Brill Building, Room 902. Ellie: "John had to leave to go do a demo and said he'd be back in a hour or so. So I just sat there playing the piano, and in walks this guy and says, 'Hi Carole'—he was expecting to see Carole King and listen to some of *her* material. When he saw I wasn't Carole he asked who I was and I told him, and I played him some songs, and he said they were 'interesting' and that I should come up and visit whenever I felt like it, to write or whatever. He said his name was Jerry Leiber and he introduced me to his partner Mike Stoller. I didn't know who they were, and then when I got home I

saw their name on one of my records, and then another, and another. All of these great records by The Coasters and Drifters, and Leiber & Stoller and Carole King. I couldn't believe it. I just started running around the house screaming."

Ellie continued to go up to the Brill Building and began to collaborate with a series of writers, including Ben Raleigh, Mark Barkan, John Gluck Jr., and most frequently, Tony Powers. Ellie was free-lancing in this manner for about a year and a half but the crazy pace just got to be too much: "We used to write songs in the morning, then record a demo and go around playing it for different people later in the day. Sometimes we'd just go into their offices and sing it for them. If they liked it, they'd pay for an hour or hour and a half at a demo studio, usually Associated or Dick Charles Recording, and we'd go cut it. If we sold the song we'd get an advance, usually something like thirty-five or fifty dollars—maybe seventy-five or a hundred dollars, if you were really lucky—and then we'd go back and write some more. But it was just too hectic after awhile. I just couldn't relate to

CHAPEL OF LOVE

45 RPM

Chapter SIX

having to write on schedule at a certain time with a certain person. I just decided I needed a place to call home. . . .'' So she signed on with Leiber & Stoller's Trio Music for a salary of seventy-five dollars a week, even though Hill and Range Music had offered her three hundred dollars. ''I just figured I could learn a lot more from Leiber & Stoller.''

At Trio Music she worked mainly with Tony Powers, and one of their first successes was with a group, The Exciters, that Leiber & Stoller were producing. The Exciters (Carol Johnson, Lillian Walker, Herb Rooney, and lead singer Brenda Reid), a quartet from Jamaica, Queens had struck gold the first time out with their recording of Bert Berns' ''Tell Him.'' Berns was a native New Yorker who later spent time at Miami University studying classical music, but gave that up to pursue his love of rhythm & blues. Unlike most of his contemporaries, he didn't get into the business until he was almost thirty but he had hits almost immediately, in 1961 and 1962, with his (now-classic) songs including ''Twist And Shout,'' ''A Little Bit Of Soap,'' and ''Killer Joe.'' Berns (who also used the pseudonyms Bert Russel and Russell Byrd) went on to create a string of brilliant records with Solomon Burke, Garnett Mimms, The Drifters, Isley Brothers, Ben E. King, Van Morrison, Barbara Lewis, Freddie Scott and many, many more.

The Exciters had reached #4 with ''Tell Him'' and now it was time for the follow-up. Ellie Greenwich was at that session: ''It was done at Bell Sound and I sat up in this little observation booth watching and listening. My father was there with me because I still lived at home on Long Island, and he would wait to drive me home. They cut about five tunes and it was about four or five in the morning when they finally finished. Then they sat there and listened to them and about five-thirty in the morning Leiber & Stoller turned to each other and said: 'The single's gonna be ''He's Got The Power.''' I just couldn't believe it. I was so excited. I was almost in a stupor. It was nerve-racking and tense, but they were healthy tensions. Decisions were made relatively quickly, sometimes right on the spot. Then the record would come out and within three weeks you'd know if you had something.''

The Exciters' records took great, natural singers and placed them in an ultra-creative and sympathetic environment. They utilized the people who were best at their individual craft: the wonderfully inventive arrangements of Teacho Wilshire, seasoned session musicians, songs by Bert Berns, Greenwich and Powers, Burt Bacharach, Leiber & Stoller, Van McCoy and others, and the brilliant production talents of Leiber & Stoller. The recordings were almost up-tempo extensions of the work of The Drifters, sporting a Latin baion beat bathed in strings, marimba, rhythmic percussion, and the ever-present triangle. ''He's Got The Power'' only reached the Top Sixty, and the groups' future recordings didn't even do *that* well chartwise, but their work was always classy and Brenda Reid's vocals were consistently emotional and utterly convincing.

Greenwich: ''Brenda had one of the best female voices I've ever heard. As far as I was concerned she could do no wrong—she would only add to the song, make it greater. The Exciters were all very nice people. They worked hard and learned quickly, as quick as anyone I ever worked with. We'd have heavy rehearsals before we'd go into the studio. We'd play the song for them, find the right key, work out the lead vocal, and then blend in interesting background vocals. Then we'd usually work with the arranger and come up with all the overdub parts as well. In the studio they were using four-track then. You'd get the rhythm track and mix that down to one track. Then you'd have voices on another, percussion and sweetening (horns, strings, etc.) on another. You always had to leave one track open so you could 'bounce' two tracks together. If you had to double the lead vocal, for instance, you'd take the one on tape and the live one and mix them together on one track. There wasn't any 'sel-sync' yet, so you couldn't punch in. You had to get a complete performance from start to finish all the way through, or else start over from the top.''

After ''Tell Him,'' and ''He's Got The Power,'' The Exciters chart impact was minimal, but they continued to be influential. Their 1963 recording of Jeff and Ellie's song, ''Do Wah Diddy'' (which only reached #78), was later covered by Manfred Mann, who took it to Number One all over the world. The Exciters also cut a Barry-Greenwich-

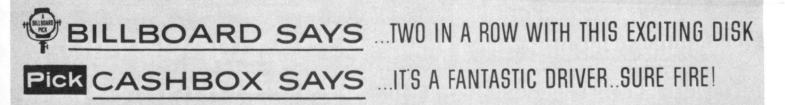

Spector song, "All Grown Up" but it was not released, as Phil Spector issued *his* production of it with The Crystals. After leaving United Artists, The Exciters continued to record, first at Roulette and then at Bang, usually under the supervision of Bert Berns. They returned to the charts early in 1966 with a version of Berns' "Little Bit Of Soap," but this Top Sixty hit proved to be their final chart appearance.

Over the first few months of 1963, two major events occurred in the life of Ellie Greenwich—events that would prove to be crucial in shaping the future of pop music for years to come. The first of these was when Mike Stoller and Jerry Leiber introduced Ellie and Tony Powers to Phil Spector. Soon the three of them would be collaborating on hits for Bob B. Soxx and The Blue Jeans, Darlene Love and others. (Greenwich's work with Spector is chronicled in Chapter Nine.) The second turning point was precipitated by her marriage to Jeff Barry, their decision to also work together professionally, and her subsequent split with Tony Powers. "I explained the situation to Tony about how Jeff and I were married and found it hard not to write with each other. Jeff was also at Trio by this time, so we were both working for the same company. It was very hard for me to do, and Tony was understandably very upset, because things had been going really well for us. Jeff was working with Artie Resnick and he had to do the same thing. I guess it caused some animosity. After that everybody considered us as a closed writing shop."

Jeff and Ellie were living in Lefrak City in Queens. One day while riding into Manhattan on the E-train, they began to write a song. "We were writing a song for The Sensations who had 'Let Me In,' and although we had started it the night before, we were actually working on it on the train. We had a session booked for ten in the morning at Associated to cut a demo, and we just got finished writing in time for the session. We brought it over to the office and played it for Jerry and Mike and they said 'Hey, this sounds interesting, let's see what we can do with this record,' and I had no idea what they were talking about. I said, 'What record?—there is no record.' Meanwhile Phil Spector was in the office and he said, 'I want that record—it's a smash.' Next thing I know Mike and Jerry got a deal with Jubilee Records for the record—and it's just a demo with piano and drums. Then we had to come up with a group name, and we wanted something visual. I loved that Dee Clark record 'Raindrops,' so we finally came up with that, 'The Raindrops.'"

The first release, their "demo" of "What A Guy," did well, reaching #41, and the follow-up, "The Kind Of Boy You Can't Forget," went all the way to #17. The Raindrops records featured Ellie's wonderfully youthful vocals and Jeff's bass-vocal line counterpoint. They were simple and incredibly melodic with hooks galore. Their third record, "That Boy John," was pulled off several

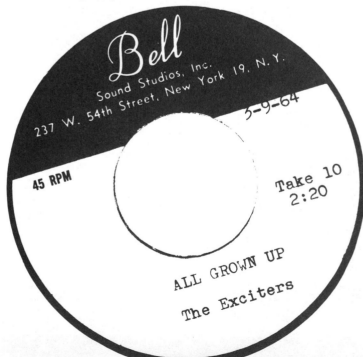

An acetate for the unreleased version of "All Grown Up" by The Exciters.

88

major stations after the assassination of John F. Kennedy. Jeff and Ellie posed for "group" pictures with the addition of a third "Raindrop," Ellie's sister. They did some TV shows and record hops with Bobby Bosco substituting for Jeff. "Jeff was real tall and a bit self-conscious about his appearance," remembers Ellie, "so he never went out on the road with us." Although the later singles were a bit more produced than their original demo, The Raindrops album was quickly thrown together: "We had some singles, and we had some demos lying around, and then we went in and did a couple of things real quick. That was the album. In total the whole thing might've cost a total of $1400. 'What A Guy' cost $140. We were in by 10 AM and out by 11:15." When Leiber & Stoller made the deal for The Raindrops with Jubilee, they gave Jeff and Ellie five points. Jeff and Ellie thought this was pretty good, since most artists only got 3 or 3 and a half percent back then. Years later, Ellie found out what the whole deal was: "We were getting five points, but Jubilee was paying a 16 percent royalty, so Leiber & Stoller and Ed Burton (of Trinity Music where Jeff had been employed) split the rest. We were the writer, the producer, the arranger, and the artist, and they were getting twice as much as us. . . ." Ellie still maintains that it didn't *really* matter all that much: "It was all fun and innocence. We were just happy to have a deal, and to get paid to do what we loved was just unbelievable. I remember the first royalty

The Raindrops with Bruce Morrow at Palisades Amusement Park. Only Ellie Greenwich (right) was involved with the recordings. The other "Raindrops" were only used for public appearances.

check we got from Jubilee was for $28,000. I just couldn't believe my eyes. I thought the decimal point was in the wrong place. But that was the right amount and that was a lot of money in those days."

The Raindrops issued a few more singles but the records weren't selling too well. Jeff and Ellie were also busy cutting demos for other artists, heavily involved with Phil Spector, and then Jerry Leiber & Mike Stoller announced that they were going to form their own label, to be called Red Bird Records.

Around this time Jeff suggested to Ellie that he should get sole credit as producer because Ellie might be having children soon and leave the business, while Jeff would have to carry on. It was important to keep his name and reputation well remembered in business, and this was the way to accomplish that. "I was a little hurt when he suggested it, because I always felt people should get credit for what they do, but I also felt it was in the best interests of our relationship and family setup—so I went along with it. . . . Who knew that we'd break up and I'd have to start all over again?" A quick examination of The Raindrops records shows the production credits for the first few as "Jeff Barry and Ellie Greenwich"; the next few as "Ellie and Jeff Barry"; and finally "Jeff Barry."

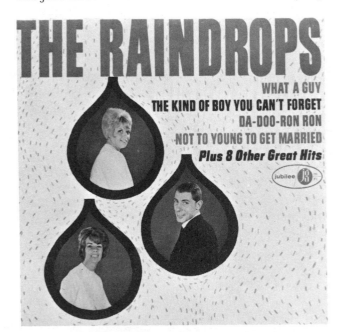

Jerry Leiber (top) and Mike Stoller in 1964 taking a break during a Red Bird recording session.

Red Bird Records was formed by Jerry Leiber, Mike Stoller, and record business veteran George Goldner, whose long-term achievements included his own labels like Rama, Gee, Gone, and End. He was a pioneer in the r&b field, and helped many artists like The Crows, Frankie Lymon, The Chantels, The Cleftones, The Flamingos, and Little Anthony & The Imperials crossover into the huge pop market. Leiber & Stoller wanted Red Bird for two reasons: to be free of their vast array of commitments, and to make money. In the two years prior to the formation of Red Bird, the team had become overloaded with assignments. Not only were they working full time at Atlantic with The Drifters, The Coasters, Ben E. King, Isley Brothers and others, but they were also busy writing, producing and licensing material to other companies with artists like Jay and The Americans, Mike Clifford, The Exciters, and Marv Johnson (all for United Artists), and several others for various other labels. On many of these records they got production royalties, but on some they just received their two cents mechanical for writing and publishing. If they only published the song, they only earned one cent. "So after a while we got to thinking," recalled Leiber, "why should we settle for two cents when we could have our own company and get twenty-one cents?" They *had* owned their own company before, Spark Records, during the mid-fifties, but after they came to New York to work for Atlantic it was absorbed and dissolved. In late 1962, they issued one record on their short-lived Tiger label, and then about a year later tried again with several releases on their own Daisy label, but these companies apparently were not serious attempts for chart dominance. (The first record on Daisy, incidentally, issued in late 1963, was a powerful Spector-type girl group record by Cathy Saint.)

George Goldner was supposed to handle the business and promotion end of things, leaving Leiber & Stoller free to pursue their own creative instincts, as well as sign up new writers, producers, and performers. One of the first artists to walk through their doors was a trio of girls from New Orleans who had been spotted at a talent contest by Joe Jones. Jones was a New Orleans music veteran who even had a hit under his own name, "You Talk Too Much," in 1960. The trio consisted of Barbara Ann Hawkins, her younger sister Rosa

Lee, and Joan Marie Johnson. They auditioned right in the new Red Bird offices, were signed up, and put together with Jeff Barry and Ellie Greenwich. Greenwich and Barry had written a song with Phil Spector called "Chapel Of Love" that Spector had first cut with The Ronettes in October 1963. He wasn't satisfied with the way it turned out, and then cut it with The Crystals. Neither version had seen the light of day. Ellie: "We always believed in that song and we called Phil and asked him, 'Are you putting it out?' He said, 'I don't know . . . I don't think so . . . no, no, never coming out. . . . ' So we said, 'We're thinking of doing it,' and he said, 'No, no, you can't do that.' He always wanted to have total control over everything he had anything to do with. I don't know how happy he was that Jeff and I were going to do something on our own on the production level without him. He wasn't totally thrilled, but he didn't stop it. Maybe Leiber & Stoller worked something out with him, I'll never know. So we took a shot with it, and went in and cut it after a lot of rehearsal." During the session the girls thought their name was going to be Little Miss And The Muffets, but just before the record came out they were christened The Dixie Cups. "After the session, I knew it was a number one record," declares Ellie. " 'Chapel Of Love' and 'Leader Of The Pack' were the only two I was dead sure about." Some copies of the record read "A Leiber-Stoller Production," and some read "Produced By Joe Jones," but, says Ellie; "We weren't getting production monies at the time, so I really didn't care that much about production credits. Today everyone is so credit conscious, but Jeff and I produced 'Chapel Of Love'. . . ."

Issued late in April of 1964, the record did indeed zoom to #1 in only 6 weeks, and remained there for almost a month, knocking off The Beatles' "Love Me Do." Next came "People Say," another Barry-Greenwich song, and this one went to #12. The Dixie Cups' records featured a clean, crisp sound which left room for special effects like bells and chimes, tack pianos, and clear acoustic guitars (unusual for the time) to add audible color to the production. While Phil Spector was busy blurring and fuzzying up his sounds, the philosophy at Red Bird was to combine a melodic tune, visual "teenage" lyrics, a tight backing track, and an interesting natural vocal into a smartly exe-

Jeff Barry, Ellie Greenwich, and The Dixie Cups.

cuted pop hit. They succeeded beyond their wildest dreams.

After two big hits with their first two releases, The Dixie Cups' fortunes slowed somewhat as "You Should Have Seen The Way He Looked At Me," and "Little Bell" respectively reached #'s 39 and 51. Then one night as the group and Jeff and Ellie were listening back to some songs they had just cut, the girls started singing an old song they knew. Ellie picks up the story: "One girl starts singing 'My grandma and your grandma . . .' and I said, 'What's that?' and they said, 'Oh, it's just some old New Orleans traditional song called "Iko Iko". . . .' And I said, 'I like that—keep singing it.' And Jeff starts hitting the wall, and I'm banging away on the console, and I told our engineer Brooks Arthur, 'Hold it Brooks, we're not done for the night yet.' So we went out into the studio and we all grabbed something—a coke bottle, whatever. We had this Jamaican box in the corner—Jeff and I had gotten it down there on our honeymoon—and that's the only real 'instrument' you hear on the tape. I said, 'Girls, let's go,' and we did. The original tape went on forever. So we picked out the best section, went back and fixed it up a little, added the background vocals and some little things here and there, and that was it. We listened to it, and said, 'I don't believe it—that should be the next single.'" Indeed it was, and a successful one at that, reaching #20. In a sense, "Iko Iko" was the purest and most beautiful record The Dixie Cups made—sparse, totally natural, and sporting wonderful call and response vocals.

The Dixie Cups only had one album, but it was issued two or three different times. First it was called *Chapel Of Love*. Next it was replastered with a sticker that said *People Say*. Then it was issued with a new cover as *Iko Iko*. But although the group was doing well, manager Joe Jones had a hankering for the "major label big time," and moved The Dixie Cups to ABC, where a series of records, lacking the Red Bird touch, all failed to make the charts. This was a pattern throughout the fifties and sixties, where groups would leave small, creative companies to go with big labels who had no real understanding of what originally gave the group their earlier hits in the first place. Perhaps they were getting low royalties (or even no royalties) at the small company, but that's not to say that the

majors were much better in that respect anyway. And to paraphrase an old music business proverb handed down from small label to successful artist: "It's better to have three percent of something, than six percent of nothing. . . ." But things were going so well at Red Bird that the loss of The Dixie Cups didn't seem to phase anyone at all.

The next group to sign with Red Bird was The Jelly Beans, four girls and a guy from Jersey City, New Jersey. They were all high school students who were discovered by Bill Downs (who then became their manager). Downs brought the group to New York songwriter-producer Steve Venet, who then marched the quintet over to Red Bird. The group consisted of Elyse Herbert, her sister Maxine, Alma Brewer, Diane Taylor, and Charles Thomas, and once again the aspiring hitmakers were put in the hands of Barry and Greenwich. Although other records were being issued on Red Bird, mostly more soul-influenced sounds produced by Leiber & Stoller, Barry and Greenwich were the ones who were making the hits and almost always with girl groups. Did the team actively solicit girl groups, or feel more comfortable with them? Ellie: "Girls were happening on the charts, so girls kept coming into the office. When teen idols were happening, every office was filled with aspiring Frankie Avalons. If the group sounded good, and looked good, we'd take a shot. We didn't think in terms of 'girl groups'—we never put a label on it. If it was a good song, or a good

The Jelly Beans.

group, we just did it. We didn't really think that much about it. . . ." As time progressed, Jeff and Ellie were fast becoming as important to Red Bird and Trio, as Goffin and King had been to Dimension and Aldon.

The Jelly Beans' first release, "I Wanna Love Him So Bad," was in fact quite similar to some of Goffin and King's Dimension creations. This was some two years after the Dimension sound had peaked, and yet with some slight variations this record showed that the public still loved the style. It went all the way to #9. Ellie continues, "I felt that Trio's strength over Aldon was that we were smaller, and also Leiber & Stoller were the best writers and producers around, so who better to learn or take suggestions from? Before Red Bird really got going and Jeff and I were still cutting demos and trying to sell the songs, we would always be in competition with someone at Aldon. If they got the record, I'd envy them, but it wasn't a

kind of negative, resentful reaction. I wish I could've gotten it, but I was happy for them, and really wished them the best. Sometimes we'd be waiting outside a demo studio for our time and Gerry and Carole would be in there cutting something, and we'd turn to each other and say 'Gee, that really sounds good.' But that only made us try harder—the competition was fierce."

The Jelly Beans' next record was "Baby Be Mine," a warmly melodic mid-tempo Barry-Greenwich-Venet composition which only reached #51. The sound here was fuller, and closer to some of Phil Spector's recordings, and it utilized a vocal that was as close as one could imagine to Ellie Greenwich's own style. An album, *Baby Be Mine,* was scheduled for release and some tracks were recorded, but it never came out. Neither were any future Jelly Beans singles, for the group was gone, and no one today really seems to remember how or why.

The Ad Libs.

BLUE CAT

Leiber & Stoller, meanwhile, had revived their Tiger label as an outlet for more r&b-influenced material. After a half dozen releases, they dropped Tiger and started up Blue-Cat as the r&b companion to Red Bird. They were looking hard for an act to kick off the label with when Bill Downs brought them a demo of a group he found in a Bayonne, New Jersey night club. On the demo was a song called "The Boy From New York City," which John Taylor, a friend of the group had written. Shortly after Jerry, Mike and George Goldner auditioned the group in person, Leiber & Stoller's solid production of The Ad Libs "Boy From New York City" was blaring out from every radio in America. It was the most r&b-flavored hit the company had, and it vaulted into the Top Ten in early 1965. But although the group, Hugh Harris, David Ward, Norman Donegan, Danny Austin and lead singer Mary Ann Thomas, issued several more records over the next year, none could match the vitality and impact of "The Boy From New York City." By 1966, they too had departed from the Red Bird roster.

Most of the hit Red Bird acts maintained a heavy touring schedule, splitting their time between the more white audience-attended package shows like Dick Clark's Caravan Of Stars, and the all-black tours which played places like The Apollo in New York and The Howard Theater in Washington D.C. The Dixie Cups' first tour in the U.S. was shared with The Crystals, Fabian and Gene Pitney, and then they toured England in late 1964 with both British and American acts. In the spring of 1965 they were part of a U.S. *Shindig* package with Gerry and The Pacemakers, Shirley Ellis, and others including emcee Jimmy O'Neil, The Shindig Dancers, and The Shindig Band. After The Ad Libs first record charted, they were added to a Chuck Berry-Dionne Warwick tour, and they went out on a Dick Clark Easter swing with Del Shannon, The Zombies and many more. The Jelly Beans did a summer 1964 Dick Clark tour, and then went over to The Apollo. In general, the Red Bird staff didn't attend the shows, as Ellie explains: "It was usually too crowded and hectic, and besides we were pretty tired at the end of a day— we also got tired of hearing those songs over and over again. We'd go down once as a courtesy, and to see what their act was like, but to us the shows weren't very important—it was always the records for us. . . ."

The inner circle at Red Bird was like a tight-knit family, with the same small group of people repeatedly working together. In the studio, Artie Butler was usually the official arranger, and Brooks Arthur was the recording engineer. Mira Sound was the preferred studio, although occasionally A&R or Bell Studios were used. ("Mira wasn't such a great studio," says Ellie, "it just had the right feeling and camaraderie. . . .") Drummers included Buddy Saltzman, Al Rogers, Gary Chester, and Bernard Purdie. Keyboards were handled by Artie Butler, Frank Owens and occasionally Ellie Greenwich. Guitars were played by Al Gorgoni, Sal Di Troia, and Charlie Macey and bassists included Dick Romaff and Russell George. The strings were in the custody of Irving Spice and his string section while Artie Kaplan who was contractor for the session, sounded up a five-piece horn section which almost always included himself. Percussion was handled by Jeff and Ellie and whoever else was around, especially George Devins who *only* did percussion. Most of the time they couldn't afford strings, but later on when they could, and did use them, it was usually seven or eight pieces: three or four violins, two violas, and two cellos.

After the song was written, the group would meet with Jeff and Ellie and rehearse their various parts. Ellie usually worked more with the girls and their vocals ("It was just easier and more natural that way—if one of the girls came in and it was that time of the month and she wasn't feeling so well, I'd understand, and she could take the day off . . . ."). Jeff and Ellie would try to get three finished rhythm tracks recorded in a three-hour session. A typical A-side would take eight to ten hours from start to finish, from basic track to overdubs, to lead vocals, to background vocals, and sweetening if needed. Mixing didn't take too long ("Mixing only four tracks doesn't leave that much to mix . . . ."). Ellie: "We usually had pretty simple charts. Getting the rhythm track and lead vocal usually took the longest. We didn't have too many choices after that as far as technology went. We used echo or reverb, maybe doubled the vocals, and that was about it. We were always well-rehearsed—we had to be to get a complete performance from beginning to end. Later on, when eight-tracks came in we could at least get a couple of performances down—occasionally we'd splice a piece of one onto a piece of another. . . ." As far as Leiber & Stoller's involvement went, it decreased as time went by. "If we were working with a new group, they'd check the first song or session —after that we'd just do it, and if there was an album we'd just fill it up however we saw fit. Before we had proved ourselves they used to come down to the sessions, then they'd just call in and see how we were doing, finally we'd just do it and play them the finished record."

The Butterflys were among the least recognized of the Red Bird groups, and that's a pity considering how memorable their two records were. Steve Venet brought the group to the label, and he worked with Jeff and Ellie on writing and producing for them. The first release, "Goodnight Baby," melded The Little Eva/Cookies sullen/breathy vocal style with a Latin-tinged, rather subdued shuffling melody. It reached the middle of the Top 100, but then inexplicably, the next one, a Barry-Greenwich-Spector song called "I Wonder" failed to chart at all. Spector had cut the song with both The Crystals and The Ronettes, but it was

Merry Xmas from RED BIRD

THE JELLY BEANS

A 1964 Christmas advertisement for Red Bird Records which identifies The Butterflys as The Jelly Beans.

never a single, and was not well-known to the public. The Butterflys' version was close to The Ronettes, wonderfully ethereal, and in that sense, by not attempting to follow the other Red Bird groups into the world of catchy pop anthems, was something quite special. It stood by itself as an emotionally honest and musically riveting recording, and it was almost as if Jeff and Ellie were sending this one out to Spector, saying in essence, "Listen Phil, we can make these records too, if we want to . . . your style is great, and you're the best at that . . . but our own brand of pop hitmaking is pretty unique too. You'll stick to your territory and we'll stick to ours. . . ."

Perhaps the most creative and fully realized Red Bird release in the girl-group mold, is the most obscure of all, a single by Ellie Greenwich herself. "You Don't Know" is the kind of record that not only transcends and expands the boundaries that come to mind when someone says, "Girl-group record," but it also can stand alone, totally unique and unmatched by any other competition. It's mature and somber, sparse and penetrating, dealing lyrically with a potential love triangle, and detailing the guilt and confusion inherent in the situation. It's beautifully arranged, moving from section to section with grace, power and a never-ending array of surprising touches. The chorus, with its dizzying strings, bottomless tympanis and wailing background leaves one breathless, and Ellie's vocals seem to speak from deep emotional experience. Ellie too, has fond memories: "I had such high hopes for that record. We did it at Bell Sound with Jeff and Shadow (Morton)—I can still picture Shadow wildly conducting the session. It took a lot of work to record that—the song really got to me. It was really quite exciting. It was going to be the pick of the week on WMCA, but then Jackie De Shannon came out with 'What The World Needs Now,' and that's the one radio went with instead. Leiber & Stoller wanted me to go on the road to promote it, and to go over to England, but Jeff wasn't too happy about that. We were busy writing, producing, doing demos, doing background vocals on other records. He didn't understand what the purpose was—was I going to become a performer and be traveling all the time? After we lost WMCA and I went along with Jeff about not touring, Leiber & Stoller lost interest, I think. They didn't push it, and I think they valued me more as a writer–producer than as a potential artist—they didn't want to lose me. It never charted, but it got me a lot of recognition in the business.

"I was really kept in the dark as far as most business practices went," continues Ellie, "sometimes a bunch of tough-looking guys would appear, and I'd be sent off to another room, while they all talked alone. There always was some kind of payola, but it was much smaller than what I hear goes on today. You know, twenty dinners in a week, a hooker for a night, maybe even a color TV, but that was it. There's always going to be payoffs and favors—just like in any big business—and this was a big buiness. Red Bird would usually hire specific promoters to work certain releases, like Bill Spitalsky, Juggy Gayles, and Herb Rosen."

Although Jeff and Ellie were drawing weekly salaries of about $275, getting their writing and performance royalties, and doing some session work as well, they did not receive producer royalties at Red Bird. They could write, arrange, rehearse, record, and produce a hit, but perhaps all they would get would be a penny a record for their writer's share. "We *would* get generous bonuses around Christmastime," recalls Ellie, "and we also got some stock in Red Bird in lieu of production monies, but then later on when I wanted to record elsewhere, I had to give my stock back to get back my recording contract—so I had no ownership after that." As far as the girls in the groups went, Ellie sees it this way, "The girls gave, and the girls took. They'd get fancy clothes, expensive dinners, all of that. Most of them didn't think in terms of a 'career.' It was just fun, and better than their alternatives, and they took what they could get. Most of them only wanted their couple of years, and then wanted to get married and raise a family. They knew there were trade-offs, but it wasn't a one-sided exploitation, that's for sure. . . ."

Red Bird was not only the most successful new independent label during the mid-sixties, they also perfected an enviable style of sound and performance. Of their first thirty releases, eighteen hit the charts, and eleven of those reached the Top Forty. But their most significant, most visible, and most influential contribution was to come from a group of white high school girls from Queens, a group that would be known as The Shangri-Las.

OUT IN
THE STREETS

45 RPM

THE STORY OF THE SHANGRI-LAS is both as crystalline and as murky as is the body of their recorded work. It is a story of users and victims. It is a story of greed, a kind of vicious avarice that reached down to the depths of honest souls and left nothing but ugly scars. It is the story of art imitating life, of life imitating art, and of a fantasy-blurred roller coaster ride where either getting off or staying on could result in painful consequences.

Sisters Mary and Betty (Elizabeth) Weiss, and twins Marge (Marguerite) and Mary Ann Ganser met at Andrew Jackson High School in Queens, New York. They began singing together because they loved to, and because the sheer exuberance they felt when they soared together let them forget about their workaday Cambria Heights existence. They loved Dionne Warwick and Little Anthony, The Four Seasons and Mary Wells, The Flamingos and Johnny Mathis. They would stand on lines at The Fox and Paramount; they would go to the record store in the afternoon and buy singles and keep a punch card so that after they bought

ten, they'd get one free; they'd call up WABC at night and vote for their favorite new releases. Then they began singing at local high school hops, and through sheer persistence got a record out on the obscure Spokane label, after meeting up with some young and hungry record biz hustlers who had a fledgling writing-producing company, Kama-Sutra Productions. No one ever heard of the record, "Wishing Well" b/w "Hate To Say I Told You So," but the songs were honest, trashy, and convincing rock 'n' roll throwaways. This was early in 1964 and the record, along with the girls (who were still in high school), were promptly forgotten. Also forgotten were some pieces of paper the girls had signed with Kama-Sutra Productions.

Meanwhile, out on Long Island, an almost equally obscure music business would-be named George Morton was told by a friend that an old acquaintance, Ellie Gaye from Levittown, was now a big hit songwriter. Morton refused to believe it until he went to a local record shop and saw that Ellie Gaye had become Ellie Greenwich and helped write "Da Doo Ron Ron," "Why Do Lovers Break Each Other's Hearts?", "Then He Kissed Me," and "Be My Baby." The next day he visited Ellie in New York and hung around the office until an exasperated Jeff Barry said, "Well, what do you do?" to which George replied, "I write songs." Jeff said, "Yeah, what kind of songs?" and Morton said, "Hit songs." And Jeff said, "Oh yeah, why don't you bring me one?" and George said, "What kind?" And Jeff said sarcastically, "How 'bout a slow one?" So George says, "OK, see ya next Tuesday."

George Morton remembers it this way: "I had never really written songs—it was a complete lie. I was just on the spot and pissed at Jeff's attitude. I left there, went back to Long Island and called a friend, Joe Monaco, who had a studio in his basement. I said, 'I've got a record company that's interested in hearing some of my material.' He said, 'You don't have any material.' I said, 'Don't worry about that.' He gave me the studio. Then I called up George Stermer and said, 'Listen I need a band.' He said, 'What for?' I said, 'I've got this record company, I've got a studio. . . .' So he got me a band. I called up another friend of mine and said, 'I need a group.' He said, 'How come?' I said, 'I got this band, I got a record company, I got a studio. . . .' He told me about some girls who were singing in Cambria Heights, Queens. So I saw them and gave them the same routine. 'I got a band, I got a studio, I got a record company. . . .' It was all bullshit, it was all a lie. So we were supposed to meet Sunday afternoon. Sunday morning I was headed for the studio, I figured I'd get there an hour early, and as I crossed the railroad tracks, it dawned on me . . . the only thing I didn't have was a song. So I pulled the car over and wrote the song. It took me about twenty-two minutes and I was finished.

"Well, I walked into the studio that day. I didn't know how arrangements went 'cause it was all in my head. I don't play an instrument or anything. So I said to the piano player, "You play bom, bom, bom. Do this, don't do that. Now sing da dat da dat . . .' and so on. Within two hours we had it down. I brought it to Jeff Barry who was sitting there ready to tear my heart out, and he heard it and said, 'Do you mind if I play this for someone else?' THEN I was frightened; up until now it was a joke. So he took it and came back thirty minutes later with a guy who had one brown eye and one blue eye who says, 'What would you like to do?' I said, 'What do you want me to do?' He said, 'I'd like you to write songs.' I said, 'OK.' He said, 'I'll give you a hundred a week, off the books.' I said, 'Do I have to come here to write?' He said, 'You can write anyplace you want to.' I said, 'I'll take the job.' He said, 'Incidentally that record you made is coming out in two weeks!' " The record was "Remember (Walkin' In The Sand)"; the group was The Shangri-Las; and the guy with one brown eye and one blue eye was Jerry Leiber.

Most of the above recollection is more or less true, but George Morton is a man known for flights of fancy, and other parties involved remember it somewhat differently. Ellie Greenwich: "I knew George from Long Island. He came by, and after he and Jeff played some verbal

OUT IN THE STREETS

45 RPM

Chapter SEVEN

games, he said he's come back in a week with a hit record. Well, he came back and played us this weird little record. It was like seven minutes long with this long narration by George in the beginning. I knew there was no way we could put out anything like that, but I thought 'Gee, that girl's voice is so strange, and the song is so interesting.' So we played it for Leiber & Stoller and they said, 'Go cut it.' George signed on with Trio and we started getting together with the girls working on arrangements and vocals and just when we were getting ready to go into the studio, all of a sudden everything came to a halt, because in walked Artie Ripp and the Kama-Sutra people, and they had contracts with the girls and there was nothing we could do about it.''

Eventually Leiber & Stoller worked out an arrangement with Kama-Sutra so that they would get some credit, some publishing and some royalties. ''So all of a sudden George and I are off the label as producers,'' says Ellie, ''and Jeff and Artie Ripp share production credits. And you know, Artie Ripp *wasn't even there.* . . .'' Released in August 1964, ''Remember (Walkin' In The Sand)'' took off like a rocket, reaching #13 within 3 weeks of its appearance on the national charts, and then stayed in the Top Ten for 6 more weeks. ''Remember'' was incredibly arranged, amazingly atmospheric, and almost painfully intense.

It was totally unlike any other kind of pop recording ever made, and at a time when new pop trends and sounds were succeeding overnight, this sound was accepted with a vengeance that for the moment eclipsed all others.

The Shangri-Las were thrown into a world of public appearances, photo sessions, and television performances. Mary later recalled: ''Our first television appearance was on Clarke Race's show in Pittsburgh. We didn't know anything about TV. We wore skirts and white shell blouses. We didn't have any makeup on and we shone like a bunch of headlights. You know, the kids in the audience can tell if you're professional or amateur, and boy, did we come on amateur. They held their breath for us. Then afterward this fourteen-year-old kid came up and said, 'Don't worry kid, you'll make it. . . .' '' Then they were hastily added to a Brooklyn Fox Show, sharing the bill with Martha & The Vandellas, Marvin Gaye, The Searchers, and others. The frilly skirts and blouses were replaced by matching pants, sweaters and black boots, and they only performed one song during their spot. Mary stood on one side of the stage and the other three stood in the middle and they acted out the song while singing with hand and body motions and ultra-choreographed moves. The kids went crazy. Apparently, The Shangri-Las did too—from what George Morton remembers: ''They went nutso. You take these kids out of Cambria Heights and all of a sudden they're the number one white female group in America, out of nowhere. One day they're eating pasta, the next day they're eating Chateaubriand, and they don't even know how to pronounce it yet!''

The Shangri-Las flew over to England for a ten-day promotional tour in October 1964, where ''Remember (Walkin' In The Sand)'' reached #14. Only three Shangri-Las made the trip—Mary ''stayed in the States because she had a bad cold,'' they told the press, but actually she was, at sixteen, still attending school. George Morton recalls what happened when it was time for the next record: ''Leiber & Stoller wanted me to collaborate with people in the business because I was an 'outsider.' I didn't have any track record or background. They were right. They were worried. All of a sudden they had a hit with a new artist and things were taking off with Red Bird Records. I didn't want to do that, so when the record hit #1 [actually it only reached #5, but it was so distinctive and popular that for all intents and purposes it was a #1 record] they walked into the office and said, 'Hey what do you want to do for the second record?' I said, 'I got an idea for a song. It's called "Leader Of The Pack."' I didn't really know I was supposed to have a second record idea all ready, so I said the first thing that came to my mind. There was no song called 'Leader Of The Pack,' but that seemed like a fancy title to me at the moment. They turned it down. They said, 'There's no way in the world we're going to release a record called "Leader Of The Pack," no one will play it. You can't make a hero out of that kind of situation.' Well, by that time Jeff Barry had become a friend, we were buddies, and he said, 'Do whatever the hell you want to do.' So I booked Ultra-Sonic Studios in Hempstead again, I booked the men. One morning the studio called me up and asked why I wasn't there, they had twenty-two men waiting . . . I knew I had something for that day . . . I said to my wife, 'Give

The Shangri-Las.

me a bottle of champagne, two cigars, and something to write with.' I went into the shower, sat down, drank the champagne, smoked the cigars, and wrote the song on a shirt cardboard with my kid's crayons. I ran to the studio, and said, 'You're singing the red, you're singing the blue. . . .' And that was it.''

Although Jeff and Ellie had helped arrange and re-work the original ''Remember (Walkin' In The Sand),'' sole writer credit was given to George Morton. For the next one, ''Leader Of The Pack,'' all three shared writer credits and Ellie remembers it this way: ''We were all sitting around wondering what we could do for a follow-up. And bikes were really in then—Jeff had a bike and George had a bike. We would all run around town. So somebody said, 'How about a song about a motorcycle?' And then somebody said, 'Where there's bikers there's always a pack,' and somebody said, 'Yeah, and there's always a leader.' So we had a pack and a leader and before we knew it, it took off from there and came up with 'Leader Of The Pack.' "

While "Remember (Walkin' In The Sand)" was still at #6, "Leader Of The Pack" entered the charts, and within 6 weeks had reached the #1 slot, knocking out The Supremes' "Baby Love" in the process. It stayed in the Top Five for six weeks, and was the most requested and most played record of its time.

It also spawned a great deal of controversy due to its lyrics dealing with bikers and death, its realistic cries of anguish, and its putdowns of parental viewpoints. Editorials and commentaries appeared in newspapers, magazines, and on television. It was unofficially banned at some stations, and in England (where it reached #11), it was banned more officially and spurred a series of articles on "teenage trash" and "death disc shocker." A British lass called Twinkle took a similarly themed record called "Terry" to #4 at the same time, as did J. Frank Wilson & The Cavaliers in the U.S. with "Last Kiss' a few months earlier. A hastily assembled group dubbed The Detergents spoofed "Leader Of The Pack" with their record called "Leader Of The Laundromat" and reached the

Top Twenty, which at least helped put the whole thing into a bit lighter perspective. But The Shangri-Las, now decked out in black vests over fluffy "Tom Jones" shirts, skintight black pants, and leather boots, were a national sensation, and Red Bird sought to cash in on the mania.

Two new Shangri-Las singles were next issued almost simultaneously at the end of 1964, with the first, "Give Him A Great Big Kiss," reaching only #19. "Give Him . . ." was written and produced solely by George Morton, and bore little resemblance to the ultra-creative, inventive, and atmospheric records it had the dubious distinction of following. The flip was a quick reworking of "Twist And Shout," and the other single, covers of The Chantels' "Maybe" and The Isley Brothers' "Shout" only reached #91 in its 2 short weeks on the chart. These three cover songs were little more than throwaways—and accurately, they were just crass attempts to cash in. The fact that they may have done severe harm to The Shangri-Las' future didn't seem to have entered into anyone's mind at the time.

By now George Morton had become Shadow Morton. Ellie: "George was never around and never could be found. He never kept appointments and was never on time. So Jeff and I nicknamed him The Shadow. 'Where's George?' 'Oh you know, The Shadow will be here soon. . . .' Shadow was about as interesting a character in a different way as was Phil Spector. He was very eccentric and he wanted total control. He created what I call these little soap operas on vinyl, and he got ultra-involved with them, and things had to be his way. He was kind of hard to deal with at times, and the only people he would listen to would be Jeff and myself—there was a mutual respect amongst the three of us. Sometimes he would drink a little too much when he was getting involved in what he was doing, and at times would totally fall asleep at the console, and we'd have to revive him before we went on with the session—sometimes eventually we just said 'let him sleep' and we'd finish up. But he had excellent ideas, and I think he was involved with some of the most interesting records that ever came out then."

At this point Ellie and the group weren't exactly seeing eye to eye: "The girls were a bunch of very nice street urchins, I called them. They were street classy I guess, and were tough. They were as they

THE SHANGRI-LAS—Red Bird—RB 20-101
Having turned in three smashes in the singles area, the Shangri-Las can't miss with their first LP effort, which includes "Remember," "Leader of the Pack," and their latest deck, "Give Him A Great Big Kiss." The second side features six tunes taped live, most of which need no introduction to the teens who will turn out in droves for this set. If these gals could displace the Britishers on the best-seller charts, this group has a tremendous selling power, and tunes like "Maybe," and "Twist and Shout" provide still more appeal.

looked; they were tough yet very vulnerable—I think that was part of the appeal. At the beginning we did not get along—they were kind of crude, and having to deal with them on a daily basis used to get me very uptight—with their gestures, and language, and chewing the gum, and the stockings ripped up their leg. We would say, 'Not nice, you must be ladies,' and they would say, 'We don't want to be ladies,' and we had a couple of rough times there until we sat down and really had it out. They told me where they come from, I told them where I was coming from, and I said, 'You need me and I need you, and we better make this work,' and we had a really big blowout in the ladies room of the Brill Building one night. We were screaming and yelling and ranting and raving. I cried and it was just horrible. After that, it was wonderful. We got along. They were on time. They wouldn't chew the gum so much. They controlled their language to a reasonable level. But they were tough girls—they really, really were.''

The group's next record was a concerted attempt to get back on track. ''Out In The Streets,'' written by Jeff and Ellie, was moody and compelling and utilized creative production touches and inventive arrangements. Blended together on the track you could hear a prominent stand-up bass, echoey distant percussive effects, alternating swirling and plucked strings, and intricately intertwined lead and backup vocals. Mary's lead vocals were sullen, wrenching, and haunting. Perhaps the combination was just a bit too real, and the record a little too complicated for mass radio consumption, for it only reached #53 in the spring of 1965. No sooner did ''Streets'' slide off the charts, than a new record, ''Give Us Your Blessings'' was issued. ''Blessings'' was a Barry–Greenwich composition that had been recorded two years earlier by Ray Peterson, and had only achieved limited success. The Shangri-Las' version was far superior, and not only played up the soap opera motif of previous Shangri-Las classics, but also marked the return of sound effects (lightning and thunder, car crashes, etc.) which had been a trademark of both ''Walkin' In The Sand'' and ''Leader Of The Pack.'' To top it off, it was another ''death disc,'' where the young couple fail to get their parents' blessing for their marriage, drive off to elope, and get killed in a rainy night car crash. It broke into the Top Thirty, something

Out in the Streets
Words and Music by JEFF BARRY and ELLIE GREENWICH

Recorded by THE SHANGRI-LAS on Red Bird Records
04347   TRIO MUSIC CO., INC.
75¢

103

#1 NEW VOCAL GROUP 1964

(Cash Box Year End R&B Survey)

Thank you
for a
great
year

THE SHANGRI-LAS

LATEST HIT SINGLES:

GIVE HIM A GREAT BIG KISS

RB 10-018

WRITTEN & PRODUCED BY SHADOW MORTON

MAYBE

RB 10-019

WRITTEN: GEORGE GOLDNER — PRODUC

WATCH FOR NEW LP SOON TO BE RELEASED

LEIBER

SHA

REMEM

(WALKIN' IN THE

RED BIRD 10-008

WRITTEN BY GEORGE MORTON
PRODUCED BY ARTIE RIPP AND JEFF BARRY

*FENWAY DISTRIBUTORS,
PITTSBURGH, PA., BROKE
THIS RECORD 1st IN THE
COUNTRY — NICK CENCI,
MGR. OF PROMOTION!

PUBLISHED BY TENDER TUNES AND TRIO MUSIC

their previous two releases had failed to accomplish.

By now the group was touring constantly. Their first long trek was on the Dick Clark Caravan Of Stars tour in the spring of 1965 where they shared the stage and the bus with Del Shannon, Dee Dee Sharp, The Zombies, The Ad Libs, The Ikettes, and Tommy Roe. It was at this point that the girls had to put together a permanent band to back them on the road.

One new recruit was drummer Joseph Alexander: "I was playing with a local high school band called The Poor Boys, and we got a spot on a Saturday afternoon Murray The K pre-holiday show. Peter and Gordon, and Cannibal and The Headhunters were also on the bill, and The Shangri-Las, who were not playing, came down backstage and just hung around. I got to talking with their guitar player, Jerry, and met the girls. Jerry said they were putting together a band, and the next week he called me, I met with him and Shadow, and the next thing I knew, I was the drummer for The Shangri-Las." Joe was just turning seventeen at the time, and he left high school to go on tour. "We did Dick Clark tours and a lot of Murray The K shows. On the Clark tours we would be on the road for three, maybe four months at a time—all one-nighters. At least the tours were routed out properly so we didn't have to travel too far between shows. Sometimes we'd do two a day, something like a state fair in the afternoon, and then drive a bit and do a show at night. Four days on, one day off, for week after week after week. We did bowling alleys, halls, dances, anything from four hundred to four thousand people. The equipment would be there when we arrived—we just carried baggage. We'd do a twenty-minute set, just four or five songs. The nighttime shows would start at around 6:30 and run for two hours or so. There was always wildness when the girls came on stage, with kids rushing and pushing up against the stage. They would grab Mary, and try to pull her hair. The sound would go off, the drums would fall over, the lights would go out—you name it—it happened. After the show kids came backstage or waited outside and always had records for us to sign. They'd give the group gifts. People respected [us] and we enjoyed seeing them.

"No matter what the gig, everyone usually only got fifty dollars, even the girls. We'd get paid anywhere from six hundred and fifty to two thousand dollars, but we only saw fifty, sometimes less. But all our expenses were paid—like hotels, travel, food, clothes, even haircuts. Our rent was taken care of."

Hefty royalties, however, were hard to come by. The miniscule three or four percent royalty the group was owed amounted to three or four cents a record, but even at that rate a million-selling record should have earned the group thirty or forty thousand dollars. But Red Bird got a piece, and Kama-Sutra got a piece, and Shadow got a piece, and the group's management got a piece, and then the group had to pay back studio costs, not only the hourly rates, but musicians, arrangers, string sections, and so on. Then there were recordings that never came out, or weren't hits, and numerous sessions for album tracks. With that kind of set-up it's a wonder they didn't wind up owing the record company money. "Nobody knew from royalties," says Joe. "It was just fun to be doing what we were doing—and when you came right down to it, what else *could* we do?"

What else, indeed, except to keep on touring. Alexander: "I guess I would call it a pre-*Magical Mystery Tour*. Eventually everyone got to know each other's idiosyncrasies, and when to joke and when to leave someone alone. Lots of times we were the only white group on the bus, but everyone always got along. Usually we'd be with groups like The Coasters, The Drifters, Marvelettes, Jive Five, Cannibal and The Headhunters, The Vibrations and The Contours. The Vibrations were really funny guys, and could always be counted upon to say the right thing or make some funny crack just at the right time when everyone was down and really needed a lift. For us in particular, it was always Marge. She was the strong one, almost like a den mother. She would talk about keeping the faith, and always had the right answer for a problem. Sometimes the bus would pull over at some park, and we'd get out to relax and have a little picnic. The girls used to have this kid's toy where you pump up a plastic rocket and shoot it into the sky. Well they varied it slightly and would attach white mice to the rocket, shoot them up, and watch the mice float down with a parachute. Then the mice would land and run away.

"The hotels were usually pretty nice, always

The red-hot Red Bird label recently gave birth to a new teen-beat sensation, a femme threesome called The Shangri-Las. In quick succession, the gals have come-up with three smash sides, "Remember (Walkin' In The Sand)," "Leader Of The Pack," flattered by a novelty answer hit, and currently "Give Him A Great Big Kiss." It's a certainty that the teen market can't wait to get its hands on the team's first LP, named after them, just marketed by the label. Within the next week or so, a new single is also due. Gals will also receive hefty TV exposure in the near future via guest appearances on "Hullabaloo" and the "Lloyd Thaxton" program.

clean, and we'd sleep two or three in a room. Wherever we went guys would always be hitting on the girls, but they all looked out for each other. But soon you're on a treadmill and the bad experiences start to outweigh the good, and you begin to get depressed and disenchanted. Then you close yourself off and start to toughen up—those scars can hurt. There was always a lot of booze . . . and pot. Five dollars worth of pot would last for a whole week back then—we'd smoke it in these little cornpipes. A bunch of people would take pills too, either to wake you up or put you to sleep, sometimes both. There'd be a lot of card playing, and informal parties—not wild orgy-like parties—just good times where we could unwind and keep our spirits up. It was like being drafted. We were altogether in the same boat, so we made the best of it. We never really thought about money—we did it for the fun and innocence and love of the art.''

Even when they returned home, it would just be for a few weeks, and then it was back out on the road for another few months. Alexander: ''Even when we were back in New York, we'd do shows. One-off live dates or TV shows like Lloyd Thaxton, Upbeat, and Clay Cole. The band would go record backing tracks, just live, really quickly on some two-track mono machine at places like Broadway Recording and Variety Sound. Then the girls would go to the show and sing live over the music. We'd go to Europe on package shows of American artists—we always seemed to go with The Coasters and Drifters. We'd play a lot of halls and get a great reception. British bands would always come down to see us and visit. Brian Jones was always around. The Small Faces. The Move. Whoever was around. But for years, everyone just lived out of a suitcase.''

But exactly who was living out of the suitcases varied from time to time. After their initial hit, Betty had left the group, and The Shangri-Las became a trio. Girls would leave and substitutes would be recruited. Then one would return and another would leave. Almost everyone concerned was ''lead singer'' on tour at one time or another. Alexander: ''I remember one time when Betty left. She just exploded. She was fed up and couldn't take it anymore. As time went on, it happened to everybody.'' Press photos were identified incorrectly, depending upon who was in the group at the moment, and interviewers who thought they were speaking to Betty were speaking to Mary, simply because it was better for appearance's sake not to let on that people were coming and going constantly. The group's ''management'' was equally as disheveled. Their first manager had been Larry Martire, but then, Alexander remembers: ''We didn't know *who* our manager was. Guys would come down to different shows and say, 'Hi, I'm your new manager,' or something like that. There was this one guy, Fat Frankie from Coney Island—we never knew his last name and it was probably better that way—who took care of business for awhile.''

Back at Red Bird, the records kept being released. In late 1965 came ''Right Now And Not Later,'' a total jump into the Motown sound, produced by Ronald Moseley and Robert Bateman. It barely scraped into the Top 100, hitting #99 for 2 weeks. Two weeks later another single, ''I Can Never Go Home Anymore,'' suddenly appeared. Written and produced by Shadow Morton, the song was the ultimate realization of The Shangri-Las' breathy spoken-word story-telling style. This time, instead of glamorizing rebellion, it preached reconciliation between mother and daughter. The last half of the record played up an eerie Yiddish-like motif against Mary's alternatingly tearful talking and anguished cries. It was unnerving and chilling and very real. Apparently it touched a nerve with the public as well because it became the group's first Top Ten record since "Leader Of The Pack." Their second album, *Shangri-Las '65*, was recalled and retitled *I Can Never Go Home* to include this latest hit. Actually their second album was repackaged at least four different times, sometimes with different artwork, sometimes with a different track or two. Joseph Alexander: "When we were on the road, we didn't care about the charts. We never looked at them, and didn't even know what records were released. We'd only find out when we'd pull into a town and there'd be a line on the poster under our name that said, 'Latest hit . . .' and there'd be a space where they'd fill in a new title. The girls would go in the studio and then things wouldn't come out until seven months or a year later. Sometimes the sessions would get crazy. People were brought in to play and then taken out. Then other people would be brought in. You never knew who played on the final record."

The next release, "Long Live Our Love," concerned a boyfriend who went overseas to fight, while the girlfriend waited nervously, and faithfully, at home. It was a bit too upbeatly patriotic and didn't ring true; a more honest and convincing song—for the Shangri-Las at least—would have had the soldier die in action. The rest of 1966 was taken up by two records, "Dressed In Black," and "Past, Present and Future." They were both depressing dirge-like narratives which seemed to not only reflect how the group was feeling at the time, but also foreshadow the future. Neither were commercial successes, and then Leiber & Stoller decided to leave Red Bird Records: "We had started Red Bird records with George Goldner because we wanted to make money and we wanted to do our thing," Jerry Leiber said later, "but after two years we got tired of what we were doing. George only wanted pop hits, and he really knew how to sell those, but we wanted to make soul records. On top of that we were spending a lot of our time taking care of the business, and that's not what we wanted to do either. . . ." One aspect of the business that was particularly unsavory and often frightening was the silent friends who helped

The Nu-Luvs were groomed as an imitation of The Shangri-Las. The plan didn't work. . . .

you take care of business. Occasionally four husky guys would appear at Red Bird's offices with bulges under their coat, and all the men would retire to a back room and talk things over. Without Leiber & Stoller, Barry and Greenwich (who went over to Bang Records with Bert Berns), and Shadow Morton and The Shangri-Las (who went over the Mercury Records), Goldner couldn't keep the company afloat. Red Bird never again had even one record in the Top 100, and within a year, the doors were shuttered. Jerry Leiber: "We made a lot of money. From March 1964 to March 1966, we were the number two publisher in the world, right behind The Beatles' MacLen Music. It was a great financial success."

Meanwhile other people were still trying to cash in on The Shangri-Las' sound and name. Shadow Morton produced The Goodies for Blue Cat, where he used two Shangri-Las songs, copied their vocal sound, and used some of their backing tracks. He also produced The Nu-Luvs for Mercury singing "So Soft, So Warm" which was basically the same song and sound as The Shangri-Las' "Dressed In Black." Mercury also bought the rights to The Shangri-Las' Red Bird classics and issued *The Shangri-Las Golden Hits* in 1967. The girls themselves did cut two singles for Mercury and these were glossy, slick, dishonest pieces of plastic which were as misdirected as the girls themselves were.

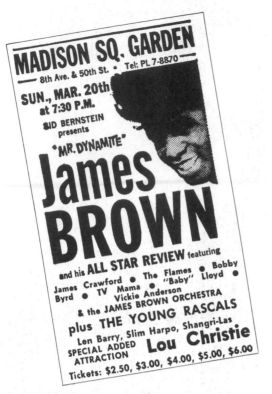

By 1966, The Shangri-Las found themselves on the bottom of the bill for their Madison Square Garden appearance.

The Shangri-Las' integrity rested in their emotional honesty. There was no pretence in what they did. "Our lines are realistic and frank. We don't put people down in our songs for what they do," declared Mary. The Shangri-Las lyrics revealed a deep commitment. When they cried it wasn't because, as in most other typical girl-group records, 'Gee my boyfriend left me,' or 'I can't go to the party.' Their sadness wasn't a sign of stereotyped female weakness, or male-controlled lives. No, they made their choices on their own terms, of their own will, and often were victims of these choices. They chose to get involved, to open themselves up, and they soared to heights and sunk to depths. There was no in-between. An in-between existence just wasn't the way to live. They admired Bob Dylan for his honesty and emotionalism, and if their lyrics were not as intellectual as his perhaps, well, they felt that the end result was the same. Their music was music of the streets, their own brand of soul music, because soul comes from feeling and communicating—and feeling and communicating is not bordered by any racial boundaries. Betty: "If you're talking right at the kids you're singing to, then the audience feels it too. Sometimes Mary will pick a kid out of the audience and she's singing to *him*. That's our soul. It's got nothing to do with color. It's when you see the audience grooving and you know everything just clicks, that's soul. They may buy The Supremes, but they listen to us. Because The Supremes come on very feminine and chic, but we come on like the average American girl who isn't just all slinky and sexy. We couldn't do all those oozy 'baby baby's,' but The Supremes couldn't get away with 'Leader Of The Pack.' "

When the girls were suddenly cut loose from their world of recording and touring, they were lost. They had been living in their own world, and when that was gone, there was no safety net or foundation for support. Having been on the road for so long, there was no time or reason to set up a home, maintain long-term stable relationships, or have a family. Being thrust into the real world saw them scatter in forty different directions. They were at a loss for what to do. Their disenchantment turned to bitterness. Although their old records were constantly being repackaged and sold, played, advertised, and exploited, they rarely saw a penny. Joe Alexander: "All the time, they never said, 'No, we won't do that,' or stood up for more money. The sadness and dramatic parts of their records were true to life. They didn't play parts. It was real. They were used. People around them only wanted to capitalize on the moment and take what they could right at that moment, regardless of the human factor. These are the rock 'n' roll parasites of the world. Bloodsuckers I call them. The girls were good people. Mary was like a high school cheerleader, Marge was the smart girl in science class, and Betty was the girl in the convertible with her hair flying. Later on, it got crazier with all these lawsuits flying around, and people came in and told them that they had no rights to the name 'The Shangri-Las'—that they couldn't get work and play under that name. Can you believe that?"

Mary's compelling narrative on the Shangri-Las' final Red Bird recording, "Past, Present and Future," contains these passages: "Past: I thought I was in love, . . . Present: Go for a walk? I guess so, but don't try to touch me, just don't try to touch me, because that will never happen again, . . . Future: I once thought I'd fall in love but at the moment it doesn't look good. It doesn't look good at all. I don't think it will ever happen again. . . ." In a music world full of phonies and charlatans, coming face to face with painful reality like this can be just as disheartening. And in the words of The Shangri-Las: "That's called sad."

IT'S MY PARTY

45 RPM

N OBODY IN THE BUSINESS REAL-ly took female performers too seriously back then," says Lesley Gore, "the system just wasn't open to women. If a man's career wasn't successful anymore, he could move into A&R or production, or into the company hierarchy—but we couldn't do that. The company would market us—put out some story, press release, or image for us—and that was it—whether it was accurate or not. To this day everyone I meet thinks I was this 'poor little rich girl' who was singing at a party and performing 'It's My Party,' when a record company executive discovered me, and made me and that song a hit overnight. It was just a fantasy tale and I resented it for years—but I had to live with it. . . ."

In actual fact Lesley Gore was discovered via a demo disc, and she never heard "It's My Party" until months later. Lesley was living in Tenafly, New Jersey, and singing with an all-male band, performing mostly current hits at local high school dances and at straighter affairs like catering houses in Queens. She cut some demo discs with the

group, and gave them to her agent, Joe Glaser, at Associated Booking. Joe played them for Irving Green of Mercury Records, and although Green didn't like the band or their original songs he did like the lead vocalist. Glaser got Green to agree to cut a few singles, and Lesley Gore became a Mercury Recording Artist. She was sixteen at the time.

Mercury staff producer Quincy Jones got the assignment to work with Lesley, and one day in February 1963 he appeared at the Gores' house in New Jersey weighted down with boxes of songwriter and publisher demos. Lesley: "He actually came over with about 250 demos. The first one he played was a song called 'It's My Party,' and I said, 'That's pretty good, let's hear some more.' I never really heard demos before, and I had no experience picking hits, so I wasn't really sure what I was doing. We put that in the 'maybe' pile, and then listened to every one of the other 249. When we got to the bottom of the pile, we went back to 'It's My Party,' and it sounded just great—so that was the one."

Quincy then worked on the song with arranger and conductor Claus Ogerman, as well as with Lesley, and then they were ready to go in and record. The session was held at Bell Sound on Saturday, March 30th, 1963, and began promptly at 2 P.M. The room was filled with musicians and everyone played and was recorded at once—there was no overdubbing. "It was just unbelievable to me. Here I was with all these people playing and I was off in a booth singing live along with them. We did four songs that day, one was the B-side, a song called 'Danny' that Paul Anka, a New Jersey neighbor, had brought to me. We did three or four takes on, 'It's My Party,' and that was it."

The following Friday, Lesley was driving in New Jersey, when she heard "It's My Party" on the radio. "It was on the radio in New York less than a week after the session—it was amazing—the record wasn't even officially pressed or released yet, and it started taking off. . . ." The record was rushed out at the end of April, and because of the pre-release air-play, demand was so great that "It's My Party" entered the national charts at #60. It soon became one of the fastest moving releases by an unknown artist ever to appear on the charts: week number one–#60; week number two–#28; week number three–#10; week number four–#1. Four weeks to a national Number One, and Lesley was thrown into a whirlwind schedule of personal appearances. "We tried to keep it down to a minimum. I was still in high school, at The Dwight School For Girls in Tenafly, and I tried to limit my career work to the weekends. I planned to stay in school, and to try to lead a normal life. My first public performance for that record was on a Baltimore teen dance show, where I lip-synced to the record. Then we made the rounds of high school dances sponsored by local deejays so we could grease them up a little. There were countless hops—they were endless—on one night I think I visited something like twelve of them."

"It's My Party" made such a strong impression with the public that Lesley was immediately cast into a rigid mold. If her first record had only been a mild hit, she would have had freer reign over image and material, but now the pressure was too intense to tamper with the formula. The formula was three-tiered: the lyrics were definitely "teenage" and usually dealt with love triangles of one sort or another; the backing track was full—with band, horns, strings, and backup vocalists combined into a professional, if somewhat antiseptic sound; and Lesley herself had a squeaky clean image and a plaintive vocal quality, both of which were exploited to the fullest. On "It's My Party," Lesley had lost Johnny to Judy, and millions cried along with her, but on the follow-up, "Judy's Turn To Cry," Lesley-the-victim got her revenge (Let Lesley rub Judy's face in the dirt a little because "now Johnny's come back to me. . . ."). "Judy's Turn To Cry" was written specifically as a sequel to "It's My Party," and the identification with Lesley's plight on her first record was so strong that when she finally got her revenge the second time around, the public supported her fully. The record went all the way to #5 and was followed similarly by "She's A Fool," a strong record that

IT'S MY PARTY

45 RPM

Chapter EIGHT

was more strident and original than its predecessor. Lesley's lyrics may have been overly simplistic but they hit home with masses of teenagers who saw things the same way. Lesley was only sixteen and seventeen when she recorded these records, and she felt that these were honest representations of how kids felt—she related to them herself. The problem arose when she matured, but the pressure was on her to continue in the same mold.

Many artists in the girl-group scene were not groups at all, Little Eva and Claudine Clark for instance, but in sound and lyric and hefty use of backup vocalists, they clearly fit the bill. Even true girl groups like The Shangri-Las, Shirelles, Ronettes, and Supremes only had one primary lead vocalist, while the rest of the group functioned merely as backup vocalists on records; their importance was felt more strongly on live shows, but on record, it was usually the lead vocal that sold the record. Lesley's voice was usually double-tracked anyway, not only to fatten up the sound, but also to align the recording more clearly with the "girl-group" genre. Unlike the true girl groups, Lesley's appearance and public pronouncements made her a person that the adult world could approve of. Ed Sullivan, a staunch enemy of the tougher girl groups, was a strong supporter and featured Lesley

on many of his shows. She was a perennial television guest, not only on the teen-oriented shows like *Shindig* and *Hullabaloo*, but also on the more adult-oriented variety shows. She appeared in films like *Ski Party, Girls On The Beach, The T.A.M.I. Show,* and was offered the lead in a Broadway show. She turned this down so she could continue her education, and this heavily touted value system was much ballyhooed in both the squeaky clean teen press and the adult media as well.

Lesley's next release, "You Don't Own Me," is in many ways her most original, powerful and fully realized record. It was an intense ballad with a stirring arrangement, but more importantly, it lyrically struck a blow for independence. On her first few records she was a victim, or a gloating winner—but either way her happiness was dependent on someone else—a boyfriend, for instance, and that was *his* choice. Her unhappiness often came at the hands of a turncoat friend—again a situation beyond her control. On "You Don't Own Me," Lesley was on the attack and let it be known that she was able to take care of herself and control her own life—even though that realization seemed to come at the expense of some painful experiences. The record was a massive hit, going all the way to #2, kept out of the top spot only by The Beatles' seven-week run at #1 with "I Want To Hold Your Hand."

''The meeting of the clan.''

''Buffee cheers me up when things go wrong.''

''What I think of boys at times-- only at times!''

''When there's nothing-- or no one--else to lean on.''

''My official fan club portrait.''

LESLEY GORE

On her first tour of England in October 1963, where she had been less successful with the record-buying public, she performed a professional and tightly conceived show. Sharing the bill with Timi Yuro, Brook Benton, Dion, and Trini Lopez, her quick set consisted of "She's A Fool," "Just Let Me Cry," "It's My Party," and "Judy's Turn To Cry." The problem was that upon her return to the U.S. and entrance into Sarah Lawrence College, she was almost completely ostracized: "At Dwight, it was a very small and personal environment. My friends and teachers were very supportive and understanding, and happy for my success. They were actually a part of the entire process. At Sarah Lawrence, the music I was known for was not very fashionable. They weren't open to me as a person, to see what I was really like and what other interests I had. They only saw a portion of me, and had preconceived notions about who or what I was. My records and performances were just a costume, but they couldn't see through that. It

really opened my eyes and was a jolt of reality and what life was all about."

That was not the end to her problems. After doing a phone interview with someone from the *Saturday Evening Post*, a story came out pointing a guilty finger at Lesley as a prime purveyor of what the writer dubbed "the dumb sound." Lesley was hurt, believing that her songs communicated with her audience and that ultimately, although stated perhaps in simpler terms, their concerns were no different than "love-lost," "love-found" songs that were made popular by such "respected" singers as Frank Sinatra, Dean Martin, or Doris Day (who in their day sang songs by composers held in wide public esteem). The Lutheran Christian Encounter publishing house issued a book on pop music—and centering in on girl-group records in particular—damned them not only musically, but lyrically as well. They synopsized "teenage popular music" as follows:

the nation's no·1

Singing Teen Sweetheart

LESLEY GORE

Get these 3 great Mercury hit albums at your local record store!

1. Things happen to me. I have no control over them and no responsibility for them.

2. Life has no discernible meaning or purpose; it is governed by an inscrutable fate: "What will be, will be."

3. I am alone in this frightening, incomprehensible world. (Although there is safety in conforming with the crowd, this doesn't alleviate my basic insecurity.)

4. If love were to happen to me—*your* love—all my anxieties would be magically resolved. You, the love object, are so incomparably wonderful (in fact, divine) that I worship you and would do virtually anything to obtain you.

5. If you withhold your love, or if, as fate might decree, you turn it off and give it to someone else, my loneliness and anxiety become unbearable.

Without entering into a lengthy debate, it would seem that American popular music for decades has revolved in some degree around these themes, and rock 'n' roll, though usually stated in a simpler, more repetitive manner, was no different than its predecessors. Additionally, these were not the only themes that popular music dealt with, and the Lutheran criticism was coming from an obviously biased point of view. Their solution to what they called this "unhealthy, false and fantasy-oriented way of thinking" was simply to place one's faith and belief in "God In Christ because this is reality." Others might argue that this merely substituted one crutch for another, but regardless of your views on that matter, it is clear that popular music was constantly under fire. Lesley Gore herself was caught between the two sides, seeing validity in both their arguments, and tried to walk a fine line between her earlier "teenage" direction, and a blander, more acceptable-to-adults traditional pop sound.

Her releases mirrored this split personality dilemma, with the sappier pop standard side often getting the record company nod. It wasn't until Lesley worked with Ellie Greenwich that she could again create contemporary and vibrant recordings. Ellie: "I had been cutting demos of other people's songs for Lesley. I sang all the voices, lead and background. When Lesley heard them she asked who it was, and she liked them a lot so I was hired to do background work on her recordings. Then we got friendly, and I wondered why I hadn't written anything for her. So I went back to the office and played around on the piano a little, and on the way home in the cab I started singing 'Maybe I know. . . .' When I got home, I kept at it and came up with 'Maybe I Know' and 'Look Of Love.' Jeff got home from another session, and I said, 'Here's what I have; I need a bridge, I need some words for the chorus—we gotta play 'em for Lesley tomorrow; and on and on. He said, 'Huh?' And I said, 'That's it—don't worry, I'm sure we'll get them.' So we finished them up, and didn't do demos, I just went over the next day and played them for Claus (Ogerman). He loved them, and Lesley loved them, and they went in the next week and cut 'em both. I sang background with Jean Thomas and Miki Harris."

Lesley: "I worked most closely with Claus on sorting through material, and then we'd present it to Quincy. We usually agreed on what we should record. The arrangements would be all worked out beforehand—there were never too many surprises waiting for me in the studio—we had it down pretty well. We'd cut three or four sides a session; sometimes we'd get an album done in four sessions. We never really had too many takes. Either it felt right or it didn't, and everyone could tell if it was right. Claus would be in the studio and Quincy would be behind the board, and we usually had Phil Ramone as the engineer. The musicians were great, both as players and as people, and everything was very professional. It all went so smoothly and wonderfully. At first my vocals were done live while the band played, because the union had some rule about overdubbing, but then we got to the point where everyone would leave, and we'd overdub my vocals after everyone had left, sort of on the sly. . . ."

"Maybe I Know" was the first of the Barry-Greenwich songs to be released, and although it did have touches of MOR pop, it was honest and compelling, sporting a wonderful melody, a riveting lyric, and a convincing vocal performance. It reached #14, and after another single flopped "Look Of Love" was released, and brought Lesley back into the Top Thirty. "Look Of Love" drove on more solidly than most of Lesley's recordings, and even used some of the obvious Spector touches. The lyrics of both Barry-Greenwich songs dealt with broken relationships, but were more intricately constructed and original than most of Lesley's previous singles. Lesley continued to release material for Mercury over the next several years, but most of it fared poorly on the charts, and the few that did score ("Sunshine, Lollipops, and Rainbows" and "California Nights") were uniformly saccharin. As Lesley grew older, her earlier leanings towards strict nightclub-type pop became more pronounced, and she eventually disappeared from the charts.

Although Lesley Gore sold millions of records, she never reaped enormous windfalls: "It took awhile until we got really serious about the business. Joe Glaser was my agent and handled most matters, while my father looked after most of the personal business. I stayed in school throughout it all, and didn't do those long Dick Clark-type tours—I might fly in for a show or two, or do some television, but I never was out on the road for an extended period of time. I pretty much had control with Claus and Quincy over my material, but what happened to it after the session was beyond my jurisdiction. "The company designed the album and single covers, and sent out publicity pictures. I never had much input there, and was often stuck with something I really didn't like. Getting accurate accountings was close to impossible. When I first signed up, I was only getting a small royalty, something like 2 or 2 and a half percent. It went up slightly over the years, but not by much. And I had to pay back all the studio costs—like musicians, tape and all the rest. I'd be having all these hits, and not be getting too much money. I never could understand that. I'm sure we were charged for everything—if they xeroxed something, we got charged for it. I did get something, enough to live on during those years and pay for school, but not much more than that. Anyone who thinks I could retire and buy a house in the South of France is badly mistaken. It was always a battle to get anything respected. Even though I was a big seller, they only cared about males. They were pushing males, and everyone was fed males. That was always clear to me. They just thought it was easier to sell males. It really got to me after a while. . . ."

Her burst of seven Top Twenty singles within a two-year period made Lesley Gore a major chart force, and her anguished classics created and perfected a unique sub-genre of girl-group records. Many imitators tried to follow her, and although several one-shot hits were secured, no one was quite so successful at galvanizing a continuing public response. In retrospect, some seem rather precious, and due to constant parodying over the years, perhaps campy, but for their time they best represented a certain aura of truthful naivete—that perhaps, it's sad to say, we'll probably never see again.

There were several other performers who worked in the style made popular by Lesley Gore. In most cases they were incredibly naive in both sound and lyric—stripping bare to the essentials of female teenage angst. For many, they were wimpy beyond belief, but teenage girls in particular found a certain camaraderie and allegiance to their stylings. Shelley Fabares was an early pioneer with the wispy "Johnny Angel" which went all the way to #1 in early 1962. (Other television spinoff recording artists like Annette and Patty Duke made their mark, but only by the widest criteria could they fall into the girl-group category. . . .) It's too bad Shelley Fabares typified the early Queen of wimpy girl groups, because she later made wonderfully solid records with the writing and production help of David Gates, Jan Barry, P.F. Sloan, and Steve Barri. Marcie Blane issued over six singles on Seville Records, but only the first, "(I Want To Be) Bobby's Girl," was a hit, reaching #3 late in 1962. Robin Ward's handful of singles for Dot were glossy Los Angeles pop-rock records written and produced by Gil Garfield and Perry Botkin Jr. "Wonderful Summer" went to #14 in (surprisingly enough) January 1964, but the follow-ups couldn't recapture the initial appeal. Her final release, "In His Car," is notable for its ethereal Beach Boys-influenced mood and lush harmonies. "Little" Peggy March was supported for years by her record company, RCA, who paired her with an endless stream of writers and producers, but only the first release, "I Will Follow Him," really impressed the record buying

Tracey Dey with producer Bob Crewe.

public. "I Will Follow Him" was about as extreme a devotional record as one could imagine, and it was a huge hit (not only in America, but around the world), in the spring of 1963. Once it reached the Top Ten, it stayed there for two months, and held down the #1 spot for three weeks, fighting off some fierce competition. Linda Scott came up with her classic (once again the first time out) with "I Told Every Little Star" for The Canadian-American label in early 1961. This #3 record was followed by a series of mild chart placings, though she did reach the Top Twenty twice more during 1961. In early 1962, the President and A & R director for Canadian-American (Neil Galligan and Bob [Hutch] Davie respectively) left the label to form their own company, Congress Records, and took Linda Scott with them. Linda was placed in the unenviable task of recording her final Canadian-American session from 10 P.M. to midnight one Friday night, and then when she legally became a Congress Records act at midnight, was rushed over to their session to record her debut for that label. Both reached the deejays and stores on the same day, and both canceled each other out on the airwaves; the confusion and split play added up to a #70 record for her old label, and a #60 for her new label. Over a dozen singles followed, first on Congress, and later on Kapp, but despite extensive touring, frequent television exposure, and occasional movie roles, Linda Scott's star had faded

permanently.

Diane Renay was a personal favorite of Bob Crewe, and he wrote and produced for her on a succession of labels. It was Bob Crewe's talents that gave Diane a shot at Lesley Gore's crown, but only "Navy Blue" (#6 in March 1964) made the grade. From 1962-1966, Crewe worked with her at Atco, 20th Century-Fox, MGM, and finally New Voice, but that second big hit just did not materialize. Crewe performed a similar role in the career of Tracey Dey, first on Vee Jay (where he cut an answer record to his own Four Seasons creation, "Sherry," called "Jerry I'm Your Sherry"), then Liberty, and finally half a dozen releases for AMY. Of the three that charted, none broke into the Top Fifty.

Ultimately, it seems that most of these solo girl-group performers tended to aspire to more long-term nightclub-type careers, and only used the girl-group medium as a means to gain a career foothold. They had pretty, if nondescript, voices but no roots or feel for rock 'n' roll or rhythm & blues. When their MOR leanings became too obvious, their relevance to the vast teenage audience disappeared. Musically, records were almost uniformly lightweight, lacking the powerful and creative stylings of the best of the girl groups. One special song that caught the public's fancy and became a hit (they almost seemed like novelty records) was usually the most they achieved. At their best, however, they could say more in two and a half minutes about the "female adolescent condition" than many psychology textbooks could manage in four hundred pages.

Linda Scott.

Chapter NINE

BE MY BABY

BY THE END OF 1962, PHIL SPECtor had finally reached the point where he felt he was in control of his musical life. He had hit #1 with The Crystals' "He's A Rebel," and wrested full ownership of the Philles label away from his partners, Lester Sill and Harry Finfer. Spector was also pleased that he had produced this number one record with session singers as vocalists; it convinced him even more that he could make a hit with whomever he wanted and that the artists themselves were of secondary importance. Darlene Love, who sang lead, and The Blossoms, who sang backup on "He's A Rebel," were merely paid a session fee. They had no share of the royalties, and they couldn't tour as The Crystals since Spector owned the rights to the name. Lester Sill recalls that when "He's A Rebel" hit the top spot, Philles gave Darlene and her friends a bonus instead of a royalty—"a nice amount. . . ." Darlene Love says the total payment she received for "He's A Rebel" was $1500.

Phil Spector was an emotional man who would do anything to help out a friend; once you penetrated inside his wall of defenses and he felt secure about the friendship, you were accepted as part of the family. But it often happened that a disagreement or hurt would penetrate the bond, and then Phil would be just as quick to completely cut off the relationship: having no relationship was preferable to having a painful one. The year of 1963 would see Phil establish several important new ties—the pain and the hurt would come later. . . .

Spector's first new hookup came with Darlene Love, an L.A.-based vocalist who had recorded for several years on numerous labels as the lead singer of the vocal trio, The Blossoms. Darlene, born Darlene Wright, also was a much-in-demand session vocalist who sang backup on literally hundreds of records cut in Los Angeles during the early sixties. Phil was taken not only with her vocal strengths and distinctive sound, but also with the confidence and ease with which she carried them off. After "He's A Rebel," Spector put together a vocal trio of Darlene, Fanita James, another Blossom, and Bobby Sheen, a Clyde McPhatter-type vocalist with whom Phil had previously cut a solo record at Liberty. They concocted a soulful version of "Zip-A-Dee-Doo-Dah," which sported one of the weirdest guitar solo sounds ever laid down—it took Duane Eddy's echoey twang to the limit—and when Phil returned to New York, a major label offered him a $10,000 advance for the master. Spector turned them down, and dubbed the makeshift group Bobby and The Holidays. By the time he issued the record himself on Philles, the group had become Bob B. Soxx and The Blue Jeans and their innovative reworking of an old standard swept into the Top Ten in January 1963.

As part of his settlement with ex-partners Sill and Finfer, Spector was required to give a portion of the profits from The Crystals' next two releases to the departed duo. The first of these was a Barry Mann-Cynthia Weil tune, ''He's Sure The Boy I Love,'' with Darlene Love once again on lead vocals. The record is drivingly melodic and soulfully visual, cut loose with ragged edges. It's pure rhythm with pounding drums carrying the beat, maracas and sleigh bells layered on top, and Darlene's vocals exhibiting as honest and heartfelt an emotion as one could ever hope for. Lyrically, the song meshed together topical social images of youthful class values (Cadillacs, unemployment checks, diamond rings, movie stars etc.), with the belief that true, deep love could rise above these worldly problems and provide real happiness. While others sang of exteriors, ''He's Sure The Boy I Love'' dug deep into the interiors of both hearts and minds.

The record reached #11 on the Top 100, #2 on the r&b charts, and then Spector decided that he really didn't want to give any more profits to his former partners. He devised a plan to fulfill his legal obligations and still not pay out one cent in royalties. He went into the studio with the real Crystals and cut a five-minute tune called ''(Let's Dance) The Screw.'' It was a hastily recorded bump-and-grind song with obvious sexual innuendos, and would clearly, by virtue of its length, music, and lyrics, not get played. Spector pressed up some deejay copies, sent them to his distributors, and promptly forgot about the record. ''The Screw,'' allegedly a new dance craze, was merely Phil's big joke—it might have also referred to the fact that Phil was possibly ''screwing'' his ex-partners out of their potential share of profits. This was the second Crystals record; it sold zero copies; therefore he would owe Sill and Finfer no money and they would have no further profit participation. As a final touch to the ''joke,'' Spector had his lawyer bellow in a deep voice on the record at various intervals, ''Do the screw.'' Ho-Ho-Ho—big joke, Phil.

Back in New York scouting around for material, Spector had a meeting set up with fledgling hit-writer Ellie Greenwich: ''I was on a 'first refusal' basis with Leiber & Stoller at this point, which meant that I played them all my songs and if they liked them, they could have them; if not, I was free to take them elsewhere. I wrote '(Today I Met) The Boy I'm Gonna Marry,' and Leiber & Stoller weren't too excited by it. I took it to Aaron Schroeder and he liked it and arranged for Phil Spector to hear that and some other songs. So in

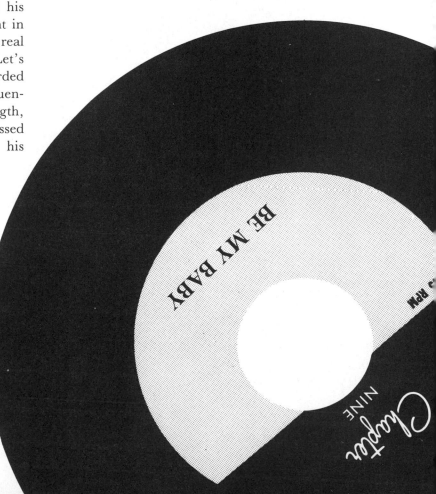

POP SPOTLIGHT
ZIP-A-DEE-DOO-DAH
Bob B. Soxx & the Blue Jeans.
Philles PHLP 4002 (M)
Bob B. Soxx and his girl friends, the Blue Jeans, are one of the hottest of the newer groups and they've scored big with their first single, the title song of this album. Other solid sides include "This Land Is Your Land" (current also for the New Christy Minstrels), "White Cliffs of Dover," "Let the Good Times Roll," and several worthy items by the album's producer, Phil Spector. Solid teen wax.

Bob B. Soxx and The Blue Jeans

(L-R): Bobby Sheen, Darlene Love, and Fanita James.

comes Phil and I'm sitting at the piano playing 'It Was Me Yesterday.' Phil was walking around the room fixing his clothes, looking in the mirror, and adjusting his hair—all the time making noises while I was playing my song. Finally I said, 'Either you want to hear my songs or you don't.' Phil exploded and stormed out of the room, and everyone in the office felt that Spector was gone for good." A short time later, Phil heard a demo of "The Boy I'm Gonna Marry" and wanted the song, and arranged to meet the writers: "I had a 2 P.M. appointment with Phil and by 2:10 I was ready to leave. But Tony Powers [Ellie's co-writer], convinced me to wait. So we hung around in the hall lobby of 62nd Street and York Avenue until 5:30 or 6:00. I didn't really know who Spector was, or the power he had in the business, and the fact that everybody usually bowed down to him, so when he came I was really mad. 'Hey Phil, if you make an appointment and can't keep it, you should let us know. You were very rude!' And I think he just liked the idea that I stood up to him, because we hit it off right away."

Ellie's early songs were written with Tony Powers, and Spector wanted a piece of the publishing if he recorded them. When he couldn't get that, he secured one-third of the writers' share and credits, an arrangement that upset Greenwich: "Morally I regret it. I felt that if you wrote a song, you wrote it. And if you produced it, you produced it. I did a lot of editing and putting together of songs for other people, but I never took writer's credits unless I actually wrote it. It was commonplace to make deals between publishers, writers, and companies, but I don't think it's right, and I just won't do it. I passed up a lot of big money deals by refusing to throw in a piece of the action." Spector shared writers' credits on the three Greenwich-Powers songs he recorded, although his input in writing was negligible. After that he became a more active participant in the writing sessions, and was credited and paid accordingly.

In L.A. he cut "Why Do Lovers Break Each Other's Hearts," and "(Today I Met) The Boy I'm Gonna Marry," both featuring Darlene Love. Spector recorded the songs first, and would decide who would be listed as the artist, only after hearing the final product, or even if the record would come out at all. "Why Do Lovers . . ." became the next release for Bob B. Soxx and The Blue Jeans, and with Bobby Sheen's deep vocals augmenting the bass line, Darlene's voice warmly but strongly selling the message, with saxophones and percussion carrying the rest of the song, the record reached #38. "The Boy I'm Gonna Marry" became the first solo release for Darlene Love. It was melodically stronger and more emotionally intense, but a bit slow-paced for AM airwaves. It only reached #39. Both these records were special, almost exceptional by 1963 standards, but not *great*—and Spector only wanted to make great records. "If I can't be better than what's around, and what's been done before, then what's the point in doing it?" asked Phil. "I'd just rather not make records."

Faced with the fact that his last two releases had barely scraped into the Top Forty, Spector decided that he needed a big hit or nothing at all. As an independent record company, Philles would get paid by a series of distributors strung throughout the country. Sometimes payments were slow, or nonexistent, and the only real leverage a company had was to hold back a new hit until the distributors paid for the last hit. Spector knew that each record had to be a smash in order to get paid and keep his distributors out there pushing his product—a string of flops could put a small company out of business before it knew what happened. He also felt that he had strayed from his original self-composed commandments: music must be emotional and honest; create a sound on record that no one can copy or cover; and make sure you get paid. He had fought for his control and freedom, and now it was time to put up or shut up. Phil Spector was not about to shut up.

Meanwhile, Ellie Greenwich and her new husband and writing partner Jeff Barry came up with a song which they called "Da Doo Ron Ron," subtitled "When He Walked Me Home." Spector felt that this was what he was looking for, flew out to L.A., and gathered up his forces. The team included engineer Larry Levine and his Goldstar Studios, arranger Jack Nitzsche, and a slew of session people including some, and sometimes most of, the following: Barney Kessel, Glen Campbell, Billy Strange, Carol Kaye, Irv Rubin, Bill Pitman, and Tommy Tedesco on guitars; Hal Blaine, Earl Palmer, and Ritchie Frost on drums; Leon Russell, Larry Knectal, Harold Battiste, Don Randi, Nino Tempo, Mike Spencer, and Al DeLory on keyboards; Steve Douglas, Jay Migliori, Lou Blackburn, and Roy Caton on horns; Larry Knectal, Jimmy Bond, Ray Pullman, and Wallick Dean on bass; and anyone and everyone on percussion, including Sonny Bono, Frank Kapp, Julius Wechter, Gene Estes, and Nino Tempo. On backup vocals he would use members of various Philles groups as well as Gracia Nitzsche, Jean King, Cher Bono, Edna Wright, and Carolyn Willis. All in all, it was the cream of West Coast session players.

Spector recorded the tracks for "Da Doo Ron Ron" in Los Angeles, but couldn't get the right vocal sound from his West Coast singers, so he flew back to New York and used LaLa Brooks of The Crystals. When he had the whole thing finished, he felt that the record just needed a little more punch and emphasis on the bottom end, but it was already recorded and there were no open tracks available for overdubs. Spector and Larry Levine came up with an ingenious solution: while they were mixing "Da Doo Ron Ron" down to the

The Crystals, 1964.

mono master, Spector had Nino Tempo out in the studio playing a bass drum with mallets for accents wherever needed—as the original tracks were mixed into mono, they also added in Nino Tempo's live drum figures—anyone looking today to find Tempo's drums on the original 3-tracks just won't find it—it only exists on the mono master, and that's it.

"Da Doo Ron Ron" itself was everything Spector wanted—it thunderously blares out from the opening, with drums, handclaps, and saxophones mixed together into what would soon become known as "the wall of sound." The vocals, melody, and story line are exhilarating; Tempo's drum overdub is stunning in its power and definition; and the whole thing is over before you can catch your breath. It's a record that exudes a life of its own and demands not only attention, but almost a total immersion into its driving, exuberant vitality. It was a huge hit both on the pop and r&b charts, and also was the first record to make the Spector sound popular around the world.

Phil followed this up with "Then He Kissed Me" which took the popular Latin baion beat uptempo at a galloping pace, and added lush, swirling strings over the top. Once again, it was a global smash.

The Crystals themselves were busy touring, but their dissatisfaction with Spector was growing each day. For one, they were unhappy about Phil's usage of Darlene Love as vocalist on so-called Crystals records. They also felt that they should be earning more money from record royalties. They also feared for their future and wanted to branch out in other musical directions and develop a night-club act, sing more middle-of-the-road fare and perform some songs with a jazz flavor to them. In the studio, they would sit for hours while Spector worked on the sound and arrangements of the musicians. He would listen to the tracks endlessly at ear-piercing volume, and ignore their boredom or their needs. He would make them sing over and over again—leads, backgrounds, even individual sections. They would record songs that would

Recording studio track sheet for an unreleased
Phil Spector-Crystals session for a song called "Please Be My Boyfriend."

124

Bill

Philles Records

440 E 62nd st

ny. ny.

①

BROADWAY RECORDING STUDIOS, INC.

1697 Broadway, New York 19, New York
Suite 1005 - Studio
Tel. CIrcle 6-3069

PHILLES RECORDS

TO: Phil Spector

DATE: 7/9/64

3 TR

7:30 – 12:30

½ hr Break

Master Number	Size	Subject
2 TR Basic Session		Please be my baby Friend
		T/ ct T ct T3 T4 T5
		T6 T7 ct T8 ct T9
		T11 T12 T13 T14 ct
3 TR →		T1 T2 T3 T4 ct
8/4/64		Please be my baby Friend
4th OD →		T1 ct T2 T3 T4 ct T5 T6
		T7 T8 ct

30 4		ST.	135.00
		Tape ¼	8.00
120		Tape ½	20.00
15			
135			163.00
			6.52
OK Billed in full 7/21/64			169.52

TOTAL NUMBER OF MASTERS: _____

RECEIVED BY: _____ TIME: _____

never be released, and their request for input on choice of material fell on deaf ears. They believed that Spector was egomaniacal and was making their records so noisy and murky that they couldn't cut through the din. Spector told an interviewer at the time: "The cloudier and fuzzier a record is, the more honesty and guts it has." The conflicting views of Spector and The Crystals were poles apart and not getting any closer.

The original quintet of Crystals was now down to a foursome, as Mary Thomas dropped out, and Pat Wright was replaced with Frances Collins. It was this quartet that made the first trip to England in early 1964, headlining an extensive and successful six-week tour with Johnny Kidd, Joe Brown, Heinz, and Manfred Mann. Manfred

Darlene Love and The Cookies backstage at a "Show of Stars" package tour date.

The Blossoms backing up Marvin Gaye in *The T.A.M.I. Show* movie.

Mann actually backed up The Crystals on their live dates, coming as close as five musicians could to approximating the Spector recorded sound. The members of Manfred Mann also took The Crystals down to a series of small rock clubs in London, where the girls mixed with the new British rock groups, all of whom loved The Crystals' records and respected the Spector sound. After a six-week tour without one day off, the girls were set to relax, sightsee, and shop around London, but they suddenly got a call from Spector in New York who told them to take the next plane home for a recording session. The Crystals, along with tour manager Arthur Pemberton, did so but were not happy about it.

Although The Crystals were coming off two Top Five hits in a row, Spector's eccentricities and disregard for their needs frayed their nerves. They wanted out. Phil refused and made their records even noisier than before. The first was "Little Boy," a recording that had some of the sound, but none of the vitality or emotional impact of The Crystals' previous hits. It only reached #92. Then came "All Grown Up," which was loosely based on an old Chuck Berry song, and this one didn't even crack the Top 100. In England, Spector pulled "Little Boy" off the market and issued "I Wonder," an adventurous track which didn't quite come together and lost the vocals somewhere in a swirling pit of background fuzz. To top it off, Spector was lavishing most of his time and effort recording a new female vocal group for Philles, The Ronettes, and The Crystals were considerably less than a priority. They ultimately bought their way out of their contract with Spector and went over to United Artists for a handful of releases, none of which ever made the charts. The Crystals had become one of the most popular and recognizable recording artists of their era, but with the massively solid foundation of Phil Spector's input pulled out from under them, they were buried by their wall of sound that now lay crumbled at their feet.

The Blossoms.

Back in Los Angeles things were not going so well between Spector and his vocal star Darlene Love either. Some of Darlene's complaints were similar to those of The Crystals, but a prime disagreement between Phil and Darlene arose out of Spector's insistence that Darlene curtail her outside career work. Darlene occasionally did make public appearances with Bob B. Soxx and The Blue Jeans, as well as solo spots of her own, but these were exceptions to the rule. Darlene was happier and more financially secure singing on record dates in Los Angeles, and backing big-name singers on their live shows. On top of the fact that these commitments often led to scheduling conflicts with Spector sessions, Phil was incensed that Darlene continued to make records for other labels with The Blossoms, and even solo records under pseudonyms. In 1964, The Blossoms sang behind several artists in the popular movie *The T.A.M.I. Show,* and then they began to appear weekly on the national TV show, *Shindig.* Here, they not only backed up most of the artists on the show, but they also had regular on-camera song spots of their own. (Many of Spector's regular session musicians played each week on *Shindig* as well—their television payments were significantly higher than their recording studio work earned.) Jack Good, producer of *Shindig,* said at the time: "These three girls (The Blossoms) are quite remarkable. They back approximately ten numbers per show, but don't have to be taught the songs. You tell them what they will be singing, and that's it. The number is polished and ready for the first run-through. They are individually great, and as a group, sensational."

In mid-1963, Spector issued what would become the final Bob B. Soxx and The Blue Jeans single, "Not Too Young To Get Married," a wildly uptempo song that echoed the sound and party-like atmosphere of earlier hits by Gary U.S. Bonds. Not very original in concept or execution, it only reached #63. Then came two solo singles by Darlene Love, "Wait 'Till My Bobby Gets Home," and "A Fine Fine Boy." "Wait 'Till My Bobby Gets Home" was a melodic teenage party record which took Darlene into the Top Thirty for the first time as a solo artist, and "A Fine Fine Boy" was in many ways even better, but lacked a memorable hook, and only reached #53. Then came "Christmas (Baby Please Come Home),"

first issued in late 1963 in conjunction with the release of Phil Spector's *Christmas* album. In actual fact the song, written by Barry, Greenwich, and Spector, was the only new original song to appear on the Christmas album, but Christmas of 1963 saw the country fixated by the death of John Kennedy, and there was no place for a new Christmas record on the airwaves. It was issued the following Christmas as well, but once again did not chart, possibly because most Christmas hits tend to be happy or at least seasonally reflective, while "Christmas (Baby Please Come Home)" delivered one of the most intensely depressing messages ever recorded. It was, however, Darlene Love's most moving and heart-wrenching performance for Spector, and Phil himself rose to the occasion with a brilliantly conceived and masterfully executed production. In the lyrics, Darlene's man is gone, and the baubles and trappings of Christmas only reinforce and increase her loneliness. The musical track intensifies as the song progresses, and Darlene's vocals become more and more frenetic. Bells, strings, pounding drums, a wailing chorus, and hammering piano trills ultimately collide with Darlene's painful anguish in what is the most moving and cataclysmic buildup of any pop record Phil Spector, or anyone else for that matter, has ever made. If only one recording could exist with the name of Phil Spector on it, this might have to be the one.

From the time Spector first used a song by Ellie Greenwich until the spurt ended, two years had elapsed, and *all eleven* of Spector's single releases during this period were written either by Ellie and Tony Powers or Jeff Barry. This consisted of two by Bob B. Soxx and The Blue Jeans, three by The Crystals, four by Darlene Love, and two by The Ronettes. Not only were most of them major hits, but by any reasonable use of the word, many of them were classics—creations that have never been surpassed, with stylings that remain greatly influential today. Simply put, the result was one of the most fertile and significant collaborative efforts that pop music has ever produced. How and why the creative energies meshed at that particular moment in time, or what course pop history would have taken if they didn't meet are impossible questions to answer, but we *can* look back at how the process itself worked.

At first, Jeff and Ellie would cut demos of their

songs; Jeff would play piano setting out the beat and chords; Ellie would add melody accents and coloring on an organ; then Jeff would overdub a simple and solid drumbeat, often using a piece of styrofoam on the snare to approximate the sound he wanted. Those three tracks were mixed together onto a single track, and Ellie would sing the lead, and overdub the backups. Sometimes Jeff would contribute a vocal bass part if it was right for the song. The whole thing would get mixed together, and the demo was complete. Spector would take the demo, work out his arrangements, and the record would be cut.

Once the trio got to be closer, both musically and personally, they would write together and no demos would be cut. Ellie describes the scene: "We would usually meet at Phil's office on East 62nd Street. I'd play piano, Phil would play guitar. We'd play and sing, someone would leave the room, then come back a while later. Jeff would be playing and coming up with parts. We'd throw around ideas, riffs, lyrical ideas. We'd take a break, then come back and work. Phil would say, 'I like that—keep that,' or 'Use the first two lines and the two from the other section,' and on and on. Stuff would just come out of our heads—I don't know why or how, but it just did. With three people you could bounce off each other and then you could sing something with three-part harmony. Someone would hook a tambourine to their foot and pound out the beat. We were just on the same wavelength, and it was great fun, really. Sometimes the writing sessions would occur over a few days, and at the end we'd have a bunch of new songs. If we got a couple of goosebumps in a

At a January 1963 BMI Awards dinner (Top, L-R): Evelyn Kingsley, Mike Stoller, Bert Berns, Zelda, Paul Case, Sam Cooke, Jerry Leiber. (Bottom, L-R): Phil Spector, Mr. and Mrs. Danny Kessler, and Barry DeVorzen.

writing session, we knew we had something."

Sometimes Jeff and Ellie would get to play the song for the group who would eventually record it, but as time went on Phil would just go out and cut the record. Ellie: "We kept a tape rolling during the writing sessions and when we were done, Phil would fly out to L.A. and work on arrangements with Jack Nitzsche. Sometimes he'd call us and say 'What were the words over here . . . how did this part go . . . play it over the phone . . . ok . . . I'm coming back in two days.' He'd come back and say 'This is the single'; the record would come out, be on the charts two days later—just bam, bam, bam. The energy and excitement were unbelievable. When he played us the finished record, it was usually bigger sounding than we expected. We were usually very, very happy with the results. After a while we felt that some of the records were getting too big and too noisy and we told him, 'Phil, listen we think this is getting a bit out of hand,' and he'd listen, but the final decision was always his."

Ellie continues: "Phil works totally on impulse without any regard for the consequences—just whatever he feels at the time. To him the artist was just the vehicle—'Please sing now, ok good, thank you very much, bye bye. . . .' I remember at one session for Darlene, the musicians came in with little short-sleeve shirts that said 'Phil Spector' across the front and they all stood up when he came in. It was like a little army. He was absolutely in charge. I don't know if they feared him or revered him, or joked with him—it was probably a combination of everything. He knew what he wanted and come hell or high water—if the meters were bulging off the scales, and everyone's saying, 'It's impossible to do this,' he would go, 'Rip up the whole studio—I want the entire studio for an echo chamber.' They'd say, 'Phil, you can't do that.' And he'd say, 'I'm doing it.' He did it his way. He did what he really believed in. He bucked a lot of things, and took the consequences—good or bad."

Darlene Love was one of the few Philles artists who was outspoken in her opinions with Phil. She might not have been happy with material, or financial arrangements, and as time went by she became increasingly irritated by lengthy sessions where she would give her all, and then records would never get released. Spector, for one reason or another, just didn't feel they were good enough, commercial enough, or right for the moment. On the other hand, Phil was still irked by Darlene's continuing non-Spector related work. They managed to patch up their differences, and decided to create a hit with a song called "Stumble And Fall." First issued in the fall of 1964, the record was quite marvelous and seemed almost guaranteed to bring Darlene back into the Top Thirty and maybe much higher, but then things fell apart. Darlene remembers: "We made this record to hit where the other ones had flopped. It had been out for about two weeks, and then Phil and I got mad at each other and he pulled it back off the market by sending out a note to the radio stations saying that the pressing plant had inadvertently put out the wrong record, and that there would be another one very soon." Others close to the scene felt that a major factor in the withdrawal of the record was that Spector's last few singles had been relatively unsuccessful, and that the initial reaction to "Stumble And Fall" was less than enthusiastic. (When Spector pulled the record back, he rushed out The Ronettes' "Walking In The Rain" in its place, and that *was* a major hit. . . .) Whatever the reason, the result was that Darlene was mad at Phil, and Phil was mad with Darlene—they split, and never made another Philles record together. First The Crystals, and now Darlene Love had left the fold, but Spector was busily immersed in a series of records with a group with whom he felt the closest emotional ties—the records and the group would come to be recognized and remembered as the pinnacle of the girl-group era. The records were many. The group was The Ronettes.

"My approach to the business has always been from an art standpoint," said Phil Spector. "The fact that it was commercial and successful was just added gravy. It wasn't part of my scheme. My scheme was to do the things I felt." Spector was driven by idealism and emotion, and his work embodies a tremendous force and conviction that his imitators and competitors just could not equal. Spector was possessed by the need to make his work bigger and better than not only everybody else, but himself as well. He had to prove himself, time and time again—the last one was never good enough or big enough. For years his work had been his life, but then there came a time when he met Veronica Bennett, and his *life* became his work.

Veronica Bennett, her sister Estelle, and their

Darlene Love.

cousin Nedra Talley were all native New Yorkers who lived in upper Manhattan. They loved rock 'n' roll and rhythm & blues and by their early teens were singing together, occasionally in public. In 1961, they were waiting on line to get into the Peppermint Lounge, the hottest night spot in town since the Twist craze had broken open, and the person guarding the door thought they were in show business—they all dressed alike and had "a look" about them. He let them in, and within a few weeks they were hired to dance on stage while the music played. They each only got ten dollars a night, but they loved it, mixing with celebrities, performing, going on tour with the Clay Cole Twist package—it was the world's biggest party and they were right there in the middle, and all this at the ages of sixteen and seventeen. Soon they became regulars at the Brooklyn Fox Shows, where they became known as Murray The K's dancing girls. By mid-1961, they had a recording contract with Colpix Records and during 1961 and 1962 had a handful of singles released, first as Ronnie and The Relatives, and later on as The Ronettes. (Their name, The Ronettes, came by combining parts of all their first names, Veronica was known as Ronnie, along with Estelle, and Nedra. They also thought it sounded like The Rockettes, which was just fine because The Ronettes were known primarily for their dancing routines. . . .) These records were rather lightweight, run-of-the-mill, early girl-group-type records—what they lacked

TWIST FROM COAST-TO-COAST

The Ronettes when they were dancers at the Peppermint Lounge.

TWISTING IN MIAMI...

The Twist has hit hard in the South! (Note that one Club even has that Peppermint flavor!) A little research shows that guys and dolls who Twist below the Mason-Dixon Line put the emphasis on knee-action, rather than hip-twisting. A Southern Twist is more of a squat than a swivel, the experts say. But no matter where you go, there's one thing everyone agrees on— that it's crazy, man, crazy!

was a sound, a great song, and a clear point of view. The girls also did some backing vocal sessions for other artists recording in New York, and got to know the studios, musicians, and producers about town.

As the story goes, Estelle was calling someone about some recording work, and mistakenly got Phil Spector on the other end of the line. He asked who they were, what they did, and so on, and then asked if they wanted to do some vocal backups on a session. They said yes, and met up at a studio on 57th Street. Phil was taken first by their appearance—they wore heavy eye makeup, tight dresses and slacks, and all had matching hairdos piled high on their heads. He quickly decided that he wanted to record them, and later on when he actually heard them sing, was surprised at just how good they sounded. In early 1963, they did do some backups on Bob B. Soxx and The Blue Jeans and Darlene Love records, and Spector also had Ronnie do a vocal on a track he had recorded previously, "Why Don't They Let Us Fall In Love," but that stayed unreleased.

Ronnie didn't possess a particularly strong voice, nor was her range anything special, but there was a unique quality to her sound. It was youthful, sultry, and best of all, honest. In an uncanny way it sounded not unlike a young Frankie Lymon, not only in tone but in phrasing as well. That was enough for Spector.

Although The Ronettes and Phil Spector claim that their initial meeting was accidental and that they had never met before, at the very least they were both aware of each other, and probably had met if only casually. Phil had visited the Peppermint Lounge where The Ronettes were highly visible dancing on stage all night. They worked regularly with Murray The K at the Brooklyn Fox Shows, and Spector and Murray were well acquainted. They recorded for the New York Colpix label using studios and musicians that Spector also used. In 1962, it was probably The Ronettes who had recorded a single for Atco under the name The Heartbreakers, produced by Bert Berns, again a close contemporary of Spector. Even Ellie Greenwich, at that moment in the middle of of a hit-writing streak with Spector, knew of the group: ''I had seen Ronnie out at Levittown Memorial High School as Ronnie And The Relatives. They were something even then, with that long hair, and those eyes—they were into some heavy-duty eye makeup. . . .'' The Ronettes had also become friendly with Gerry Goffin and Carole King; Carole had written a song for the group (''You Bet I Would'' on Colpix), and The Ronettes had sung backup on a Little Eva session.

In actual fact, it appears to have been Georgia Winters of *16 Magazine* who set up the initial meeting between Spector and The Ronettes. Phil wanted to sign the group, but they were under contract to Colpix. They devised a plan where The Ronettes would go up to Colpix and tell the folks at the company that they didn't want to be in show business anymore—that they wanted to go back to school and be teachers and nurses. This subterfuge worked and the girls got their release from Colpix. Although Phil had been working with the group since early 1963, and continued working with them while they were seeking their release from Colpix, it wasn't until August of 1963 that Spector sent out a press release announcing that The Ronettes were signed to Philles. (He had let the dust settle so it didn't appear that he had enticed the group away from Colpix, which was precisely what he had done).

Spector had one track in the can already on the group, and it was certainly good enough for a debut release, but Phil seemed to take The Ronettes first release more seriously than he had done with any of his other groups. He even visited with Ronnie and Estelle's mother several times, and assured her that the Ronettes would have a number one hit with their first Philles release. During the early summer of 1963, Spector spent all his energies recording two tracks out at Goldstar Studios—''Be My Baby'' and ''Baby I Love You''—both written with Jeff Barry and Ellie Greenwich. Phil's 'wall' was not so much the specific *sound* that people thought, but more accurately a *style* of recording. It was the style that stayed the same; the sound could and would vary significantly from record to record.

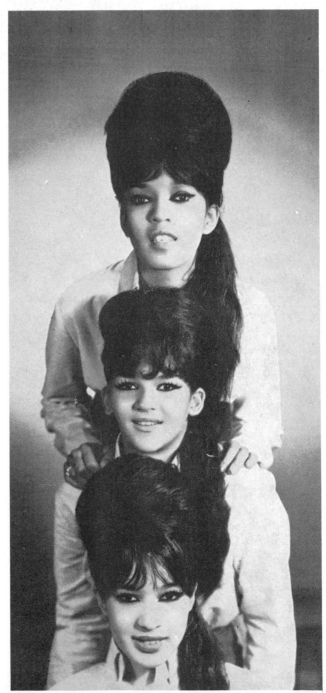

The Ronettes.

The Ronettes sign with Phil Spector, 1963.

For starters, Spector would take as long as necessary to get what he wanted. It may have taken hours for the drum sound, or hours for the blend of guitars, but Phil would stick at it. Sometimes it would come quickly, but often the sessions went on for sixteen hours straight or until everyone just couldn't play or listen back anymore. Sometimes he would record the same song with different arrangements or at different tempos, or use the same track and try out different vocalists until just the right combination was found. Often-finished or close-to-finished recordings would never be issued—despite the fact that everyone close to Phil said they were hits—because they just didn't meet Phil's standards.

At Goldstar, the control room was roughly 10 feet by 15 feet, while the recording room (which would sometimes contain some twenty musicians and all their equipment) was 22 feet by 30 feet. All of Spector's records during this time were made on 3-track machines, and then mixed down to mono for singles releases. Spector did not like stereo, and his recording style was not geared to make stereo masters. He wanted everything to blend together, to rise and fall together without the prominence of any one sound or instrument; others would try to get a clean sound on all their instruments, to try and isolate those individual sounds—Spector wanted just the opposite.

Once the arrangements for the song were written out and learned by the players, Spector would start by working with the guitarists, and there were usually three to five. Each guitarist would have a mike and they'd play through the song over and over again while their positions or the microphones would be moved, and changes in the sound would occur. The guitars usually stuck to straight rhythm; there were rarely any leads. Then Spector would repeat the process with two or three pianos, and two basses. Then everyone would play together and they'd work on the sound balance again. The horns, usually two trombones, two saxes, and two trumpets would be next, followed by a group of percussionists (maracas, tambourine, triangle, bells, shakers, glockenspiels, and castanets) who would work on their sounds. Then the drums, usually played by Hal Blaine, would enter into the picture, with one microphone on the bass drum and one over the top of the kit.

Most of the time was not spent in actual recording, but in getting sounds, balances, microphone placements, and so on, all blended just the right way. With twenty or so musicians playing at once, this was a tedious process and the movement of one player or sound might mean that the others would have to be readjusted as well. When it was time to record, all the music would be recorded on one track. The guitars, basses, pianos, horns, percussion, and drums would be blended together on that track incorporating the amp sounds, room leakage sounds, and Goldstar's own echo chambers. If Phil could get one musical track recorded in one lengthy session, he was satisfied. Another day and a second track would be used for the vocals, and another day and the final track would be used for strings.

Then the mixing would begin. One would think that with only three tracks to mix together, it would be a simple process, but mixes took hours, and sometimes days. Phil would talk it over with engineer Larry Levine and then Levine would try to get what Phil wanted. Phil would listen, give Levine some more suggestions, go out for a while, then come back and listen. He'd make more suggestions and the process would continue until Phil was totally satisfied. Spector would listen over and over again to small sections of the mix, or the entire thing, usually at ear-splitting volume, and even when he got a mix he liked, sometimes the whole thing would have to be done over because the fade out wasn't just right. Spector was a nut for fades and it had to be just at the right moment and just at the right pace. When it was all over, everyone waited to see when, and if, the record would come out.

When Spector returned to New York in July he had three finished Ronettes recordings with him: "Be My Baby," "Baby I Love You," and "Why Don't They Let Us Fall In Love." He played two of them for Jeff Barry and Ellie Greenwich and asked which they thought should be the single. Ellie recalls what happened: "Phil played us 'Be My Baby' and 'Why Don't They Let Us Fall In Love,' and I said to go with 'Why Don't They. . . .' I really loved that song, and also thought it was very commercial. Jeff said he didn't know for sure, that either one of them could be hits. But Phil was really sold on 'Be My Baby,' and he went with that."

Beginning in late 1962, every Philles release had the inscription "Phil and Annette" etched in the runoff grooves. The romantic coupling referred to Phil and his wife, Annette Merar. Now, almost a year later, Spector's debut record for The Ronettes was released. It was called "Be My Baby" and the lack of any inscription on the inner vinyl was most conspicuous in its absence.

Upon its release "Be My Baby" became one of the fastest-selling Philles records to date, and ultimately became the company's unqualified biggest hit. It moved so swiftly that The Ronettes were still playing The Riptide Club in Wildwood, New Jersey, backing up Joey Dee, during the three weeks their debut moved from #90 to #20 on the national Top 100. It stayed in the Top Five for well over a month, and resounded from every single radio in America.

In the year 2063, when a time capsule is found, the discoverers will find a copy of "Be My Baby." Enclosed in plastic, there will be a plaque on the outside that reads: "An Example Of The Perfect Pop Record." If any vestige of the human spirit remains in their chemically irradiated brains, they cannot fail to be swept up in its swirling sonic majesty; in its cry for the most true and eternal love; and in its unbridled faith in life. Phil Spector's *musical* philosophy was based on the belief that the whole was much greater than the sum of its parts. With "Be My Baby" he showed us, and perhaps himself as well, that the same philosophy might hold for our lives as well.

★★★★★★★★★★★★★★★★★★★★★★★★★★★★

Spector always desired to find a sound so strong, so special, that it could be successful purely on the strength of that element alone. On "Be My Baby" he found not only the sound, but the message, the voice, and the melody as well. To try to equal or surpass that one-in-a-million combination the next time around is something mere mortals cannot ac-

The Ronettes and The Rolling Stones party at the Gold Bug nightclub.

complish. (Do you know which painting da Vinci created *following* the Mona Lisa?) And though Phil Spector's work may qualify him as a genius, he was also, like every other genius this planet has produced, a mere mortal. He followed ''Be My Baby'' with ''Baby I Love You,'' another brilliant record that somehow only reached #24. It wasn't as unique as its predecessor, but it certainly should have had more of a chart impact than it did.

Perhaps one reason that it didn't go further was that Spector refused, for the most part, to play the payola game; to glad-hand and dine with the dee-jays and programmers; to take page after page of trade advertisements; to say just how wonderful everyone else in the business was. He told a British interviewer in 1964: ''I was in business for myself. I did all my own promotion and everything. We've been successful purely on the strength of our discs. I'm proud of that. Just the girls and I. No office staff, no advertising, no nothing. . . .'' An exaggeration perhaps, but not very far from the truth.

In 1964, things began to get complicated for Spector. He suddenly ceased collaborating with Ellie Greenwich and Jeff Barry, and teamed up with Pete Anders and Vinny Poncia, two young writers signed to Hill and Range publishers. (Ellie: ''There was no argument or blowout. It just stopped. Out of the blue. There was never any 'why' with Phil. He just decided to work somewhere else, and would go do it. That's just the way it was. . . .'') Phil was managing The Ronettes, and he was also dating Ronnie. When The Ronettes went over to tour England in early 1964 with The

Phil Spector conducts the orchestra in the film, *The Big T.N.T. Show.*

American International Pictures

Rolling Stones, they were the toast of the town, and became close with The Stones and The Beatles. Phil flew over to keep his eye on things. A disintegrating marriage created emotional pressures and a blossoming new love only intensified matters.

Almost all of Spector's previous hits—"He's A Rebel," "Uptown," "He's Sure The Boy I Love," "Da Doo Ron Ron," "Then He Kissed Me"—were lyrically constructed with universal, second person imagery. In a sharp turn, Phil's lyrics for The Ronettes were specific and in the first person. "Then He Kissed Me" would have been "Then You Kissed Me," and "He's Sure The Boy I Love" would have become "You're Sure The Boy I Love" had Spector done them with The Ronettes. With "Be My Baby" and "Baby I Love," Phil was expressing how he felt for the first time, sending these musical love letters out to Ronnie, and perhaps gaining pleasure by hearing Ronnie sing the words directly to him. (About this time Spector recorded a hopeful love song entitled "Pretty Girl (You're So Fine)," which he sung emotionally. It was created purely for private consumption. Phil was always best at expressing his feelings through music.) As a final touch, he entitled The Ronettes' debut album, *Presenting The Fabulous Ronettes.*

Perhaps one reason that Spector decided not to collaborate with Jeff Barry and Ellie Greenwich after such great success was that as his relationship with Ronnie intensified and his lyrics became more personal, he was not comfortable revealing his bare emotions to friends. Phil was a loner, in business and in his personal life, and would bottle up any feelings of unhappiness, insecurity or loneliness to the outside world. Ellie: "Phil kept everything pretty much separate. He did not allow us to befriend his acts—he never divulged what was going on—who he was recording, what songs he was cutting, business dealings. Whatever was going on was kept very, very quiet. Everything was his decision." For his part Spector said: "I only worked with a few sets of writers that were really good: Barry and Cynthia, Carole and Gerry, and then Jeff and Ellie. It was more important that they understood me than anything else. Jeff and Ellie *really* understood me, really knew what I wanted, and were able to deliver. The others understood, but not as much as Jeff and Ellie did."

In 1964, Spector began his collaboration with Pete Anders and Vinny Poncia, and issued two new Ronettes singles. "(The Best Part Of) Breakin' Up" came first and was a solidly romantic, evocative record, but it only reached #39. Then came "Do I Love You," which was even better, more rhythmically driving, and intricately arranged. It only reached #34. Spector was musical director at this time for a film entitled *The Big T.N.T. Show.* It spotlighted a wide range of pop talent and also highlighted performances by The Ronettes. Distribution problems kept it from being a major success. Spector started up a new label called Phil Spector Records and issued two singles by Ronnie under the name Veronica. Although they were only test-marketed, and not pushed as much as Philles releases, neither one made the charts. By the end of 1964, in the face of decreasing record sales, Spector made a concession in his attitude toward promotion and hired the well-respected and powerful promotion man, Danny Davis, to work full-time at Philles.

The first release that Danny Davis and Spector promoted together was a new single by The Ronettes, written by Spector, Barry Mann, and Cynthia Weil, entitled "Walkin' In The Rain." For this release, Spector not only hired Davis, but also issued the record in a picture sleeve—a first for Philles—another concession to commercial considerations. "Walkin' In The Rain" was one of Spector's most unified and distinctive productions since his chart slide had started, and it musically and lyrically meshed images of earthly love and devotion with the power of heavenly-sent downpours. Although it has remained popular over the years and gained stature and recognition, it only reached #23 at the time of its release. It also gave Spector and his engineer Larry Levine their only Grammy Award: a special citation for "Special Effects."

Ronnie: "I remember the session for 'Walkin' In The Rain'— which is actually my favorite recording—Barry and Cynthia were there with Phil and I did one vocal take. I came into the control room and said I wanted to work on it, do some more, because I felt I could do better and be more comfortable. They said, 'No, what you did was exactly what we want. That's the one.' So we kept it that way . . . just one take." Barry Mann: "Spector is a great producer. He enhanced things, created a sound. He was a star. You could write a

Cynthia Weil and Barry Mann, 1963.

good song and give it to a producer who'd fuck it up totally. I mean half of our demos were better than the records that were out on them. There were very few really good producers around at that time—Leiber & Stoller, Jerry Wexler, Phil Spector . . . that was about it.''

Ronnie: ''Those days when we were recording were great, really fantastic. The recordings were done so differently. I sang all of my songs in the dark—sometimes we'd be in the studio twenty-four hours in a row, recording. We had so many great people involved with those records: Sonny and Cher, The Blossoms, Leon Russell, Nino Tempo, Harry Nilsson, lot of others. We'd have fifteen people in the studio at once. Sometimes we have five people sing backup vocals, and then double or triple it so it would sound like fifteen voices. Phil would teach me a song, and I'd learn it very quickly. Then he'd go work with his arranger, usually Jack 'Specs' Nitzsche, and they'd work it out. He'd call me and the band in to see how it sounded together. Then the entire process would begin—the band would be on one track, the vocals on another, and strings, which were recorded at a different time would be on the third. We recorded so much stuff that wasn't released, it wasn't funny. ([Like] 'I Wish I Never Saw The Sunshine,' which me and everybody else flipped out over at the time it was done.) Like Larry Levine would say, 'Phil, what's wrong with you? These are great, put 'em out.' But it was always something personal with Phil, that he didn't let it out—or else he didn't think it was going to be a hit—if it was going to be on Philles Records it had to be a smash. There were others: 'Chapel Of Love,' 'Paradise,' 'Baby Let's Be Lovers.' I must have had about an album's worth, maybe more, of stuff that never came out. . . .''

In 1965, two new Ronettes singles did come out. The first was another Spector–Mann–Weil collaboration, ''Born To Be Together,'' sporting a typically tremulous lead vocal from Ronnie layered on top of a musical track that was so dense that much of it remained buried somewhere in the grooves. It didn't crack the Top Fifty, and the follow-up, ''Is This What I Get For Loving You?'' (written by Spector–Goffin–King) did even worse, only reaching #75. Even though he was having a tremendous success with the first male group on Philles, The Righteous Brothers, he was upset and resentful at the lukewarm reception his Ronettes releases received. Phil felt that he was creating emotional, innovative, artistic records, and that the programmers just didn't understand them. They were more interested in selling trash. The deejays felt that Spector's Records were too noisy, murky, and complicated. With all the new sounds jumping into the charts, many also felt the Spector sound was a throwback and out of touch with the times. This criticism hurled at a man whose motto was stamped on each release—''Tomorrow's Sound Today''—was particularly ironic.

At the bottom, the industry was not so much irked by *what* Spector did, but rather *how* he did it. His cocky attitude, his often disparaging remarks about trends in music and the way business was conducted, coupled with his refusal to glad-hand, offer thanks, or play the game *their* way turned off many people. He snubbed convention in the way he looked, dressed, and acted. The response was: ''Phil needs us—we don't need him.'' Spector didn't see it that way, and by this point, whether they played his records or not, Phil didn't really need them anymore. He had been so much in control and so successful (obvious factors that contributed to jealous backlashes), that by the time he was twenty-five, he was a millionaire several times over. He had sold millions of records through his

. . .and in 1965.

137

own company, one that was run with minimal bureaucratic overhead, and wrote and published some of the biggest hits of the era. His writing and publishing income alone at this time was well over one hundred thousand dollars a year. Of the twenty-five or so official Philles releases, over half were smash hits, and another quarter of them were respectable chart items. He had invested wisely in real estate, and had even received a percentage of monies for sales of several early Rolling Stones albums by acting as a middleman and dealmaker between their British and American companies.

Other events that made Phil wealthy were more upsetting but no less lucrative. The Crystals had to buy out their contract to leave the label. The Righteous Brothers tried to leave Philles at the height of their popularity because they wanted more artistic control. Spector sued and won, and The Righteous Brothers' new label, MGM, was forced to pay an enormous cash settlement to Spector. And then other problems began to mount up with increasing frequency.

In 1965, the Musicians Union shut down Spector's recording operations for violating archaic rules regarding overdubbing. After a few weeks stand-off, Spector had no choice but to pay a large penalty fee to the union, and take out a conciliatory trade ad. Under a copy of the telegram reinstating Philles in good standing with the Musicians Union, Spector wrote: "Conform to norm society; Won't stand for impropriety; In the extreme of which you dream; You must always join the team."

He lost The Crystals, Righteous Brothers, and Darlene Love, and then tried to sign several new acts, including The Young Rascals and The Lovin' Spoonful. He lost them to big money offers and promises, was incensed at the growing sums paid by companies as advances to new groups, and also hurt that his creative reputation alone had not been sufficient to land the acts. There were offers to buy out his operation, and thoughts of Philles going public, but all these were refused. Members of The Crystals instituted a lawsuit regarding royalties, a suit that was settled in favor of Spector after meandering through the courts for several years. Spector was unhappy with the trends in popular music and the disreputable business practices that accompanied them. As an independent, he had to deal with organized crime who wanted to muscle in for a piece of the action. Spector said in 1969: "What Mafia? What record business? I wouldn't say anything I knew anyways. I just try to hire them all, that's all. No, I wouldn't say a word about them."

By mid-1966, the output at Philles was grinding to a dead halt. Promotion man Danny Davis had nothing to promote and no reason to stay. Spector tried to keep him on by increasing his salary, and by starting up a new label called Phi-Dan which issued non-Spector produced masters in conjunction with Davis, but it was not a full-fledged operation, and did not succeed. When Davis tried to leave with time left on his contract, Spector was hurt, and sued. In the meantime, Spector had promised to invest funds in a new movie venture, *The Last Movie*, produced by Dennis Hopper.

Estelle Bennett and Paul McCartney
on the 1966 Beatles American Tour.

and pressures that had occured over the previous few years. Phil had accomplished so much artistically, was financially secure for the future, and saw no reason to try and fight on. Spector had become close friends with Lenny Bruce in 1965, and despaired as Lenny sunk deeper and deeper into a pit of desperation and decline. When Bruce died in August of 1966, Spector was shocked and the hurt jolted his very being. Lenny was killed by outside forces that had tried to silence his existence, and Spector did not want to become society's next victim. Real or imagined, Spector felt persecuted and overwhelmed, and the best option was to withdraw from view and seclude himself in his palatial home. When Lenny died, a Los Angeles police official visited Spector and showed him a series of official police photographs of the gruesome death scene. For a fee, he said, Spector could buy the photos and negatives and they would never get published. Spector paid five thousand dollars to keep the photos away from public exploitation, but the whole transaction left him sickened and disgusted. It was the final corrupt event that convinced Spector to cut himself off from the sick and parasitical society he saw all around him.

Disagreements arose between the principals, Spector pulled out his financing, and Hopper's company sued Spector. In order to get Danny Davis to testify on his behalf, Spector dropped his suit against Davis; Davis testified; and Spector won in his court confrontation with Hopper. Phil was soured on the business, soured with people, and soured with life. In the past he had fought back—this time he withdrew.

In the summer of 1966, The Ronettes were scheduled to go on tour with The Beatles across the United States. Spector wanted Ronnie to be with him, and offered her a choice. Either go on tour and continue your career, or marry me. Ronnie chose the latter, and shortly thereafter Phil and Ronnie became Mr. and Mrs. Phil Spector. (The Ronettes–Beatles tour went on as scheduled, however. Ronnie's cousin Elaine took her place for the appearances, and no one was the wiser.)

Many people point to the commercial failure of Spector's production of Ike and Tina Turner's "River Deep Mountain High" as the reason for his exit from the record business. This was a factor, but it was really the total culmination of the myriad problems, lawsuits, rebuffs, corruption,

A holiday greeting card from Phil and Ronnie, Winter 1968.

After Phil and Ronnie were married, they retired to Spector's Los Angeles mansion, where Phil settled in and rarely left. Ronnie had given up performing, something she loved, and Spector tried to keep her at home with him. Ronnie: "After we were married, I simply did nothing. It was Phil's choice. I felt left out in the cold. My first love was entertaining, and you just can't take someone's love away. I came from a large family and was used to having lots of people around all the time. When we got married it was just servants. They were much older than me and called me 'Mrs. Spector,' and I'm calling them by their first names. It was just . . . stupid, really. It was such a big house; it was like living in a mausoleum. Phil, as everybody knows, is moody; nice, but very moody. We had twenty-three rooms, and he never wanted to go out. I'd say I want to go play pool or go bowling—so he would buy me a bowling alley or something. There was nothing to go out for. If there was something special I liked, like hard peaches, he would make sure the cook got everything, so I had nothing to do. I had no career, and I couldn't even be a housewife. We stayed home and I had no choice. I had a baby boy, that was a good thing, and helped. But we had cooks, servants, nurses, governesses—I just got so bored. . . ." Phil occasionally tried to pacify Ron-

nie, and issued two singles, one in 1969 on A & M, and one in 1971 on Apple, but they slipped out, barely noticed by the public. Philles was gone, the girl-group sound was gone, many of Spector's friends were gone, and by 1973, even Ronnie would be gone.

Musically, there was no place for Spector to go at the time he retired. He had been hungry for success and recognition. He got that..He tried to make the records bigger and bigger, to put more and more onto vinyl, but the tiny grooves just couldn't handle the overload. He had said it all in a handful of records, maybe even just one like "You've Lost That Lovin' Feeling," but imitation was not for Phil Spector. Ellie Greenwich: "Those records had a Wagnerian power and intensity. Phil got so wrapped up in those recordings. Then everything got bigger, bigger, and bigger until there was no more record. But he wanted to go further, get bigger and bigger, *but there was no bigger. . . .*"

The bigness that Spector wanted only got smaller as the murky wall of sound imploded. This ironic fact hit Spector deeply, and when he found he couldn't go higher, couldn't attain perfection, he cut himself off. There was no ultimate solution to life, no magic key that unlocked the door to utopia. He had paved the way for individual expression and the search for the better, the other, the different. Now in the late sixties, the rest of the world caught up with him. The intense explosive effect of all those new clothes, hairstyles, sexual styles, uses of language and image, battles for ethnic and sexual freedom, and widespread drug experimentation simply stunned him. Images of assassinations, riots, and Asian wars flickered day after day and night after night. The other side, even the darker side, once seemed attractive: the harsh reality of 42nd Street and its misfit inhabitants, Lenny Bruce's rebellious image, language, and drug use; the deals, crime, violence and corruption that frequently permeated the music business. Spector alternated between attraction and repulsion, exhilaration and fear. The dream was one thing, the reality was another. In the end there was no right way. No best way. No only way. No ultimate way. It was a matter of individual solutions, of individual satisfactions. That was what Phil Spector's music had tried to show us all along. Eventually, he too, would hear its message.

Chapter
TEN

5 RPM

EASIER SAID
THAN DONE

THE MASSIVE POPULARITY OF
the girl groups, and in particular, the
rhythmically driving sounds of Phil
Spector and Motown, set the music industry on its ear, and dozens of producers and artists decided to follow suit. Most didn't have the
creative brilliance or financial resources of a
Motown or Phil Spector, and their records usually
came out as a curious hybrid of various girl-group
trademarks. In the same way that one appreciates
the look and feel of a B-movie, one can enjoy these
records—they are strangely unique, extracting only the essential elements from that which has
already been successful. In the course of this con-
densation, a familiar but still different entity was
created. For the first time, "girl-group" records
were being produced with assembly-line techniques.

When Gerry Goffin and Carole King created
"The Locomotion," it was not a *"girl-group"* rec-
ord. When Phil Spector produced "Da Doo Ron
Ron" it was not a *"girl-group"* record. When
Tamla issued "Please Mr. Postman," they

weren't promoting a *"girl-group"* record. There
simply was no such thing as a girl-group record.
They were great records with female singers—it
was only after the media tagged these various successes with a label that people began to think in
terms of *"girl-group"* records. Once something is
labeled, people see it in a different fashion. A Roy
Lichtenstein painting is just a work of art, until it's
called "Pop Art"—after that we are looking at *pop
art*, and we bring certain preconceptions, values,
and reactions to it. Then other artists decide to create "pop art." That further distorts the original in-
tentions of the art, until finally we only create and
see what "pop art" is supposed to be. Frequently
even the originators of what becomes a labeled
movement get caught up in the rules or trademarks
of their art, and consciously or subconsciously
limit the scope of their future work. By falling into
the trap of formula and repetition, the movement
loses vitality and soon becomes archaic.

Such was the case with the girl-group sound, and
only those who broke through the parameters of
the ordained rules, like Motown, survived. Perhaps that's why we rarely heard male singers performing over a backing track and beat like the ones
used on "Locomotion," "Be My Baby," or
"Leader Of The Pack." The sound had first been
successful with girls, was labeled as such, and then
became their exclusive turf. This is an ironic twist,
because many of the girl groups (most notably The
Chantels and Ronettes) were inspired by Frankie
Lymon. Granted Lymon's young voice was in a
high range, but it still seems inconceivable that
such a popular sound (and the backing tracks were

142

an essential ingredient) was not grafted on male voices. The few that did try were almost universally sung by young, high register vocalists ("Killer Joe" by The Rocky Fellers for instance), so that for all intents and purposes, they were just girl-group records. (The closest girl-group sounding record sung by males from this period that I've heard, is an obscure release by The Aubrey Twins —Tyrone & Jerome. These brothers must have been thirteen-year-olds because they sound just like young girls. Perhaps one reason for their failure was that programmers or listeners may have thought that girls were indeed singing the song, and with that in mind it would have qualified as the first major label lesbian pop recording. Such confusion would not lead to commercial success in 1964. . . .)

The impact of the girl groups did lead to a significant tilt in the balance of white and black performers on the charts. Most of the popular girl groups were black, and their acceptance on the national charts forged a level of integration that was never before, and never again, equaled. Since the advent of rock 'n' roll, blacks had never accounted for more than 30 percent of the year's biggest hits. In 1960, their share was roughly 25 percent, but by the end of 1962—the year of The Crystals, Dee Dee Sharp, Little Eva, The Shirelles and so on—that figure had broken through the 40 percent mark. By 1965, when the sound had lost its popularity, their chart share had fallen back down to 25 percent.

In fact, with all the talk about racial progress and integration that we've heard over the last decade, the music charts are more segregated today than in 1963. Today we have talk of "black-oriented records," and the "black-music" charts in the industry's trade papers are almost 100 percent black. In 1963, artists such as The Four Seasons, Neil Sedaka, Elvis Presley, Bobby (Boris) Pickett, Lesley Gore, Jan & Dean, Lonnie Mack, and many others scored highly on what was called the "R & B Chart." Some might argue that today's system gives blacks their own music and culture, but that kind of stereotypical labeling only closes doors and limits expression. Blacks are told that this is a black record and you should like it, or this is a white record and you shouldn't like that. In 1963, people didn't see their work as black or white—they were just good records and good music. And if masses of blacks and whites could share the experience, the enjoyment, and the message of the same record, communication and understanding could only increase. That was one of the great hopes and promises of early rock 'n' roll—a vibrant, jubilant sound that transcended racial barriers. [As this is being written, the week's

EASIER SAID THAN DONE

Chapter TEN

national Top 100 (December 1981) finds *14* percent of the Top Fifty spots filled by blacks; the same week in 1962 finds the level at almost *40* percent. For the time being at least, this most vital of rock 'n' roll promises seems to have fallen far short of its goal.] Similarly, the impact of the girl groups placed more females on the chart than ever before. [In December 1981 the Top Fifty contained records by only *nine* female artists—a similar week in 1963 finds double that amount.]

The impact of the girl groups was not only an American phenomenon. Their records were hits all over the world, and many indigenous girl groups sprang up to fill local needs. In England, there were American girl-group clones like The Orchids, The Breakaways and The Liverbirds, but record buyers usually preferred to buy the "real thing" rather than the native imitations. (Occasionally, a British artist would have a hit with a cover of an American recording, like Billie Davis did in 1963 with her version of The Exciters' "Tell Him," but this was more the exception than the rule.) In a mid-1963 reader's poll in *Melody Maker* for favorite artist, male or female, British or American, The Crystals, Shirelles, and Chiffons all placed in the Top Ten. In 1964, a *Record Mirror* poll on favorite female artist, U.S. or U.K., found The Crystals, Ronettes, Shirelles, Martha & The Vandellas, Dixie Cups, Chiffons, and Marvelettes all lodged in the Top Ten. Much of the early material recorded by such British stars as The Beatles, Hollies, Manfred Mann, and Herman's Hermits consisted of their versions of American girl-group songs, and the chart success of such British performers as Dusty Springfield and Sandie Shaw owes more to their adherence to the girl-group sound than to their association with the British Invasion. While the whole world was busily embracing the girl-group sound, here in America, the beat went on.

In the same way that Phil Spector had taken what had previously been a "boom, boom-boom" backing beat and brought it way upfront, so did The Chiffons on their first record. The group's "He's So Fine" took a backing vocal sound prominent on many doo-wop records, brought it to the forefront, and then built a song around it. When the record begins with "Doo-lang Doo-lang Doo-lang, . . ." you're hooked immediately and can't escape. No one did escape it either—it reached #1 in only 6 weeks on the charts.

Judy Craig, Barbara Lee, Patricia Bennett and Sylvia Peterson met at high school, where the top of Manhattan meets the South Bronx. Here they would sing in the lunchroom or after school out in the streets. A local boy, Ronnie Mack, played piano and wrote songs. He'd rehearse with the girls, and then take them down to Manhattan where he had enough money for exactly one hour of studio time. He played the piano, the girls sang, and they recorded as many songs as they could get through in the allotted time. The girls forgot about their hour of fun, but Ronnie Mack made the rounds of company after company, knocking on door after door. The only door that opened after weeks of rejection was the one occupied by Phil Margo, Mitch Margo, Hank Medress, and Jay Siegel. This quartet of Brooklynites had been knocking around the music business for years (they had even become famous as The Tokens) and set out to write, produce, and sing on as many records as possible. They hung around with the Sedakas and Goffin-Kings, hustled production deals, practiced their craft, and even had a few hits, but their work was often uneven and usually uninspired. They would hop on any bandwagon, any trend that could be exploited, and when Ronnie Mack came through that door with that song and those girls, the slot machine dollar signs rolled around their collective eyes. One guy's eyes said "Girl group"; another guy's eyes said "Hit song"; the third guy's eyes read "Lotsa money"; the fourth fellow closed his lids blissfully revealing two final words: "Do It."

Margo, Margo, Medress and Siegel took the group into the studio and recorded "He's So Fine." Hank Medress said later: "We didn't try to copy Spector or Carole King—we just tried to copy the hooks. . . ." "He's So Fine" was *all* hooks, laid on top of a solid, simple accompaniment and natural spontaneous vocals from the girls. They first tried to sell the master at Capitol where they had a production deal, but when Capitol passed on the record, it went over to the New York-based independent, Laurie Records. The record not only went to #1, but stayed in the Top Ten for over 2 months.

Laurie was the kind of company not known for its restraint in attempting to capitalize on a fortuitous event, and they rushed out a follow-up just as "He's So Fine" was anchored in the Top Ten. When the new release appeared to flounder, Margo, Margo, Medress and Siegel, now going

under the company name of Bright Tunes Productions, contacted Carole King, who brought them over a finished master. It was a recording of a Goffin–King song called "One Fine Day" and it was sung by Little Eva. Little Eva and Dimension records were going through a down period, so the Bright Tunes people erased the original vocals, and put The Chiffons' voices on in their places. "One Fine Day" took off and went all the way to #5. The record was simply marvelous—a driving shuffling drum beat, a classic melody, heartfelt lyrics, and best of all, a riveting stuttering piano line.

Now with two Top Ten girl-group hits to their credit, the Bright Tunes folks began to churn out the imitations. In homage to themselves they produced "The Doolang" for Andrea Carroll, and issued recordings by The Parlettes, and The Summits. (Two years later they were still at it with The Cinnamons and The Bitter Sweets.) And at the height of The Chiffons' popularity, they issued two records by The Chiffons under the name The Four Pennies for the Laurie subsidiary, Rust. One of these, a Jeff Barry–Ellie Greenwich composition

entitled "When The Boy's Happy," was a beautiful song—and Bright Tunes merely tried to copy it off Jeff and Ellie's version recorded as The Raindrops. They even used Greenwich and Barry's studio (Mira) and engineer (Brooks Arthur). So much for originality.

Meanwhile, the next two official Chiffons releases charted, but failed to break into the Top Thirty. The next one didn't even enter the Hot 100, and the girls were quite unhappy. For one, they were dissatisfied with their choice of material—in fact they had no choice whatsoever over songs, arrangements, cover artwork or anything else considered "the creative end." When they received their royalty statements they found that a huge amount of money was being deducted for studio time: Bright Tunes was running endless sessions, and employing significant numbers of studio musicians in an attempt to record as much material as possible and create *their* version of the Spector sound. Unfortunately, while the producers experimented and recorded, The Chiffons were paying for it. Shortly thereafter, The Chiffons entered into a lawsuit to free themselves of their con-

THE CHIFFONS

tract, and after a lengthy court battle, came out on top, primarily because they were minors when they had signed their initial contract. (They were sixteen and seventeen when "He's So Fine" hit #1.)

But the victory was rather an empty one, because no label wanted to touch a group that had sued to get out of their contract, and on top of that they had no producer or songwriter to create new hits. Eventually the group went back to Laurie, and signed directly to the label. In mid-1965 they released an adventurously ethereal record, "Nobody Knows What's Goin' On In My Mind," which became their first Top Fifty record in a year and a half, but then it was another year before "Sweet Talkin' Guy" swept them back into the Top Ten. This record was more Motown-influenced than their previous releases, but in 1966 if there was a sound to emulate, Motown's was the one. The Chiffons continued to record, and toured incessantly, but there were no more hits. Although their chart life was longer than many of the other girl groups, at the end of the line they had little to show for it.

There were many producers who should be noted for their girl-group work, despite the fact that most of them didn't score too many hits. These were their learning years, and many went on to greater success with other artists. Several of the people who worked closely with Phil Spector also moonlighted as producers themselves, and more often than not, their recordings were patterned after Spector's. Jack Nitzsche made several wonderfully atmospheric records with Joni Lyman, Karen Verros, The Satisfactions, Ramona King, Pat Powdrill, and Merry Clayton (the latter just missing out with the original recording of "It's In His Kiss" which was later taken to #6 by Betty Everett). Spector associate Jerry Riopell made his best record with Bonnie and The Treasures ("Home Of The Brave") and also worked with Ramona King and Clydie King. Steve Douglas, one of Spector's most notable session musicians, created strong girl-group records with The Girls ("Chico's Girl") and Toni Jones ("Here Comes My Baby"), as well as with The What Four and Yolanda and The Charmaines. These were almost all recorded on the West Coast and were usually more glossily arranged and produced than their New York counterparts. Also on the West Coast was David Gates, who wrote and produced some tremendous girl-group records with Dorothy Berry, Shelley Fabares, The Blossoms, and the thundering mid-chart hit, "My One & Only Jimmy Boy," recorded by The Girlfriends. Gates also wrote "Popsicles & Icicles" which Kim Fowley produced for The Murmaids (Carol Fischer, Terry Fischer, Sally Gordon) in late 1963. The record,

The Murmaids.

an updated simplistic variation on the sound of The Paris Sisters, went all the way to #3 for the small Chattahoochee label, but none of their follow-ups even broke into the Top 100. Brian Wilson, a staunch Spector fan, made a handful of girl-group records that grafted the Beach Boys' California sound onto the emerging girl-group styles. His records with Sharon Marie and The Honeys were quite interesting, especially "He's A Doll" and "The One You Can't Have," both of which were superbly powerful.

Producers best known for their work in the soul area also ventured into the girl-group arena. Robert Bateman, who had done much of work at Motown, struck out on his own and worked with The Bouquets, Candy Carroll, Jill Harris, and Roddie Joy. His Motown-influenced productions with The Bouquets (on Blue Cat), and Roddie Joy (on Red Bird), were intense and atmospheric. Bert Berns flirted with the girl-group sound, but usually preferred to stay closer to the soul idiom. Good records were made with Linda Laurie, The Flamettes, and Baby Jane and The Rockabyes, while his best work resulted in hits for Betty Harris and Barbara Lewis. Frequently a Berns associate, Jerry Ragovoy wrote and produced for The Pandoras, The Pirouettes, Debbie Rollins, and The Tran-Sisters, records which placed the girls in a solid soul-inspired groove. Curtis Mayfield, Sylvester Stewart (Sly Stone), and Richard Barrett also mined the girl-group soul vein, and Henry Glover, Teacho Wiltschire, and Rudy Clark featured prominently on many girl-group records as writers, producers, and arrangers.

The Girlfriends.

Jackie DeShannon, Joe Yore, Jack Nitzsche.

Back on the East Coast, Kama-Sutra Productions turned out a series of girl-group records with Stacy Cane, The Juliettes, Ann Marie, The Petites, and The Pussycats. Based in Philadelphia, the writing and production team of John Madera and Dave White contributed material to several Cameo-Parkway acts, and created their own lightweight girl-group records with Maureen Gray, The Pixies Three, The Sherrys, and Ann D'Andre. One of their biggest successes came when they wrote "You Don't Own Me," which Lesley Gore took to #5. Paul Simon learned his craft in the early sixties, often cutting demos with Carole King, and he also wrote and produced for The Cupcakes and The Fashions. Artie Resnick and Kenny Young did uniformly strong work with The Charmettes, The Johnston Sisters, Bernadette Peters and The Goodnight Kisses. Other more mainstream acts tried to integrate the girl-group sound into their previously MOR leanings, and frequently called upon New York's talents to perform the surgery. The most successful of these operations was Skeeter Davis' "I Can't Stay Mad At You" (Goffin-King), and Connie Francis' "Don't Ever Leave Me" (Barry-Greenwich), both of which not only charted, but were also marvelous records. Still other producers not only tried to recreate a general sound, they went one step further and attempted to copy a specific group or record. The Victorians' "What Makes Little Girls Cry" could easily be mistaken for a Bob B. Soxx and The Blue Jeans record, and Alder Ray's " 'Cause I Love Him" invokes the spirit of The Crystals/Darlene Love most dramatically. The Shangri-Las were imitated (but never equaled) by The Pussycats, Nu-Luvs, Bitter Sweets, and most

effectively of all by The Whyte Boots. In early 1969, The Goodees revived The Shangri-Las' legacy with "Condition Red," and broke into The Top Fifty on the small HIP label. Even with what sounded like a mediocre Phil Spector-Ellie Greenwich demo, Alice Wonderland's "He's Mine," hit the charts in late 1963, but was washed away by the real McCoy. Perhaps the strangest of all hit-bound girl-group records was created by Abner Spector (no relation to Phil). He worked with The Patty Cakes and The Hearts on his own Tuff label, but his weirdest concoction came with "Sally Go Round the Roses" by The Jaynetts. This intensely ethereal and atmospheric record, sporting strangely cryptic lyrics, went all the way to #2 in late 1963, and must rate as one of the finest victories of sound-and-beat over content to ever conquer the American charts. Perhaps destined to be a one-time-only affair, all The Jaynetts' follow-ups failed to even break into The Top 100.

The Honeys.

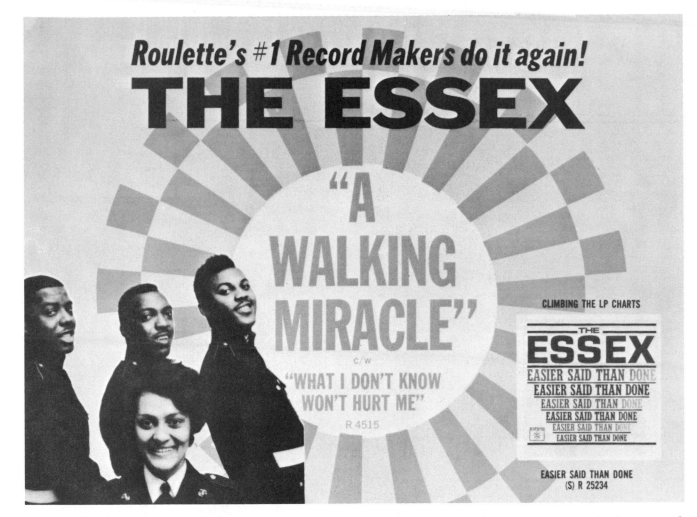

The direction and fate of three other girl groups who hit the charts point up the strengths as well as the failures that plagued many of the female performers. The Essex were four men and a woman who were all members of the Marine Corps stationed at Camp Lejeune, North Carolina. The men, Walter Vickers, Rodney Taylor, Billie Hill, and Rudolph Johnson, sang together on the base to entertain their fellow troops. They soon enlisted the vocal talents of Anita Humes, and cut a demo record which was heard by Roulette Records. Roulette was in the process of absorbing George Goldner's End-Gone-Gee complex, and Goldner chose The Essex as one of the first acts he would work with at Roulette. He was taken by Anita Humes' vocal quality, as well as by the original songs on the demo which were written by members of the group and Marine friend William Linton. Goldner hooked them up with producer-arranger Henry Glover, who put together an all-star session band, and then worked and reworked their tunes into a slickly formulaic mold. The first release, "Easier Said Than Done," took off in the spring of 1963 and by mid-July had hit #1. A quick follow-up, "A Walkin' Miracle," was rushed out, and despite the fact that it was little more than an inferior rehash of "Easier Said Than Done," it went as far as #12. From there on it was downhill, with a handful of albums and singles failing to excite the public. By 1964, the group was going under the name, "The Essex featuring Anita Humes," or "Anita Humes and The Essex," and then during 1964 and 1965, Roulette made her a solo act and issued a few records by "Anita Humes," but the initial spontaneity and interactive magic was gone. The company forgot about the group, the group forgot about each other, and after two quick Top Fifteen hits, their careers in the music business were over. The formula had been employed, succeeded for a moment, and then no new formula was forthcoming. Next stop: Camp Lejeune, North Carolina. What had appealed to Goldner on the group's demo was their human, somewhat amateurish vocal qualities and their true-to-life songs, but by trying to fit the group into an already established genre, both those qualities—and ultimately what had made the group promising in the first place—were lost.

Reparata and The Delrons (Sheila Reilly, Carol Drobnicki, and Mary Aiese—who played the part of Reparata), grew up in Brooklyn and in 1964 came to the attention of Bill and Steve Jerome, who operated a makeshift production company out of their home in Bay Ridge, Brooklyn. The Brothers Jerome would try to appropriate any given style of popularity using whatever came through the door. Such was the case with Reparata and The Delrons, who would be "just perfect" for the Jeromes' foray into the world of girl groups. First step was to dump a fourth Delron, Kathy Romeo, because the Jeromes figured that she was a bit too overweight to present the right public image. So much for the group sound.

After a false start at Laurie Records, the group went over to World Artists in late 1964, where they successfully imitated the sound and feel of Ellie Greenwich and Jeff Barry's work at Red Bird with a song called "Whenever A Teenager Cries." The record was a huge hit in the New York area, but only reached #60 nationally. Their hastily conceived album consisted primarily of covers of girl-group hits like "Do Wah Diddy," "Dedicated To The One I Love," and "I Have A Boyfriend," along with other "original" tracks which were little more than barely disguised copies of still other girl-group hits.

Flushed with this slight success, the Brothers Jerome began using real studios and real musicians, and augmented Reparata's sound with session singers. They also began writing and producing for other new groups, and almost without fail,

they simply tried to use the same studios and personnel that had created the original hit that they were trying to copy. Such was the case with Reparata and The Delrons—whose numerous singles and albums were uncomfortably imitative and just as uncomfortably unsuccessful. The group had no control over material, monies, or much else of substance, and though they recorded for years under a variety of names, they never again made the charts. Looking back, it seems apparent that this would be inevitable, but during the time it was happening, fast talk, big promises, and a little taste of fame blotted out perspective. Perhaps their career alternatives at the time seemed like less appealing choices, but finding only darkness at the end of five years of tunnel digging is a tough way to see the light.

By the end of 1965, the girl-group ranks had thinned from the charts, with The Supremes almost singlehandedly holding up the banner of the sound. Producer Bob Crewe had been in business since the mid-fifties as a writer, producer, manager, and artist in his own right. In the early sixties he teamed up with The Four Seasons and produced and often wrote their string of hits. He was an admirer of Phil Spector and often used Spectro-esque touches for his work with The Four Seasons. He then began churning out girl-group records, once again with an hommage to Spector. Crewe's records were solid, well arranged, catchy and more often than not, a notch above the rest of the girl-group bandwagon jumpers. He produced Tracey Dey, Diane Renay, Linda Laurie, The Shepherd Sisters, Calendar Girls, Rag Dolls, Beach-Girls, and made some standout recordings with Shirley Mathews. In 1965 he formed two labels, Dyno-Voice and New Voice, and immediately scored hits with Mitch Ryder, Norma Tangea, and Eddie Rambeau. The manager of Diane Renay, Vince Marc, had used a vocal trio to back up Diane, and brought them to the attention of Crewe and his staff writers and producers Sandy Linzer and Denny Randell. The group, lead vocalist Barbara Harris, Barbara Parritt, and June Monteiro, were dubbed The Toys, and with Linzer and Randell at the helm came up with a variation of a Bach melody called "A Lover's Concerto," which became their first single. The formula employed strong honest vocals, a Supremes-like musical set-

The Toys.

ting, and the added pinch of classical themes, which when blended together resulted in an appealing sound. ''A Lover's Concerto'' zoomed up the chart in late 1965, reached #2 for 3 weeks, stayed on the charts for almost 4 months, and was a huge hit worldwide (in England, for instance, it reached #5).

The Toys were fortunate to have an experienced manager (Vince Marc), a well-connected Bob Crewe, and the professional team of Linzer and Randell behind them. They got good bookings, good photos, creative album packaging, and thoughtful productions for their records. The follow-up to ''Lover's Concerto'' used similar ingredients, perhaps a bit too similar, as the record topped at #18. Once again, everyone concerned merely tried to repeat the initial formula without improving or expanding upon it, and although The Toys were more talented and their producers more creative and more diligent than most of the second-line girl-group purveyors, their moment of fame was all they achieved.

In some ways, when people were actively recording ''girl-group'' records, perhaps the most they could achieve was a moment of fame. They were making records, not building careers of ''supremely talented artists,'' and if one slight twist of the already established format brought them a hit, that was great, but there would always be new bandwagons to jump on after that. Not all girl groups deserved or were destined to achieve long-term careers, and the legacy they leave rests almost entirely on a few wonderful minutes of plastic that captured a mood, a moment, and a message unique to their times. Such was the case with the groups discussed in this chapter, and perhaps exemplified best by The Angels, whose recording of ''My Boyfriend's Back'' remains indelibly etched in the consciousness of anyone who heard it, probably a hundred times or so, in the fall of 1963.

151

"MY BOYFRIEND'S BACK" THE ANGELS AND FELDMAN-GOLDSTEIN-GOTTEHRER TELL THEIR OWN STORY

✦✦✦✦✦✦✦✦✦✦✦✦✦✦✦✦✦✦✦✦✦✦✦✦✦✦✦✦✦✦✦✦

Jiggs Allbut: "My older sister, Barbara, was the driving force of the group. She played piano and wrote songs and taught us how to harmonize. We lived in New Jersey, and got two other local girls together and started a group. At first we were called The Starlets, and with some help from some Jersey friends we made a record for the local Astro label. The A-side was the old standard, 'P.S. I Love You,' and on the back was one of Barbara's songs, 'Where Is My Love Tonight?' It did okay locally, but actually served as a demo for us to bring around to major record companies. Then we came up with the idea and arrangement for a song called ' 'Til,' and sang it for a guy in New York at Caprice Records who signed us up, and we recorded it. We were a quartet then, with a girl called Linda Jansen who sang with us. We looked through magazines for a group name, and then we put a bunch into a hat one day when we were up at the offices of Caprice. The first choice was The Blue Angels, but we changed it and shortened it to The Angels. Caprice really worked hard on ' 'Til'—they never gave up—it took almost six months of constant work, all through the end of 1961. Finally the record caught on and went all the way to #14. Then we needed a follow-up, and the company sent us down to Philadelphia where a songwriter played us song after song for hours. The one we liked was 'Cry Baby Cry,' so we did that and that got into the Top Forty. We made some singles, and an album for Caprice, but nothing much really happened. We cut demos for people, sang backup on a lot of records, did commercials and radio promos, including a couple for Murray The K on WINS."

Richard Gottehrer: "I had gotten together with Bob Feldman and Jerry Goldstein, and we began writing songs and cutting demos for a lot of people. We were under contract to publishers and then went out on our own—we'd write, produce, whatever was necessary. We met The Angels towards the end of 1962; they did demos and background work for us. Jerry was going out with Jiggs, and we had even written their last single for Caprice. Then we came up with 'My Boyfriend's Back,' which we wrote specifically for them. They were just a trio then: Jiggs, Barbara, and Peggy. We went in and recorded it, and then Doug Moody from Mercury-Smash Records got turned on to the record and passed it on to Charlie Fach. We sold the master for a large amount—at least for those days—something like eight thousand dollars. The girls were still under contract to Caprice—so we had to give Gerry Granahan an override. We got something like 8 percent from Smash—we got some, Gerry Granahan got some, and the girls got some . . . 3 percent or so."

Jiggs: "When we finished 'My Boyfriend's Back,' I just knew it was a hit. And there was a real buzz around town on the record. It came out in late July 1963, and just took off like crazy—within a couple of weeks it was #1 all over the country. The first TV show we did to promote the record was on Buddy Deane's dance show in Baltimore. Peggy did the intro, and we all turned our backs and started shaking. They started yelling at us, 'You can't do that!' and they cut to a shot that only showed us from the waist up. The switchboard lit up, and some mothers called in to complain that it was obscene. To us it was just fun—not a business. It was just great fun. We'd run all over town, and do a lot of great shows. We played at the Apollo—they didn't know if we were black or white and they didn't care—with Bobby Bland, Erma Franklin ? d The Corsairs. We went on a lot of tours; we did demos and background sessions for everyone from Lou Christie to Anthony Newley, and Frank Sinatra, Neil Diamond, Lesley Gore, and Eydie Gorme. Barbara really kept it all together and looked after everything—without her, we never would have done it all. . . ."

Gottehrer: "We were really influenced by the Spector sound and all those songs like 'Da Doo Ron Ron' and 'Wait 'Till My Bobby Gets Home.' We just took off from that. We recorded a little differently than most people. We would first do the tracks, usually at Associated Recordings, and then we'd take the tapes over to Stea-Phillips in the Hotel Victoria Ballroom where we'd do the vocals. We just liked each place for different things. We tried as much as possible to mix at Columbia with an incredible guy, Stanley Weiss. We'd spend a lot of time mixing. On 'My Boyfriend's Back,' we even had a couple of different versions—one with extra handclaps, one with horns, one with a longer instrumental break. Lots of different releases and reissues have these different versions. We'd try to

The Angels.

153

The Angels receive a #1 Record Award for "My Boyfriend's Back" from *Billboard's* Ren Grevatt.

do four songs in one session. Lots of times we'd use the same musicians: Herbie Lovelle on drums; Billy Butler and Bobby Comstock on guitar; we'd use both a stand-up and electric bass with Bob Bushnell; and Leroy Glover did a lot of the arrangements. 'My Boyfriend's Back' sold over a million copies, but the groups never sold too many albums in those days—if you did 50,000, you were doing really well. We used a fourth girl, Bernadette Carroll, on a lot of The Angels records (she worked with Bob Gaudio too)—she had that kind of Jersey nasal sound we wanted. We'd always double the vocals, both the leads and the backgrounds. After 'My Boyfriend's Back' hit, we just started writing and producing like crazy. . . .''

Jiggs: '' 'My Boyfriend's Back' was just such a big hit. We'd turn on the radio and it would be on, and then we'd switch to another station and it would be on, and then the next one would be playing it too. You just couldn't escape it. It was an immediate smash. We'd do the Murray The K shows —five shows a day—and it was great because we used to go to The Alan Freed shows and watch; now we were doing it ourselves. The first time Murray booked us—he had heard 'My Boyfriend's Back,' and knew it was going to be a hit—so he booked us before it came out. By the time the show came around, we were #1, but we still had to play

for the little money he had signed us for. We were getting a little record royalty, but we had to pay back all the studio costs, so we never made much money off our record sales. That's the way it was, what can I say?''

''My Boyfriend's Back'' was pure fun, with a big beat and a message of lovers' retribution that almost everyone identified with. But like so many of the other girl-group classics, its uncanny synthesis of form and feeling could not be repeated. The next two Angels follow-ups reached #25 and #41 respectively, and then a series of singles during 1964 and 1965 failed to chart. The Angels had no solidified management, and Feldman-Goldstein-Gottehrer were busy pursuing anything and everything. First they cut an answer record with Bobby Comstock called ''Your Boyfriend's Back,'' and then churned out an endless stream of girl-group records. They cut Nancy Baron (later one of The Angels) for Diamond; Patti Lace and The Petticoats (Paula, Peppie and Pixie) for Kapp; and Diane Christian for Smash and Bell. They even tried to revive the girl-group careers of Little Eva and Mary Wells. They scored some marginal chart action, and often created interesting, upbeat records, but the trio was often too scattered in their obligations to build a long-term success. Their songs were, more often than not, topical teenage novelty excursions—whatever the craze or fad, they'd have a record out within weeks: "Treat Him Tender Maureen," and "Little Beatle Boy" explored Beatlemania; there were songs about surfing, dancing, hairstyles, and so on. If there wasn't a theme in the news, they'd create one. They'd record with legitimate self-contained groups; they'd make records with session singers; they'd combine members of various groups on one-shot records—whatever struck their fancy or was available at the given moment. They formed publishing companies and signed up writers, including ex-Cadillac member Robert Spencer, whose songs they often recorded. They'd record and then try to sell the finished master to whoever gave them the best deal. (They even recorded themselves as The Strangeloves, and took "I Want Candy" into the Top Ten during the summer of 1965). The Chic-Lets ("I Want You To Be My Boyfriend") were actually Patti Lace and The Petticoats with Diane Christian singing lead; The Beach-Nuts ("Out In The Sun") were The Angels and Strangeloves together; Angie and The Chiclettes ("Treat Him Tender Maureen") were session singer Jean Thomas on lead with other studio session singers backing her up; and The Powder Puffs ("My Boy-friend's Woody") were Jean Thomas and members of The Angels. They wrote a song for The Angels called "Looking for Boys," but since the girls were going through their problems, and were unhappy with the Feldman-Goldstein-Gottehrer business arrangements, they refused to do it. So the F-G-G trio formed their own label, Stork Records, and as Gottehrer recalls: "Dennis Lambert went down to Brooklyn, found a bunch of girls, and we did it with them." The record took the "My Boyfriend's Back" formula one step further in female sexual aggressiveness, and was pure solid, campy fun, but the small label couldn't do much with the record.

The Angels tried to make a go of it as The Halos during 1966, but time had passed them by and they soon faded from the scene. Feldman, Goldstein, and Gottehrer soon went their separate ways as well when it became obvious that their musical era and freewheeling style would no longer be accepted. Says Gottehrer: "We did anything in those days. It was wild—we were crazy. It was a period of trial and experimentation, but everyone went in different directions and that was that. Eventually, it was just over. . . ."

The Angels at WGR Radio, Buffalo, N.Y.

NOWHERE TO RUN

OF ALL THE FEMALE GROUPS who recorded for Motown, none has left as soulful a body of music as Martha & The Vandellas. It was ironic, though, that at Motown, style always won out over soul. Unlike Mary Wells, and The Marvelettes, whose rather hot vocals were offset by the cool production of Smokey Robinson, or The Supremes, whose cool vocals were offset by the heat of Holland–Dozier–Holland, Martha & The Vandellas, and their producers H–D–H, fought fire with fire. For four years of their association, the writing trio framed lead singer Martha Reeves' piercing, but never shrill, vocals with their most gospel-like, energetic arrangements. The result was as fresh and durable a testament as any other Motown artist ever carved out.

Reeves was no newcomer to the music business when she gained entry to the Motown organization as an A&R secretary. Singing tenor in a group called The Del-Phis, she gained experience in the studio backing up local soul singers like J.J. Barnes and Mike Hanks, and they had even cut a single of

their own for Check-Mate, Chess Records' Detroit affiliate. After that label folded, Reeves went to Motown to audition as a singer, but the only offer was for a secretary, and Reeves accepted that. This position soon gave her the opportunity to bring in her fellow group members Annette Sterling, Rosalind Ashford, and lead singer Gloria Williams for work as background singers on Motown recording sessions. Among their most notable sessions were "Stubborn Kinda Fellow," "Hitch Hike," and "Can I Get A Witness," all backing up Marvin Gaye. The Del-Phis got their break when Mary Wells failed to show up for a session. The record Wells was scheduled to sing, "There He Is (At My Door)," was, according to Freddy Gorman, who co-wrote the tune with Brian Holland, an overt attempt to get a Spector-type girl-group sound. Since The Del-Phis were technically signed to Check-Mate, they changed their name to The Vels, and the record was released on a short-lived Motown subsidiary, Mel-O-Dy (not to be confused with the Motown country music label subsidiary of the same name, which was activated a few years later). The record flopped, and Gloria Williams, a mother of two with a secure city government job, decided to leave the business. Reeves, an accomplished singer whose vocal experience ranged from gospel to opera, was then enlisted to sing lead. At the same time Berry Gordy presented her with a name she didn't care for, and given fifteen minutes to come up with a name of her own choice, she fused the names of her favorite singer—Della Reese—and a street near her home—Van Dyke Avenue—to come up with Martha & The Vandellas. The group was signed to Motown's Gordy subsidiary. Their roster at the time included The Temptations, whose first two releases had flopped, and The Contours, who had just scored a national hit with "Do You Love Me?" The Vandellas' first release, "I'll Have To Let Him Go," offered ample evidence that Martha's vocal chops were to be reckoned with, but was framed by a Mickey Stevenson production cast in Motown's most typical cha-cha-type mold, and the record flopped. About this time, Gordy, who already was having success with The Marvelettes and Mary Wells, continued to pursue girl groups. He issued numerous records by Debbie Dean, The Darnells (a second-rate Spector imitation), and several other genre records as well.

In early 1963, Martha & The Vandellas were paired with the Holland–Dozier–Holland team, and in April cracked the pop charts for the first time with "Come And Get These Memories." The record moved steadily into the Top Forty, where it stalled. For weeks it hung between #30 and #40, moving up and down, but it never quite broke through to the next level, topping at only #29. "Memories" is a Motown oddity whose sound seems to have no precedent or successor in the organization's catalog—it was the "There Goes My Baby" of its genre. With its oddly tonal high-pitched vocal hook and chord changes, only its light shuffle groove, a bit reminiscent of Mary Wells' "My Guy," even remotely recalls any other Motown record. Still, it did well for the group, kicking off an artist-producer relationship

that would yield many more satisfying records, and it sent The Vandellas on the road with a Motortown Revue tour that consisted of ninety-four one-nighters.

With the next release, "Heat Wave," the H–D–H team crystallized one of the most exciting sounds in rock history. "Heat Wave" was a perfect extension of Phil Spector's classic girl-group sound, particularly the more uptempo numbers like "Da Doo Ron Ron" by The Crystals. But while Spector's writers used occasional gospel chord changes to spice up their essentially pop melodies, the H–D–H team pushed the church influence to the forefront, both in their use of hymnal melodies and a way-upfront tambourine-charged percussion sound. Finally, the unbeatable duo of James Jamerson on bass and Benny Benjamin on drums had coalesced to provide an utterly unique and incomparable bottom. Although the record was actually recorded in the winter of 1963, its release was delayed until that July to coincide with the onset of summer. During a bona fide national heat wave in August, the record shot to #4

NOWHERE TO RUN

45 RPM

Chapter
ELEVEN

Martha and The Vandellas at their earliest recording session where they backed Marvin Gaye.

on the pop charts, and pounded out from every beach, bar, and radio in America.

The group's next record, "Quicksand," maintained Motown's marketing pattern of thinly disguised soundalike follow-ups, but people had not yet tired of that sound; it reached #8 in December of 1963. Two more soundalikes, "Live Wire," and "In My Lonely Room," failed to crack through the Top Forty, and each one sold less than its predecessor. At that point, says Martha, "that was enough of that."

"Dancing In The Streets" came next and is perhaps Martha & The Vandellas' most memorable record. It also marked the beginning of a successful collaboration with Mickey Stevenson, Motown's A & R chief. Stevenson recalls that when she was his secretary, "I liked Martha because she knew about music and was tuned in." Reeves helped ease the pressure of Stevenson's numerous responsibilities among the administrative and sales departments, as well as with the artists themselves. In addition, Reeves proved capable of "hanging with" Stevenson during his long work days, eventually, "helping out on demos, and singing harmony parts" on tunes Stevenson was writing.

Of "Dancing in the Streets," both Stevenson's and The Vandellas' biggest record, Stevenson recalls that "I was successfully writing with Marvin Gaye, things like 'Hitchhike,' 'Stubborn Kind Of Fella,' and 'Pride And Joy.' Ivy Jo Hunter had just joined the company. He was a frantic writer, but was also a very different kind of writer. But I knew he had it so I signed him to Jobete Publishing and we started writing together, and the three of us collaborated on the tune. The funny part of the story is that we were going to give the song to Kim Weston, but I had Martha sing the demo, and said to myself, 'Martha sounds pretty good on this.' So when I presented the song to Kim and her first response was that she didn't like it, I didn't give her a chance to think about it twice. I immediately grabbed Martha and did the song. If you listen carefully, you'll hear me and Ivy Jo singing in the background, as well as me on cowbell and Marvin Gaye on piano."

The intention of "Dancing In The Streets" was to diffuse the smoldering tensions in the black community; with its stately introductory horn riff and opening line serving notice "around the world to get ready for a brand new beat," "Dancing" came

The first Martha and The Vandellas group photo.

Lamont Dozier, Brian Holland, Eddie Holland.

across like shofars at the walls of Jericho. It clearly struck a responsive chord with the public, shooting to #2 within 2 months of its release in the summer of 1964. (The copycat follow-up, "Wild One," failed to get into the Top Thirty.) "Wild One" was suitably tailored to the pop market, but the lyrics and overall effect appeared to be overly contrived. Their momentum was not lost, however, and "Nowhere To Run," a variation on their recent sound, brought The Vandellas back to the Top Ten in early 1965. Attempting to exploit the success of "Nowhere to Run," an inferior imitation was rushed out, but "You've Been In Love Too Long" didn't take off; the flip-side, "Love Makes Me Do Foolish Things," was played by some deejays instead. Split air-play sealed the record's fate as a non-hit. Still, while "Love Makes Me Do Foolish Things" may not have set sales records, the torchy blues ballad demonstrated the breadth of the rapport between Reeves and the H-D-H team: for Diana Ross & The Supremes, H-D-H painted pretty pictures; for Martha Reeves, they wrote soul songs.

But Reeves' career began to lose momentum when she was shuttled from top producers to competent, if not particularly inspired producers. A painful year and a half out of the Top Ten went by for the woman with the incomparable voice, while she watched hit after hit by Marvin Gaye, The Temptations, The Miracles, The Four Tops and Stevie Wonder leap up the charts. Martha & The Vandellas also looked on as Berry Gordy lavished his time and best efforts on his favorites, The

Supremes, while the label's other girl groups were not priority.

It wasn't until late 1966 that the group rebounded with "I'm Ready For Love," another H-D-H creation that sported that trio's latest hit beat—a brisk double-time that also scored well for The Temptations ("All I Need"), and The Supremes ("You Can't Hurry Love"). While the group's follow-up was again graced by an H-D-H production, the song, "Jimmy Mack," had actually been in the can for several years, its "Baby Love" era sound was little more than a pleasant anachronism, although Martha provided wonderful vocal touches.

A relative stiff, "Love Bug Leave My Heart Alone," was followed by the Richard Morris production of "Honey Chile," which reached #11 late in 1967. "Honey Chile" also marked the debut of the group's newly appended name, Martha *Reeves* & The Vandellas, changed, Martha said, because the Motown administration sensed she would react on the heels of similar honors proferred Smokey Robinson and The Miracles, and Diana Ross and The Supremes. But ironically, though numerous records were released, Martha Reeves and The Vandellas would never again enter the Top Forty.

Motown had made a fuss about their new signing, Gladys Knight & The Pips, and was working hard to secure hits for that group. By 1971, Martha had disbanded the Vandellas, an action that had little meaning at that point—the group had changed personnel six times over the years. It

meant more in a symbolic sense, almost like a dying tree whose leaves are first cast off before the tree itself is left to wither away. (The personnel changes had begun as early as mid-1963, when Annette Sterling left and was replaced by Betty Kelly. In 1968, Martha's sister Lois replaced Betty Kelly, and by 1970, Rosalind Ashford departed to be replaced by ex-Velvelette Sandra Tilley.)

Why was the career of this most talented singer and performer neglected? The answer seems to lie more in the realm of company politics than in the area of talent. Martha's personality had the fire that matched her vocals. According to a close observer on the scene, "Martha was too harsh; you couldn't tell her what to do all the time, or she'd tell you where to go. She wasn't a puppet, and sometimes she'd even go to a record hop and not sing the song exactly like the record"—a violation of a Motown commandment. "She was simply not the girl that Berry Gordy was looking for."

NOWHERE HIGHER

Martha and the Vandallas returned from the Tamla-Motown European junket just in time to help radio outlet WOOK-Washington shift the position of their Gordy outing "Nowhere to Run" into the top spot in the area. Happily accepting their help at the station's top ten board is spinner Bob King. The Detroit trio's deck follows a long string of hits, which include "Dancing in the Street" and "Heat Wave."

The girl-group sound that swept America and the world arrived in 1961 and was gone by 1965. What happened after 1965 was left primarily to Motown, and with Berry Gordy and his staff coming up with new twists and turns at pivotal junctures, Motown was able to keep most of their girl-group acts in the charts until 1968. For the most part, these chart placings were not notched with girl-group records, any more than the success of Charlie Rich or Jerry Lee Lewis on the country charts could be credited to rockabilly; Motown's later female records were slickly commerical pop, often with adult appeal. Gordy would usually drop an act if they didn't break big after a series of releases, but Motown's biggest success story would come with a group whose career wouldn't take off until their seventh release, and whose development would chart the course of the girl-group sound from its beginnings to its end.

★ ★

At the start of their career, The Supremes were merely prototypes for Motown's "Sound Of Young America," but they soon came to represent Berry Gordy's aspirations to the ultimate pop crossover: a group appreciated by adults as well as by teenagers; by blacks as well as whites—in short embodying and pursuing the Motown ethos. Under Gordy's personal tutelage and direction, the personal and professional lives of three teenage girls became indistinguishable. Gordy took total control of their image from the minute they walked into a studio to the moment they left the stage. At the height of their success, there wasn't much in-between. The results were formidable; the group became one of the most striking phenomena of the '60s—a decade that was not short on striking phenomena. Easily the most sophisticated act to emerge from a r&b scene, The Supremes achieved worldwide notoriety on the strength of *11 #1 records* during their years together. The group's original teenage qualities would soon be supplanted in an attempt to personify Berry Gordy's quest for unending upward mobility. They became cute yet sophisticated in a manner that both embraced the chi-chi and made it larger than life (in fact, unwittingly caricaturistic). Diana Ross, in particular, was the symbolic frontispiece on Berry Gordy's Cadillac, and the most striking emblem of Motown's penchant for style over soul.

The group's early recordings offer ample evidence that Ross was perhaps one of the least gifted singers in the Motown stable. On recording after recording in their first album, *Meet The Supremes*, a collection of their earliest singles, Ross is noteworthy only for her inability to stay on key. Instead, her talent lay in her relentlessly aggressive pursuit of stardom, and similarly, in her superior understanding of the needs, aims, and values of Motown as defined by her boss and pygmalion, Berry Gordy. As the body of her work progressed, Ross was most impressive for her unequaled ability to project so uniquely a stylized persona that it served to both crystallize and transcend Holland–Dozier–Holland's most original—if not most exciting—writing and production ideas.

Unlike the other women of Motown, The Supremes, despite their average age of sixteen, had been bonded together both professionally and personally for several years. The group's earliest origins trace to an elementary school talent show where both Mary Wilson and Florence Ballard performed. "I borrowed my brothers doo-rag and his black leather jacket, put a comb in the back of my blue jeans, and did a version of Frankie Lymon & The Teenagers' 'I'm Not A Juvenile Delinquent,'" recalls Wilson. Both she and Ballard were encouraged by good responses and began talking about singing together in a group. Their plans were temporarily interrupted when a member of a local doo-wop group, The Primes, an early incarnation of The Temptations, recruited Florence to join a group that would be their female counterpart, called The Primettes. But the group fell apart, leaving Ballard and another member, Betty Travis, to pick up the pieces; they then contacted Wilson. Again intervening on the girls' behalf, one of The Primes, future Temptation Paul Williams, recruited Diana Ross (then called Diane) to round out the group. While the girls had never sung together before, they had seen Ross, who "had what it took," on neighborhood street corners. The girls began rehearsing regularly, and were also taught choreography by The Primes. When Betty Travis left to go steady with her boyfriend, Ross recruited Barbara Martin to replace her. A guitarist, Marv Tarplin, was added on to accompany the group.

The Primettes began working locally, often foregoing payment for the simple chance of exposure and experience. With the assistance of Bill Williams, who dj'd for the local r&b station, WCHB, The Primettes came into contact with professional entertainers. After one gig at the 20 Grand Club with Mel Carter, Wilson recalls that "we decided we wanted to make records. We were doing it for fun and these people were making money. We thought, 'Why can't we?' "

The group decided to audition for the hottest label in town—Motown—though they had heard that "the label will rip you off. Since we didn't have anything to rip off, we went for it," recalls Wilson. Ross lived down the block from Motown recording artist William "Smokey" Robinson. His group, The Miracles, was one of the hottest acts in town, and he was able to arrange an audition with the label chief, Berry Gordy. It was a less than productive experience for the sixteen-year-olds. Not only were they told that he wasn't interested in the hassles of dealing with such a young girl group who hadn't finished school, but Robinson, impressed by the playing of the group's guitarist, Marv Tarplin, "borrowed" him for a gig, and soon made Tarplin a permanent member of The Miracles' ensemble. But all was not hopeless. On their way out the door, a Motown employee told the girls about a smaller label, Lu-Pine, that might offer them a better opportunity. The label owner, Robert West, signed the girls. They did background session work for Eddie Floyd, and record hops with The Falcons, then fronted by Wilson Pickett. They even recorded four sides for the label, and one, "Pretty Baby," featured Mary on lead. It was a measure of the label's ineffectiveness that the girls never knew that the records were released. When Lu-Pine suspended operations, the teenagers returned to Motown.

They began by simply hanging around, hitchhiking to the label's offices every day, gradually getting rides home from Berry's father, "Pops" Gordy. Eventually the girls were used for backup vocals as part of large choruses and for handclapping, for which they were each paid $2.50. But it was through another connection that The Primettes were able to further entrench themselves in the Motown operation. His name was Freddie Gorman. He had been a mailman whose route included the homes of The Primettes; after work, he'd spend time at Motown's offices writing songs with Eddie Holland. He felt that his song, "I Want A Guy," would be right for the girls, so he rehearsed it with them, and auditioned it for Berry Gordy. This time Gordy decided to sign them to his Tamla label.

By this time the group had changed its name. Berry Gordy didn't like the name The Primettes, and at contract time the name "Supremes" was picked by Florence Ballard from a list of names she was given to choose from. "I Want A Guy" was not a great record; its cha-cha groove was filled with soon-to-be-dated Motown devices like upfront flutes and guitars playing fragmented chords. Diana Ross' unformed, excessively nasal voice didn't help either. But while this first release, issued in mid-1961 flopped, it gave The Supremes a foothold at Motown that they would not relinquish. Gorman recalls that "from the very beginning, when they went out and did the record hops, they were always real ladies. The way they carried themselves impressed Berry and everybody else." It was the impression made on Gordy that would see them through a long period of failure that few as unproven as they were would be allowed to endure. The Supremes became "the girls" at Motown, even after The Marvelettes and Martha & The Vandellas beat them to the top of the charts. When Berry Gordy said he wanted to see "the girls," he meant his pets, The Supremes.

Even at this early stage of their career, a quiet, but real, dichotomy existed between the women who were bonded to each other, and the man, Berry Gordy, who demanded the personal fealty of each. Wilson recalls that while the group was still a quartet, their chaperone, John O'Den, along with his wife, gave the girls a driving lesson, and while Barbara Martin was behind the wheel, she got into an accident. O'Den told the relieved girls that his wife would take the blame for them, but unknown to The Supremes, the couple had quarreled en route to the office, and Gordy had already been told the truth. The unwitting Mary Wilson was the first called into Gordy's office to recount the incident. After she blamed Mrs. O'Den, Gordy told her that he knew the real truth and that he didn't like liars; Wilson was expelled from the group. Not knowing who had turned her in, Wilson walked aimlessly down West Grand Boulevard, her eyes filled with tears. Eventually Gordy sent someone to get her and she was reinstated into the group. When Gordy asked her why she didn't tell him the truth, she told him that there was just no way that she was going to turn one of her girls in. It was a subtle conflict that would later magnify beyond anyone's expectations.

Around the time of the release of "I Want A Guy," Barbara Martin left the group and was not replaced. The Supremes were now recording under the aegis of Gordy's number one son, Smokey Robinson, and he had them do a version of an old Miracles ballad, "Who's Loving You." While Ross' still unimpressive lead failed to bring the song home, another portentous situation developed. The flip-side of the record, "Buttered Popcorn," started to overtake "Who's Loving You" in popularity. An unassuming little song with a New Orleans-inspired "Popeye" beat, the record might have stepped up The Supremes' entry to the major league marketplace by a year, but for one

factor: it featured the lead vocals of Florence Ballard. By this time, Gordy had already decided that it would be the lean, style-conscious Diana Ross who would front the group. Mary Wilson recalls seeing arguments between Gordy and Motown's head of sales, Barney Ales, over the marketing of the record. Gordy ultimately overruled Ales, and decided "not to go for it," recalls Wilson.

For The Supremes' next release, Gordy decided to move the group from Tamla to Motown. With Robinson still at the helm, the group released "Your Heart Belongs To Me," and although the production values had improved considerably, extending the lilting Latin groove Robinson had perfected with Mary Wells, the record still flopped. While Berry Gordy had always maintained a personal involvement in Supremes' sessions—by that time "if you wanted to do anything with the group, you had to check with Berry," recalls Wilson—he personally stepped back to a writer's role

WHERE DID OUR LOVE GO
HE MEANS THE WORLD TO ME

to pen their next record, "Let Me Go The Right Way." Gordy took a page from the Brill Building songbook—specifically Bob Crewe's Vee-Jay productions for The Four Seasons—and used the more rigid, if still Latinized, groove to give The Supremes their first chart entry. In late 1962 and early 1963, "Let Me Go . . ." topped only at #90, but at least it was a start. Gordy wanted this record to happen, partially because his girls had several previous flops, and partially because he had written this new release and wanted to be a hero. He pushed and pushed for this record, with trade advertisements, and on the radio. It first charted in December for only one week and then dropped off. Five weeks later it reappeared for a month and then dropped off once more. Two weeks later it entered the Top 100 for one more week, and that was as far as it got—but certainly not for the lack of trying. The group had graduated to inclusion in the Motown Revues, but their regular producer, Smokey Robinson, still could not find the hit formula for them. They flopped once more with another Mary Wells soundalike, "Breathtaking Guy."

The turning point in the group's career came when they hooked up with the team of Holland–Dozier–Holland. That trio had already perfected a pristine blend of Phil Spector-styled wall of sound arrangements overlaid by gospel chord changes and rhythmic devices, and they'd applied them with great success to Martha & The Vandellas on songs like "Heat Wave," and to Mary Wells with "You Lost The Sweetest Boy." Taking no chances, H–D–H strengthened the sound by using members of The Four Tops to beef up the harmonies, while Eddie Holland threw in some warrior-like shouts. The result, "When the Love Light Shines," restored the group to the charts—this time into the Top Thirty for the first time. H–D–H's brilliance lay in their ability to tailor their music to the strengths and limitations of their artists. While The Supremes at that time measured themselves by Martha and The Vandellas, Motown's most successful girls, the H–D–H trio realized that The Supremes were made of vastly different stuff.

The follow-up, "Run Run Run," was cast squarely in a pure pop, Spectoresque girl-group mold. But despite the record's flop, and the girls' growing impatience—other Motown artists had by now nicknamed them the "no-hit" Supremes—the H–D–H trio was steadily intent on honing a sound suited to Ross' forming vocal style. At this point, early in 1964, she was a more fully realized—if entirely stylized—vocalist; her sound a stable mix of cutesy-poo delivery and highly articulated diction with histrionic theatricality. "Diane was a composite of a lot of people," remarks one of her peers. Word has it that Ross' vocal style was earnestly a matter of crash study, and that Gordy had once recorded an entire album of Brenda Holloway that sat in the can only to be played repeatedly for solo listening sessions by Ross.

With the release of their next record in July 1964, "Where Did Our Love Go," the H–D–H team would find the perfect formula they had been

The Supremes rehearse with Holland-Dozier-Holland.

America's No. 1 Recording Artists

The SUPREMES

TOPS ON CAMPUS

College Dates Thru April '66

CORNELL UNIVERSITY

UNIVERSITY OF VERMONT

DUKE UNIVERSITY

UNIVERSITY OF ROCHESTER

DENISON UNIVERSITY

RUTGERS UNIVERSITY

NOTRE DAME UNIVERSITY

looking for, and initiate one of the most successful collaborations in pop music history—and in the process The Supremes would turn into 1960's pop icons. Ironically, none of the group was impressed with the song. Mary Wilson recalls pleading with Eddie Holland ''not to give us this kiddy-bop stuff.'' But Holland was convinced it was a hit, and they recorded it. ''Where Did Our Love Go'' returned the group to the groove of ''Let Me Go The Right Way''—but with a difference. The phenomenal bass–drum team of Jamerson and Benjamin had by now developed its own unique groove which served as a well-spring for so many of Motown's records—it was simplistically rigid on top so that any bubble-gummer could clap along, but also had a funky tension on the bottom that could plug into any black street corner. At the same time, H–D–H developed their own clock-work-coordinated system of teamwork and rehearsals. According to Wilson, the team presented their songs to The Supremes ''as is''—''the way you hear them is the way we got them. . . .''

After Lamont Dozier would work out the melody on the piano, Eddie Holland would develop the lyrics and craft a vocal interpretation that Diana Ross would follow to the letter. Lamont Dozier supervised the vocal backgrounds, allowing Wilson and Ballard some flexibility, though making sure that Wilson's husky alto was closer to the mike than Ballard's piercing tenor. Finally, Brian Holland supervised the session from the engineering booth, periodically suggesting changes that

On a tour of Japan with Berry Gordy.

Supremes became America's own hottest act and a top international attraction as well. While Mary Wells, The Marvelettes, and Martha & The Vandellas had between them a total of two Top Twenty hits in England by the end of 1966, The Supremes by themselves had five, all of them Top Ten.

While the fifth soundalike record, "Nothing But Heartaches" only reached #11, the next one, "I Hear A Symphony," took them back to the top spot as 1965 came to a close. In 1966, the group bowed with "My World Is Empty Without You," featuring H–D–H's new double-time groove—it hit #5. The next record, "Love Is Like An Itching In My Heart," peaked at #9, and that was followed by 2 successive #1 hits, "You Can't Hurry Love," and "You Keep Me Hanging On." At this point, the still pioneering H–D–H production team had eschewed the pounding drill-press groove that had carried them through so many hits, and replaced it with a more kinetic sound and beat, more like a teletype machine. It provided a subordinate framework for Ross' now distinctive and commanding vocals.

But records had become only one facet of Gordy's plans for the group's upward mobility. The group's appearance on the cover of *Time* and almost every other international magazine of consequence; command performances at the London Palladium; an endless stream of well-designed appearances on *The Ed Sullivan Show*; and audiences with kings and queens in Europe suggested that at least as recording artists, there were no worlds left to conquer. Perhaps an ironic parallel could be drawn from the fact that The Supremes had their own brand of white bread named after them, and they actively promoted it. But Gordy quested for even more trappings of highly visible success—the most traditional notions of the kind of broad-based stardom for the group that would encompass theater, and specially, film.

would be adhered to. As always the final decisions about the release of the material were made by Berry Gordy.

The success of "Where Did Our Love Go" was abetted in no small way by the group's concurrent appearance on Dick Clark's prestigious "Cavalcade of Stars" revue in the spring of 1964, affording The Supremes a precious opportunity for a massive broad-based exposure that the Motortown Revues couldn't match. Although Motown had to beg Clark to include the group on the tour at the outset, he gladly renegotiated their contract by the tour's end. By the mid-summer, the record had shot to #1. It stayed in the Top Five for 2 months, and stood at #1 for 4 consecutive weeks, an amazing move at this time in pop history. The Supremes became unstoppably hot; within a 10-month period the group would achieve the incredible feat of hitting #1 with their next 4 releases: "Baby Love," "Come See About Me," "Stop In The Name Of Love," and "Back In My Arms Again." This came at a time when the British Invasion and other new sounds were almost totally dominating the American charts, and The

It was not entirely coincidental that at about the same time what many observers felt was a love affair gradually began to develop between Gordy and Ross. One observer described their relationship as one "between the man to whom she owed everything and the woman who would keep him 'out there' forever." Be that as it may, it became ineluctably clear to all concerned that a solo career for Diana Ross was in the process of being fashioned.

On a British TV show.

168

"I don't know whether it was Berry or Diana's idea for her to have a solo career," demures Wilson, "but I do know that it hurt Florence and myself to begin hearing about it from other people, and this was the start of The Supremes' problems."

Soon, the attention that Gordy had previously distributed evenly among the three began to shift dramatically in Ross' direction. Gordy and Ross would attend affairs together, while Wilson and Ballard were required to show up together later. "It used to bug Florence," recalls Wilson, "and rightfully so. But I knew that there was no way of stopping it, and I knew another thing—that I was still a Supreme." But at a meeting Gordy held with the three, the possibility was raised that the group might have to pack it in on the heels of Ross' solo career, to which the immediate prelude was a name change to "Diana Ross and The Supremes."

The strain of this continuing series of traumatizing events forced Wilson, and especially Ballard, to depart from their previous roles as puppets. The relationship between Ross and Ballard had already been tinged with a real, if not serious, friction, but it began to escalate. Ballard put on weight, missed radio interviews, and even missed several performances. Finally, Berry Gordy called the group together in a private meeting held in the winter of 1967 to determine whether Ballard's acting out

should affect her future as a Supreme. Regardless of their sympathy for Ballard's motives, Wilson and Ross dutifully reported that Ballard's level of professionalism was no longer up to standard. By then, the proud Ballard had decided she could no longer go along with "the program" anyway, and Gordy's choice was clear: Ballard was told to leave the group. This decision was even more traumatizing for its real implication that she was also being expelled from the extended Motown family; Ballard was dropped as a Motown artist. Within nine years, she had, according to Wilson, "wilted away." Forgotten by many former associates whose livelihood she had helped support, she embarked on a commercially unsuccessful solo career at ABC Records, and later lost a suit against Motown that charged she had been "maliciously ousted from the group." Whatever severance pay she was given by Motown was eaten up by lawyer's bills, she later stated, and as time passed, she went through a painful divorce, and continuing problems caused her to sell her home. For a time, she was even forced to collect welfare.

It would not be until December 1969 that Ross would officially leave the group for a solo career, but in April 1967 when The Supremes became "Diana Ross and the Supremes," that was for all intents and purposes, when the music died for The Supremes and all the innocence they seemed to represent to their public.

THE GIRL-GROUP SOUND EVENtually vanished from the charts. It was not due to any single event, but rather to a series of events that, when linked together, resulted in the demise of not only the sound, but of the artists and producers as well.

The British Invasion is often cited as the main reason that the girl-group sound was washed off the airwaves. This is a broad oversimplification, and for the most part, not accurate. During 1964, the year of Beatlemania, The Dave Clark Five, Zombies, Rolling Stones, Manfred Mann, and many more, girl-group records did tremendously well on The U.S. charts. *Number One* records were scored by Mary Wells, The Dixie Cups, The Supremes, and The Shangri-Las; the Number One spot was held by girl groups for 25 percent of the entire year (about the same percentage as the previous year), and other major hits were recorded by The Ronettes, Martha & The Vandellas, Lesley Gore, The Jelly Beans, and numerous others. But the British Invasion did herald the era of new sounds and of self-contained groups that wrote and played their own material. Most popular trends or genres in music run their course within three years, partly because they capture the tenor of their times so well, and partly because dozens of second-rate imitations flood the market and the public soon overdoses on the particular sound. If the girl groups *were* beaten away by a sound, it was not only the British sound, but also surf, Motown, folk-rock, and blue-eyed soul.

More importantly, it was the writers and producers who voluntarily dropped out of the scene, fearing that they could not compete with the new sounds. Don Kirshner sold Dimension Records and took his staff in different directions. Many of the writers and producers like Gerry Goffin and Carole King, and Jeff Barry and Ellie Greenwich were going through personal life changes. Writing teen anthems was not satisfying enough for them anymore. Leiber & Stoller abandoned Red Bird because they made enough money and were tired of the endless syndrome of the pop churn-em-out machine. Phil Spector made his mark and became disenchanted with the business, and went into semi-retirement. Motown changed their sound to a slicker mode, and began working with new artists. Many of the groups themselves were involved in lawsuits, or simply tired of the eternal grind of the road, and chose to build families instead of hit records.

Artists who varied their sound to stay relevant to the times did find success. The Toys' dose of classical themes took them to the top in 1966; Jackie DeShannon continued to make vibrant and exciting recordings throughout the sixties; Evie Sands recorded wonderfully contemporary girl-group flavored records during 1966 and 1967; and many soul artists whose star ascended in the mid-sixties—like Aretha Franklin, Barbara Lewis, Dionne Warwick and Fontella Bass—took many of their cues from girl-group stylings. Cher, both as a solo artist and with Sonny Bono, had hit after hit by combining the twang and message of folk-rock with the beat and sound of Phil Spector's girl-group records. Spector recalled in 1969: "It also happened that everyone got frightened over here, got guitar groups together and killed off the Negro sound. If the Negro group had stayed dominant and really pushed forward, like The Drifters and Coasters, you might not have had this massive English surge. See everybody got really frightened after The Beatles . . . the record companies, etc. . . . but every big English group has a tremendous black flavor to it. . . ."

The late fifties and early sixties were optimistic, seemingly simpler times. The Kennedy years ushered in a spirit of youthful exuberance, hope for the future, and a clear sense of right and wrong. It was a period that is remembered in terms of black and white images: the ending of the McCarthy era and the Eisenhower years; the black and white look of the Beat Generation; television shows, from dramas to sitcoms to *American Bandstand*; and the burgeoning progress of the civil rights demonstrations. The music echoed these times and themes, and perhaps it is painfully ironic that *Phil Spector's Christmas Album*—the culmination of hope, joy, spirit, rhythm, and optimism—was issued the week before John Kennedy was assassinated.

Almost from that moment on, we began to live in a world of color, where simple honest solutions and ideas would become blurred visions, and where the music had to respond to and reflect upon these new times. The mid-sixties are all in color: the Zapruder assassination footage; the Mod clothing explosion; war footage from Vietnam and from the battle-scarred streets of America's cities. There was no room for the mood and message of the girl groups in this new world—things just weren't that simple anymore. Morals and institutions were being uprooted with a disorienting frequency, and with drug usage, changing sexual values and beliefs, and the role of women and blacks in our society becoming prime social issues, the girl groups were thus linked in the public consciousness with the past. If the sixties were about anything at all, they were about the present and the future. Girl groups simply did not fit into this picture.

The ironic truth of the sixties is that the calls for free expression and understanding of others often drowned out what many purported to defend. Sweeping generalizations both then and now failed to distinguish the good from the bad. The creative from the derivative. The honest emotions from the processed pap. Girl-group records must be heard on an individual basis. Broad-based criticism or praise just does not hold up. There are hundreds of results, and more importantly, hundreds of motivations. Most of the girl groups were black. Most of the producers were white. Berry Gordy wanted to be accepted in the white world. Phil Spector and Leiber & Stoller wanted to reach the black world. To some this reeks of exploitation. To others it exhibits racial harmony. Girl-group music, in its voice, lyric, and sound, teaches us only one simple truth: there is no such thing as a simple truth.

In recent years, the legacy of the girl groups has been revived by contemporary hitmakers. The songs themselves are constantly being recorded successfully, by both male and female artists: Carole King with "One Fine Day"; Grand Funk Railroad with "The Locomotion"; Manhattan Transfer with "The Boy From New York City"; Linda Ronstadt with "Heatwave"; James Taylor with "Will You Still Love Me Tomorrow"; Shaun Cassidy with "Da Doo Ron Ron"; and "Chapel Of Love," "Be My Baby," "It's My Party," "Please Mr. Postman," and many more by a variety of artists.

The Motown and Spector sounds are constantly recreated by dozens of performers like Bette Midler, Dave Edmunds, Hall and Oates, Bruce Springsteen, and even such seemingly disparate artists as The Ramones and Meatloaf. Established hitmakers such as Eric Carmen, Roy Wood, John Lennon, Rockpile, and Billy Joel ("Say Goodbye To Hollywood") have all recorded affectionate

tributes to the sound; big hits by Abba, The Pointer Sisters ("He's So Shy"), and others have been strongly influenced by the girl groups of the past. Many new stars like Blondie, The Go-Go's, and the B-52's all cite girl groups as a major influence, and incorporate not only the music, but the mood, message, and look of the era into their current activities. And on the horizon, even more new artists use the girl-group era: The Waitresses, Kirsty Maccoll, Rachel Sweet, Joan Jett, Robin Lane, Holly & The Italians, Louise Goffin, Blue Angel and The Revillos are some of the most promising.

Ultimately, however, the sound belongs to an era and a style of recording that shall never come again. Today's performers are most successful when they use the past as a jumping-off point for their own creativity, and most note-for-note recreations merely come off as campy, or worse yet, uninspired formulaic hack jobs. Many of the writers, producers, and performers from the girl-group era are still active today, and they too come off best when they are creating vibrant, honest music true to these times.

It is a sense of commitment that makes all music stand the test of time, and if you lose faith and honesty, all that remains is artifice. Ellie Greenwich puts it best when she reflects upon the disappearance of the girl-group sound: "When something hits really big out of nowhere, you say, 'Uh oh.' When the Beatles and the entire British Invasion came in, we were all ready to say, 'Look, it's been nice, there's no more room for us—it's now the self-contained group; males; certain type of material—what do *we* do?' And I think mortal fear set in to the writers, so we didn't know what to write. We didn't continue to write because we thought 'what will we do with it?' I think everyone of us panicked, from the labels to the producers to the writers—so we ourselves made that transition happen, because we didn't know what to do; we became afraid. We said, 'Ok, we're being invaded, we either have to fight them or join them.' So we either joined them, or walked away. We didn't fight back, that's for sure. And the few people that had the resources or the wisdom—Motown for example—went on. We got scared and rushed the cycle. I don't know why, we just did. Maybe if we had fought back, things would have been different. . . ."

Discography

THERE ARE 1000 GIRL-GROUP RECORDS:

Here are 131 of The Best . . . .

Ad Libs   *(Blue Cat)*
"The Boy From New York City"

Angels   *(Smash)*
"My Boyfriend's Back"

Dorothy Berry   *(Challenge)*
"You're So Fine"

Blue-Belles   *(Newtown)*
"I Sold My Heart To The Junkman"

Bob B. Soxx & The Blue Jeans   *(Philles)*
"Zip A Dee Do Dah"; "Why Do Lovers Break
Each Other's Hearts"

Bonnie & The Treasures   *(Phi-Dan)*
"Home Of The Brave"

Bouquets   *(Blue Cat)*
"Welcome To My Heart"

Butterflys   *(Red Bird)*
"Goodnight Baby"

Chantels   *(End; End; Carlton)*
"Maybe"; "He's Gone"; "Look In My Eyes"

Charmettes   *(Kapp)*
"Please Don't Kiss Me Again"

Chiffons   *(Laurie)*
"One Fine Day"; "I Have A Boyfriend";
"Nobody Knows What's Goin' On In My Mind"

Cinderellas   *(Dimension)*
"Please Don't Wake Me"

Claudine Clark   *(Chancellor)*
"Party Lights"

Merry Clayton   *(Capitol)*
"Usher Boy"

Cookies   *(Dimension)*
"Chains"; "Don't Say Nothing Bad About My
Baby"; "I Never Dreamed"

Crystals   *(Philles)*
"Oh Yeah, Maybe Baby"; "There's No Other";
"He's A Rebel"; "Then He Kissed Me";
"Uptown"; "He Hit Me"; "He's Sure The Boy I
Love"; "Da Doo Ron Ron"; "I Wonder"

Cupcakes   *(Diamond)*
"Pied Piper"

Skeeter Davis   *(RCA)*
"I Can't Stay Mad At You"

Tracey Dey   *(AMY)*
"I Won't Tell"

Dixie Cups   *(Red Bird)*
"Chapel Of Love"; "People Say"; "Iko Iko"

Earl-Jean   *(Colpix)*
"I'm Into Something Good"

Essex   *(Roulette)*
"Easier Said Than Done"

Betty Everett   *(Vee-Jay)*
"It's In His Kiss"

Exciters   *(United Artists)*
"Tell Him"; "He's Got The Power"

Shelley Fabares   *(Colpix; Colpix; Dunhill)*
"Football Season's Over"; "He Don't Love Me";
"Pretty Please"

Connie Francis   *(MGM)*
"Don't Ever Change"

Girls   *(Capitol)*
"Chico's Girl"

Girlfriends   *(Colpix)*
"My One And Only Jimmy Boy"

Lesley Gore   *(Mercury)*
"Look Of Love"; "Maybe I Know";
"Hey Baby"

Ellie Greenwich   *(Red Bird)*
"You Don't Know"

Honey Bees   *(Fontana)*
"She Don't Deserve You"; "One
Wonderful Night"

Honeys   *(Capitol; Warner Brothers)*
"The One You Can't Have"; "He's A Doll"

Jaynetts   *(Tuff)*
"Sally Go Round The Roses"

Jelly Beans (Red Bird)
"I Wanna Love Him So Bad"; "Baby Be Mine"

Toni Jones (Smash)
"Here Comes My Baby"

Roddie Joy (Red Bird)
"If There's Anything Else You Want"

Little Eva (Dimension)
"The Locomotion"; "Keep Your Hands Off My Baby"

Darlene Love (Philles)
"Today I Met The Boy I'm Gonna Marry"; "Wait 'Til My Bobby Gets Home"; "A Fine Fine Boy"; "Christmas (Baby Please Come Home)"; "Stumble And Fall"

Joni Lyman (Reprise)
"I Just Don't Know What To Do With Myself"

Martha & The Vandellas (Gordy)
"Come And Get These Memories"; "Heatwave"; "Dancing In The Streets"; "Nowhere To Run"; "Jimmy Mack"

Marvelettes (Tamla)
"Please Mr. Postman"; "Beachwood 4-5789"; "Twistin' Postman"; "Don't Mess With Bill"

Shirley Mathews (Atlantic)
"Big Town Boy"

Murmaids (Chattahoochee)
"Popsicles And Icicles"

Orlons (Cameo)
"Wah-Wahtusi"; "South Street"; "Don't Hang Up"

Paris Sisters (Gregmark)
"I Love How You Love Me"

Pin-Ups (Stork)
"Lookin' For Boys"

Raindrops (Jubilee)
"What A Guy"; "The Kind Of Boy You Can't Forget"; "When The Boy's Happy"

Alder Ray (Liberty)
"Cause I Love Him"

Reparata and The Delrons (World Artists)
"Whenever A Teenager Cries"

Rev-Lons (Reprise)
"After Last Night"

Ribbons (Marsh)
"Ain't Gonna Kiss You"

Ronettes (Philles)
"Be My Baby"; "Baby I Love You"; "Walkin' In The Rain"; "Best Part Of Breaking Up"; "Do I Love You"

Cathy Saint (Daisy)
"Big Bad World"

Evie Sands (Blue Cat)
"I Can't Let Go"; "Take Me For A Little While"

Shangri-Las (Red Bird)
"Leader Of The Pack"; "Walkin' In The Sand"; "Give Him A Great Big Kiss"; "Out In The Streets"; "I Can Never Go Home Anymore"; "Past Present Future"; "Give Us Your Blessings"

Dee Dee Sharp (Cameo)
"Mashed Potatoes"; "Ride"

Shirelles (Scepter)
"I Met Him On A Sunday"; "Tonight's The Night"; "Will You Love Me Tomorrow"; "Mama Said"; "Baby It's You"

Dusty Springfield (Phillips)
"I Only Want To Be With You"; "Stay Awhile"

Supremes (Motown)
"Where Did Our Love Go"; "Baby Love"; "Come See About Me"; "Love Is Here And Now You're Gone"; "You Keep Me Hanging On"

Toys (Dyno-Voice)
"Lover's Concerto"

Veronica (Phil Spector)
"So Young"; "Why Don't They Let Us Fall In Love"

Victorians (Liberty)
"What Makes Little Girls Cry"

Mary Wells (Motown)
"Bye Bye Baby"; "The One Who Really Loves You"; "You Beat Me To The Punch"; "My Guy"; "Two Lovers"

Whyte Boots (Phillips)
"Nightmare"

EXCITERS

HONEYS

About The Author

ANGELS

PHILIPS

434 546 BE

GETHER

126
A Division of Phil Spector Productions

Alan Betrock has pursued his love of rock 'n' roll as a writer, editor, publisher, and record producer. He has written extensively on both the past and future of popular music for numerous publications and has compiled and annotated historical reissues for several record labels. He was founder and editor of *The Rock Marketplace*, the first contemporary record collector's magazine, and *New York Rocker*, America's leading new music publication. He has published *Rock 'N' Roll Movie Posters* and *Girl Groups: An Annotated Discography* and produced records by The dB's, Richard Hell, and Marshall Crenshaw. His pop culture archives, including girl-group music, are among the most extensive in the country.